Strategic Transitions for Youth Labour in Europe

Youth employment

The STYLE Handbook

Editors:
Jacqueline O'Reilly
Clémentine Moyart
Tiziana Nazio
and **Mark Smith**

Youth Employment: The STYLE Handbook

Edited by Jacqueline O'Reilly, Clémentine Moyart,
Tiziana Nazio and Mark Smith.

Published by CROME.
STYLE is an EU FP7 funded large scale integrated research project coordinated by CROME. This project has received funding from the European Union's Seventh Framework Programme for research, technological development and demonstration under grant agreement no. 613256.

www.style-research.eu
www.style-handbook.eu

The overarching aim of the STYLE project has been to conduct high quality research to develop theory and knowledge, inform policy-making and public debate, and engage users of research within the field of youth employment.

ISBN 978-1-4473-5034-7 (paperback)

Cover design: JacksonBone
Design and typesetting: JacksonBone

Introduction

Young people's attitudes and values

Which countries perform best and why?

What can we learn about policy innovation?

Skills and education mismatch

Migration and mobility

Family matters

Flexible working and precariousness

Inspirational music and film

Contents

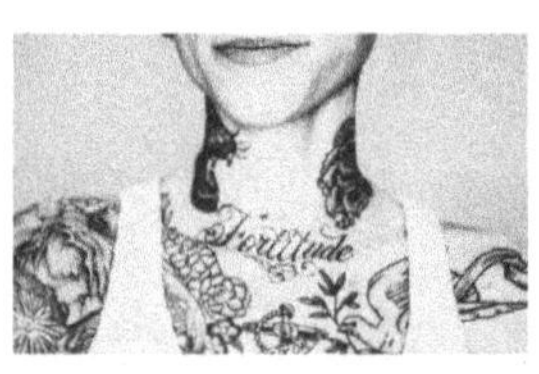

Acknowledgements viii
Authors xi
Acronyms xiii
Country abbreviations xv
Endorsements xvi

Introduction

Strategic Transitions for Youth Labour in Europe 3
Jacqueline O'Reilly, Mark Smith, Tiziana Nazio and Clémentine Moyart

Young people's attitudes and values 13

Introduction: Young people's attitudes and values 15
Jacqueline O'Reilly and Clémentine Moyart
Do you have an invisible cape? 16
Sharon Dodua Otoo
Who do young people trust and why? 18
Niall O'Higgins and Marco Stimolo
Are young people's work values changing? 21
Gábor Hajdu and Endre Sik
'One Step Forward': Resilient strategies supporting the aspirations of vulnerable young people in foster care 24
Ross, Jaymi, Sunneka, Amy, Matt, Sitara, Raija, Rosa, Katy, Chloe, Lorna, Laura, Sam, Katarina, Lefteris, Angie Hart, Claire Stubbs, Stefanos Plexousakis, Maria Georgiadi and Elias Kourkoutas
What matters to young mums? 27
Emma Mckay and Emma Feasey
Are young people outsiders and does it matter? 30
Alessandro Arrigoni and Emanuele Ferragina
The STYLE SQUAD @ European Parliament: European Youth Event (EYE) 33
Clémentine Moyart and Jacqueline O'Reilly
Boingboing Beyond Borders: Testimony from the EYE 35
Simon Duncan
Getting involved in politics 38
Edward Badu
Working with the STYLE SQUAD: A Spanish perspective 40
Fermín López
Youth voice at the ballot box and in the economy: Lost or unheard? 44
Mark Smith and Genevieve Shanahan
Music as a platform: Grime cuts through 47
Stuart Hedley
How can trade unions in Europe reconnect with young workers? 49
Kurt Vandaele
Getting your message across: How can a press agency help? 53
Natalie Sarkic-Todd and Irene Marchi
Emerging policy lessons from research on youth attitudes and values 56
Angie Hart, Niall O'Higgins, Martin Seeleib-Kaiser and Endre Sik

Which countries perform best and why? 59

Introduction to comparing country performance 61
Kari Hadjivassiliou
What drives youth unemployment? 68
Kari Hadjivassiliou, Laura Kirchner Sala and Stefan Speckesser
What policies are effective in combatting youth unemployment? 74
Francisco J. Gonzalez Carreras, Laura Kirchner Sala and Stefan Speckesser
Comparing youth transition regimes in Europe 80
Werner Eichhorst, Kari Hadjivassiliou and Florian Wozny
Policy overview of school-to-work transitions 84
Kari Hadjivassiliou
Further reading on comparing school to work transitions in Europe 88

What can we learn about policy innovation? 91

Introduction: What are the barriers to and triggers for policy innovation? 93
Maria Petmesidou and María C. González Menéndez
Policy learning, networks and diffusion of policy ideas 97
Maria Petmesidou and María C. González Menéndez
Gender inequalities in the early labour market experience of young Europeans 100
Gabriella Berloffa, Eleonora Matteazzi, Alina Şandor and Paola Villa
Policy-making and gender mainstreaming 104
Fatoş Gökşen, Alpay Filiztekin, Mark Smith, Çetin Çelik and İbrahim Öker
Ethnicity and gender differences of being employed in the UK: Policy implications 107
Carolina V. Zuccotti and Jacqueline O'Reilly
What works? Exploring a database inventory 109
Kari Hadjivassiliou
Learning from the Dutch case: innovating youth (un)employment policies in Amsterdam, Eindhoven and Tilburg 113
Marc van der Meer, Ruud Muffels and Sonja Bekker
What have we learnt about policy innovation and learning? 116
Maria Petmesidou, María C. González Menéndez and Kari Hadjivassiliou
Further reading on policy innovation, learning and transfer 121

Skills and education mismatch 123

Introduction: Skills and education mismatch 125
Seamus McGuinness
Is there a role for higher education institutions in improving the quality of first employment? 128
Seamus McGuinness, Adele Whelan and Adele Bergin
Are student workers crowding out low-skilled youth? 130
Miroslav Beblavý, Brian Fabo, Lucia Mýtna Kureková and Zuzana Žilinčíková
How different are youth and adult labour market transitions? 133
Vladislav Flek and Martina Mysíková
What are the drivers of overeducation? 136
Seamus McGuinness, Adele Bergin and Adele Whelan
Skills and education mismatch: Policy themes 139
Seamus McGuinness, Lucia Mýtna Kureková and Vladislav Flek
Further reading on skills and education mismatch 143

Migration and mobility 145

Changing patterns of migration in Europe 147
Mehtap Akgüç and Miroslav Beblavý
East2West and North2North: Youth migration and labour market intermediaries in Austria and Norway 149
Christer Hyggen, Renate Ortlieb, Hans Christian Sandlie and Silvana Weiss
Four stories of migration 151
Christer Hyggen, Renate Ortlieb, Hans Christian Sandlie and Silvana Weiss
What happens to young people moving to Germany, Norway and the UK to find work? 155
Janine Leschke, Martin Seeleib-Kaiser and Thees Spreckelsen
How well integrated are young EU migrants in the UK workforce? 159
Thees Spreckelsen and Martin Seeleib-Kaiser
Gender and migrant workers' fragile transitions from education to employment 163
Fatoş Gökşen and İbrahim Öker
Return Migration to CEE after the crisis: Estonia and Slovakia 167
Jaan Masso, Lucia Mýtna Kureková, Maryna Tverdostup and Zuzana Žilinčíková
Emerging policy lessons for youth migration 170
Lucia Mýtna Kureková and Renate Ortlieb
Further reading on youth labour mobility and migration 175

Family matters 177

Introduction: How do families matter in helping young people find work? 179
Tiziana Nazio and András Gábos
Does families' working behaviour affect their children's school-to-work trajectories? 183
Gabriella Berloffa, Eleonora Matteazzi and Alina Şandor
Workless parents, workless children? 187
Gabriella Berloffa, Eleonora Matteazzi and Paola Villa
What a difference a mum makes 191
Mark Smith and Genevieve Shanahan
Is any job better than no job? 194
Marianna Filandri, Tiziana Nazio and Jacqueline O'Reilly
The luck is in the family: Continued financial support after leaving the nest 197
Marianna Filandri and Tiziana Nazio
Leaving and returning to the parental home during the economic crisis 200
Fatoş Gökşen, Deniz Yükseker, Alpay Filiztekin, İbrahim Öker, Fernanda Mazzotta and Lavinia Parisi
When do you start your own family? 204
Elena Mariani and András Gábos
Policy themes on family matters 207
Tiziana Nazio and András Gábos
Further Reading on family matters 212

Flexible working and precariousness 213

Introduction: Balancing flexibility and security for young people during the crisis 215
Raul Eamets, Katrin Humal, Miroslav Beblavý, Ilaria Maselli, Kariappa Bheemaiah, Mark Smith, Mairéad Finn and Janine Leschke
The quality of young Europeans' employment: A dynamic perspective 219
Gabriella Berloffa, Eleonora Matteazzi, Alina Şandor and Paola Villa
Youth school-to-work transitions: From entry jobs to career employment 223
Gabriella Berloffa, Eleonora Matteazzi, Gabriele Mazzolini, Alina Şandor and Paola Villa
How has the recession affected young people's well-being in Europe? 226
Helen Russell, Janine Leschke and Mark Smith
Is self-employment a solution to young people's employment problems? 229
Renate Ortlieb, Maura Sheehan and Jaan Masso
Flexicurity policies to integrate youth before and after the crisis 232
Mark Smith and Paola Villa
The strange non-death of ALMPs 235
Magnus Paulsen Hansen and Janine Leschke
Work please, but poverty no thanks: How to avoid the rise in the working poor? 238
Mark Smith and Genevieve Shanahan
Do young people want Universal Basic Income? 241
Mark Smith and Genevieve Shanahan
'Career opportunities the ones that never knock': Are some employers more 'youth friendly' than others? 244
Jacqueline O'Reilly, Raffaele Grotti and Helen Russell
Further reading on flexible employment and precariousness 249

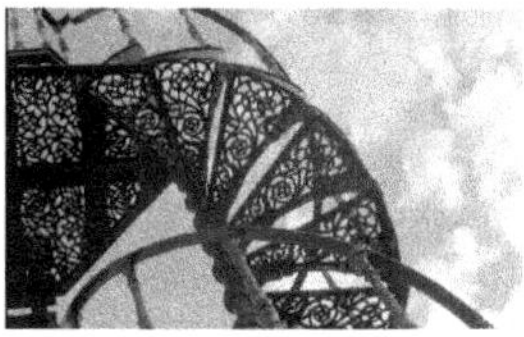

Inspirational music and film 251

Music 253
Film 256

Acknowledgements

The European Union
This book would not have been made possible without the generous investment provided by the European Union's Seventh Framework Programme for research, technological development and demonstration under grant agreement no. 613256. Our project officers at the European Commission, Dr. Georgios Papanagnou and Marc Goffart, provided excellent support on many dimensions throughout the project.

The views expressed here are those of the authors and do not necessarily reflect the official opinions of the European Union. Neither the European Union institutions and bodies nor any person acting on their behalf may be held responsible for the use that may be made of the information contained therein.

The contributions in this book are only a small part of the vast quantity of work produced over the course of the project. An extensive round of Working Papers, Policy Briefs and videos are available on the project website, Strategic Transitions for Youth Labour in Europe (**www.style-research.eu**), via EurActiv, and in contributions to the forthcoming book *Youth Labor In Transition* (New York: Oxford University Press).

The partners
It has been an enormous privilege and pleasure to work with so many intelligent, diligent and good-humoured people on this project from across Europe from 19 countries and 25 research partners, alongside external academic reviewers and policy stakeholders. The editors appreciate the contributors' patience in responding to numerous requests for revisions to their original manuscripts.

Our support team
An enormous thank you to: John Clinton, Francesca Anderson, Chris Matthews, Alison Gray, Rosie Mulgrue, Andrea Mckoy and Prof. Aidan Berry from the University of Brighton Business School, who kept us all on track in the management and completion of the project. Niamh Warde provided outstanding English editing support going well beyond the call of duty. And, Mariette Jackson and Andy Bone added the final creative panache in designing the ebook website and print copy. Thank you very much - you have all made an invaluable contribution to this rich and varied project.

Critical reviewers
The editors and authors would also like to thank the following individuals for participating in STYLE project meetings and providing critically constructive feedback on earlier versions of these contributions that were part of the working papers series:

Brendan Burchell (University of Cambridge, UK), Günther Schmid (Berlin Social Science Center (WZB), Germany), Colette Fagan (University of Manchester, UK), Maria Jepsen (ETUI), Glenda Quintini (OECD: Organisation for Economic Cooperation and Development), Jochen Clasen (Hertie School of Governance, Germany), Mark Stuart (University of Leeds, UK), Bent Greve (University of Roskilde, Denmark), Marge Unt (Coordinator of EXCEPT, Tallinn University, Estonia), Chiara Saraceno (Collegio Carlo Alberto, Italy), Paweł Kaczmarczyk (Centre of Migration Research at the University of Warsaw), Jan Brzozowski (Krakow University of Economics, Poland), Claire Wallace (University of Aberdeen, UK), Traute Meyer (University of Southampton, UK), Nigel Meager (IES, UK), Marc Cowling (University of Brighton, UK), Eskil Wadensjö (SOFI, Stockholm University, Sweden), Ute Klammer (University of Duisburg-Essen), Jale Tosun (Coordinator of CUPESSE, University of Heidelberg, Germany), Katarina Lindahl (European Commission, DG EMPLOY), Thomas Biegert (Berlin Social Science Center (WZB), Germany), Zeynep Cemalcilar (Koç University, Turkey), Torild Hammer (Norwegian Social Research, Norway), Agata Patecka (SOLIDAR, Belgium) Ramón Peña-Casas (OSE European Social Observatory, Belgium), Karen Roiy (Business Europe) and Giorgio Zecca (European Youth Forum).

We are also grateful for the further comments on earlier drafts provided remotely by: Jose Luis Arco-Tirado (University of Granada, Spain), Jason Heyes (University of Sheffield, UK), Anne Horvath (European Commission), Maria Iacovou (University of Cambridge, UK), Russell King (University of Sussex, UK), Bernhard Kittel (University of Vienna, Austria), Martin Lukes (University of Economics, Prague, Czech Republic), William Maloney (Newcastle University, UK), Emily Rainsford (Newcastle University, UK), Bettina Schuck (University of Heidelberg, Germany), Peter Sloane (Swansea University, UK), Nadia Steiber (University of Vienna, Austria), Robert Strohmeyer (University of Mannheim, Germany), Mihaela Vancea (Pompeu Fabra University, Spain), Jonas Felbo-Kolding (University of Copenhagen, Denmark), Mihails Hazans (University of Latvia, Latvia), Felix Hörisch (University of Heidelberg, Germany), Øystein Takle Lindholm (Oslo and Akershus University College of Applied Sciences, Norway), Magnus Paulsen Hansen (Copenhagen Business School), Tiiu Paas and Andres Võrk (University of Tartu, Estonia), and the Q-Step Team (University of Kent, UK).

International meetings

Earlier versions of these contributions were written as project deliverables and working papers, and they were presented and discussed at project meetings kindly hosted by the following partner organizations: CROME, University of Brighton (UK), Koç University (Turkey), Grenoble École de Management (France), Institute for Employment Studies (UK), Copenhagen Business School (Denmark), University of Turin (Italy), and the Krakow University of Economics (Poland). Thank you for all the work you put in to making these events so convivial for some very serious discussions.

Some of these contributions have been presented at numerous international conferences including: the International Sociological Association in Yokohama, 2014; a mini-conference at the Society for the Advancement of Socio-Economics held at the London

School of Economics, July 2015, in conjunction with the EU funded cupesse.eu project; a special session at the Council for European Studies meeting in Philadelphia with the former EU Commissioner László Andor, 2016, and held in conjunction with the EU funded negotiate-research.eu and Livewhat projects; a special session at the Work, Employment and Society conference at the University of Leeds, 2016, held in conjunction with the EU funded except-project.eu and cupesse.eu; and a special stream at the European Social Policy Association conference (ESPAnet) at the Erasmus University, Rotterdam, 2016, held in conjunction with the EU funded negotiate-research.eu.

Local Advisory Boards

In addition to this expert academic advice, authors also benefited from discussing their early findings with Local Advisory Boards across Europe; these boards were composed of a number of NGOs, charities, public policy-makers and trade union and employers' organizations. In particular we are grateful for the regular participation and discussions with Christine Lewis (UNISON), Katerina Rudiger (CIPD), Edward Badu (North London Citizens, UK), Menno Bart and Even Hagelien (EUROCIETT), Alvin Carpio (Young Fabians, UK), Abi Levitt and Ronan McDonald (Tomorrow's People, UK), Liina Eamets (Estonian Agricultural Registers and Information Board), Tomáš Janotík and Mária Mišečková, (Profesia, Slovakia), Aime Lauk (Statistics Estonia), Anne Lauringson and Mari Väli (Estonian Unemployment Insurance Fund), Martin Mýtny (Oracle, Slovakia), Tony Mernagh (Brighton and Hove Economic Partnership). Supporting this communications platform, Natalie Sarkic-Todd and Irene Marchi have been wonderful partners in helping promote the results of this research through EurActiv. We thank you all very much for your participation in this project, it has really enriched our discussions.

Style babies

Last but not least the fecundity of our research team was evidenced not only in their numerous publications, but also in the arrival of eleven babies born to researchers on this project (2013-17): a vibrant testament to the youthfulness of our researchers, and their ability to combine academic careers with making transitions to having families of one, two, and, in some cases, three children.

We hope that some of the findings from this research will be of benefit to young people making their way through the challenging transitions from youth to adulthood in Europe and further afield.

This has been an enormously rewarding project, and we feel very privileged to have had the opportunities to contribute some of our energy to understanding and explaining the problems that need to be addressed concerning youth employment.

Jacqueline O'Reilly, **Clémentine Moyart**, **Tiziana Nazio** and **Mark Smith**
Brighton, Brussels, Turin and Grenoble, August 2017

Authors

Adele Bergin, Economic and Social Research Institute, Ireland

Adele Whelan, Economic and Social Research Institute, Ireland

Alessandro Arrigoni, University of Oxford, UK

Alina Şandor, University of Trento, Italy

Alpay Filiztekin, Ozyegin University, Turkey

Amy, associated with Boingboing.org.uk, Brighton, UK

András Gábos, TARKI Social Research Institute, Hungary

Angie Hart, University of Brighton, UK

Brian Fabo, Centre for European Policy Studies, Belgium

Carolina V. Zuccotti, University of Brighton, UK

Çetin Çelik, Koç University Social Policy Center, Turkey

Chloe, associated with Boingboing.org.uk, Brighton

Christer Hyggen, NOVA, Norway

Claire Stubbs, University of Brighton, UK

Clémentine Moyart, European Youth Forum, Belgium

Deniz Yükseker, Koç University Social Policy Center, Turkey

Edward Badu, Executive Council, Citizens, UK

Elena Mariani, PhD student, LSE, UK

Eleonora Matteazzi, University of Trento, Italy

Elias Kourkoutas, University of Crete, Greece

Emanuele Ferragina, Sciences Politiques, Paris, France

Emma Feasey, Young Women's Trust, UK

Emma Mckay, Young Women's Trust, UK

Endre Sik, TARKI Social Research Institute, Hungary

Fatoş Gökşen, Koç University Social Policy Center, Turkey

Fermín López, University of Oviedo, Spain

Fernanda Mazzotta, University of Salerno, Italy

Florian Wozny, IZA, Germany

Francisco J. Gonzalez Carreras, Institute for Employment Studies, UK

Gábor Hajdu, TARKI Social Research Institute, Hungary

Gabriele Mazzolini, University of Trento, Italy

Gabriella Berloffa, University of Trento, Italy

Genevieve Shanahan, Grenoble École de Management, France

Hans Christian Sandlie, NOVA, Norway

Helen Russell, Economic and Social Research Institute, Ireland

İbrahim Öker, Koç University Social Policy Center, Turkey

Ilaria Maselli, Centre for European Policy Studies, Belgium

Irene Marchi, EurActiv, Belgium

Jaan Maaso, University of Tartu, Estonia

Jacqueline O'Reilly, Sussex Business School, UK

Janine Leschke, Copenhagen Business School, Denmark

Jaymi, associated with Boingboing.org.uk, Brighton

Kari Hadjivassiliou, Institute for Employment Studies, UK

Kariappa Bheemaiah, Grenoble École de Management, France

Katarina, associated with Boingboing.org.uk, Brighton

Katrin Humal, University of Tartu, Estonia

Katy, associated with Boingboing.org.uk, Brighton

Kurt Vandaele, European Trade Union Institute, Belgium

Laura Kirchner Sala, Institute for Employment Studies, UK

Laura, associated with Boingboing.org.uk, Brighton

Lavinia Parisi, University of Salerno, Italy

Lefteris, associated with Boingboing.org.uk, Brighton

Lorna, associated with Boingboing.org.uk, Brighton

Lucia Mýtna Kureková, Slovak Governance Institute, Slovakia

Magnus Paulsen Hansen, Copenhagen Business School, Denmark

Mairéad Finn, Trinity College Dublin, Ireland

Marc van der Meer, University of Tilburg, the Netherlands

Marco Stimolo, University of Salerno, Italy

María C. González Menéndez, University of Oviedo, Spain

Maria Georgiadi, University of Crete, Greece

Maria Petmesidou, Democritus University of Thrace, Greece

Marianna Filandri, University of Turin, Italy

Mark Smith, Grenoble École de Management, France

Martin Seeleib-Kaiser, University of Tübingen, Germany

Martina Mysíková, Metropolitan University of Prague, Czech Republic

Maryna Tverdostup, University of Tartu, Estonia

Matt, associated with Boingboing.org.uk, Brighton

Maura Sheehan, Napier University, Scotland

Mehtap Akgüç, Centre for European Policy Studies, Belgium

Miroslav Beblavý, Centre for European Policy Studies, Belgium

Natalie Sarkic-Todd, EurActiv, Belgium

Niall O'Higgins, University of Salerno, Italy, & International Labour Office, Switzerland

Paola Villa, University of Trento, Italy

Raija, associated with Boingboing.org.uk, Brighton

Raffaele Grotti, ESRI, Dublin, Ireland

Raul Eamets, University of Tartu, Estonia

Renate Ortlieb, University of Graz, Austria

Rosa, associated with Boingboing.org.uk, Brighton

Ross, associated with Boingboing.org.uk, Brighton

Ruud Muffels, University of Tilburg, the Netherlands

Sam, associated with Boingboing.org.uk, Brighton

Seamus McGuinness, Economic and Social Research Institute, Ireland

Sharon Dodua Otoo, Black British Mother, Activist, Author & Editor, Berlin, Germany

Silvana Weiss, University of Graz, Austria

Simon Duncan, Project worker for Boingboing.org.uk, Brighton

Sitara, associated with Boingboing.org.uk, Brighton

Sonja Bekker, University of Tilburg, the Netherlands

Stefan Speckesser, Institute for Employment Studies, UK

Stefanos Plexousakis, University of Crete, Greece

Stuart Hedley, DJ, UK

Sunneka, associated with Boingboing.org.uk, Brighton

Tiziana Nazio, Dept. of Culture, Politics and Society, University of Turin and Collegio Carlo Alberto, Italy

Vladislav Flek, Metropolitan University of Prague, Czech Republic

Werner Eichhorst, IZA, Germany

Zuzana Žilinčíková, Slovak Governance Institute, Slovakia

Researcher profiles are available on the project website:

www.style-research.eu/researchers-a-to-z

Acronyms

ALMP Active Labour Market Policy

BHPS British Household Panel Survey

CCI Cultural and Creative Industry

CEE Central and Eastern Europe

CSRs Country Specific Recommendations

CVET Continuous Vocational Education and Training

DG Directorate General

DG ECFIN Directorate General for Economic and Financial Affairs

DG EMPL Directorate General for Employment, Social Affairs & Inclusion

EC European Commission

ECB European Central Bank

EES European Employment Strategy

EFTA European Free Trade Association

EMCO European Commission Employment Committee

EPL Employment Protection Legislation

EPL-P Employment Protection Legislation – permanent/regular contracts

EPL-T Employment Protection Legislation – temporary contracts

EPSCO European Employment, Social Policy, Health and Consumer Affairs Council

ESF European Social Fund

ESL Early School Leaving

ESS European Social Survey

EST Employment Status Trajectories

ETUC European Trade Union Confederation

EU European Union

EU-LFS European Union Labour Force Survey

Eurostat Statistical Office of the European Union

EURES European Employment Services

Eurofound European Foundation for the Improvement of Living and Working Conditions

EU-SILC European Union Survey on Income and Living Conditions

EU2 2007 accession countries to the EU: Bulgaria and Romania

EU8 2004 accession countries to the EU: Czech Republic, Estonia, Hungary, Latvia, Lithuania, Poland, Slovakia, and Slovenia

EU28 European Union 28 countries

EVS European Values Study

EWCS European Working Conditions Survey

FTE Full-Time Equivalent

GDP Gross Domestic Product

HAPC Hierarchical Age-Period-Cohort (regression model)

ICT Information/Communication Technologies Sector

ILO International Labour Organisation

ISCED International Standard Classification of Education

ISCO International Standard Classification of Occupations

ISEI International Socio-Economic Index of Occupational Status

KM Kaplan-Meier (estimator)

LABREF Labour Market Reforms Database

LFS Labor Force Survey

LIFO last-in first-out

LLL Life-Long Learning

LMI labor market intermediary

LMP Labour Market Policies

MISSOC Mutual Information System on Social Protection

NACE Statistical Classification of Economic Activities

NCDS National Child Development Study

NEET Not in Employment, Education or Training

NGO Non-Governmental Organization

NRP National Reform Program

OECD Organisation for Economic Co-operation and Development

OLM Occupational Labor Markets

OM Optimal Matching

OMC Open Method of Coordination

ONS-LS Office for National Statistics Longitudinal Study

PES Public Employment Services

PIAAC Programme for the International Assessment of Adult Competencies

PLMPs Passive Labour Market Policies

PPS Purchasing Power Standards

R&D Research and Development

SES Structure of Earnings Survey

SMEs Small and Medium-Sized Enterprises

STW School to Work

STYLE Strategic Transitions for Youth Labour in Europe (FP7 project)

TAW Temporary Agency Work

TCN Third-Country National

TLM transitional labor market

UK-LFS UK Quarterly Labour Force Survey

VE Vocational Education

VET Vocational Education and Training

VoC Varieties of Capitalism

WVS World Values Survey

YEI Youth Employment Initiative

YG Youth Guarantee

Country abbreviations

AT Austria

BE Belgium

BG Bulgaria

CH Switzerland

CY Cyprus

CZ Czech Republic

DE Germany

DK Denmark

EE Estonia

EL Greece

ES Spain

FI Finland

FR France

HR Croatia

HU Hungary

IE Ireland

IS Iceland

IT Italy

LT Lithuania

LU Luxembourg

LV Latvia

MK Macedonia

MT Malta

NL Netherlands

NO Norway

PL Poland

PT Portugal

RO Romania

SE Sweden

SI Slovenia

SK Slovakia

TR Turkey

UK United Kingdom

US United States

Endorsements

"The inter-European discourse on policies that work, or do not work, regarding youth unemployment is not yet well developed. Most of the analytical work is one-dimensional in terms of disciplines or approaches. The European policy discourse, if any, is dominated by mainstream economics, which sees the youth unemployment problem only either in macroeconomic failures (EU-fiscal crisis) or in wage distortions unfavourable to youth (e.g. minimum wage, insider-outsider cleavages). This book is quite different and therefore a must read: It will stimulate mutual learning both in terms of policy exchanges as well as interdisciplinary fertilization."

Prof Günther Schmid, Professor Emeritus Free University Berlin, and Director Emeritus of the Research Unit "Labor Market Policy and Employment", Berlin Social Science Center (WZB)

"Presented in a rigorous yet easily accessible form, written for busy people, this book is essential reading for policy makers and researchers. Statistical analyses of large datasets are skilfully interwoven with detailed analyses of European institutions and descriptions of individuals' lives – sometimes harrowing, sometimes uplifting. It is the clearest guide yet as to how the last 10 years have affected young peoples' transitions into adult life and work."

Dr Brendan Burchell, Reader at the Faculty of Human, Social, and Political Science at the University of Cambridge and a fellow of Magdalene College, Cambridge.

"It is an anthology of contemporary youth experiences and provides imaginative ways of telling about young people's worlds in contemporary Europe."

Prof Claire Wallace, University of Aberdeen and former President of the European Sociological Association

"This volume offers great discoveries for a very broad audience as it summarizes conceptually rich and methodologically rigorous analysis of causes of youth unemployment in an accessible format. It represents collaborative research at its very best."

Prof Marge Unt, Coordinator of EXCEPT (except-project.eu), Head of Institute of International Social Studies, Tallinn University

"Extremely wide-ranging in scope and yet detailed in analysis and evaluation this book offers plenty of lessons for policy makers and anyone else interested in improving employment opportunities for young people in Europe today."

Prof Jochen Clasen, Professor of Comparative Social Policy, University of Edinburgh

Introduction

Strategic Transitions for Youth Labour in Europe

Jacqueline O'Reilly, **Mark Smith**,
Tiziana Nazio and **Clémentine Moyart**

Introduction

Youth transitions to employment and economic independence have become increasingly protracted and precarious. Following the Great Recession of 2008 youth unemployment rates soared, although the effects varied significantly across Europe. In countries hit hardest by the recession, young people have faced some of the largest obstacles in finding stable employment, or any kind of employment. But even in countries with a better performance record of getting young people into work, there were still significant pockets of youth, categorised as not in employment, education or training (NEETs), who struggled to make successful and sustainable transitions into employment. This was not altogether a new feature of European labour markets, but the Great Recession exacerbated problems, and in some case reversed previous successes.

Five distinctive characteristics of the recent period of youth unemployment

There are some distinctive characteristics of the current phase of youth unemployment relating to the consequences of increased labour market flexibility, skills mismatch, new patterns of migration and family legacies, as well as an increasing role for EU policy (O'Reilly et al. 2015).

First, the expansion of labour market flexibility through the liberalisation of temporary work, new forms of zero hour contracts and self-employment have made it increasingly difficult for young people to secure a stable foothold in good quality employment.

Second, the reduction in early school leaving and the expansion of higher education have made European youth more qualified than they were in previous decades. However, debates about skills and qualification mismatches illustrate how the expansion of education has been poorly aligned to the changing structure of skills required by employers.

Third, young people are more mobile and more likely to migrate to find work within the EU than in previous recessions. While this may result in reducing unemployment rates in their home countries, there are concerns about the effects of 'brain drain' on the domestic labour market. Further, relatively little attention has been given to what happens to those who return home: do they experience a bonus from having worked abroad, or is it more difficult for them to reintegrate?

Fourth, our research indicates the importance of taking account of the influence of families on contemporary youth transitions. The legacy of parental work histories, their social background and resources impact on the type of transitions their children make. Evidence suggests that these legacies are associated with new forms of polarisation for younger generations.

And, fifth, policy-making has seen a growing influence from EU institutions expanding their role in promoting and investing in policies to support national and regional initiatives, and in encouraging a greater degree of learning and policy transfer to address these problems.

The STYLE project

Against this background the EU funded STYLE project set out to examine how strategic transitions for youth labour in Europe have been taking shape in the shadow of the Great Recession. The STYLE project examined the obstacles and opportunities affecting youth employment in Europe.

This involved 25 research partners, an international advisory network and local advisory boards of employers, unions, policy-makers and Non-Governmental Organisations from 19 European countries. The aim of the project was to provide a comprehensive understanding of the causes of very high unemployment among young people and to assess the effectiveness of labour market policies designed to mitigate this phenomenon. The contributions to this volume are intended to provide an accessible summary covering the breadth of research conducted in the project.

The structure of the book

The book includes over 90 authors and more than 60 individual contributions. These contributions are a mixture of summaries from the research working papers, along with individual contributions from a number of young stakeholders who have been involved in different ways with the project. The chapters here have been organised into eight key sections.

Young people's attitudes and values

The first part of the book is a deliberately eclectic range of contributions reflecting a spectrum of voices included in the project at different stages. This has sixteen contributions from young authors, DJs, community activists, journalists, and charity and social enterprise workers, alongside academic researchers.

Policy debates are often discussed as something that happens to 'others', while the voice of those 'others' is rarely heard. This section of the book seeks to redress this imbalance. These contributions focus on how young people's attitudes and values are expressed and interpreted.

The key messages coming out of these contributions illustrate that regardless of different backgrounds and age, young people still value the importance of work as part of their life. However, finding jobs that are rewarding and satisfying is not always easy, especially for those who are less advantaged or are living in countries where youth unemployment is very high. Even under these challenging conditions, with appropriate support they have a valuable contribution to make. Hart et al. (2017) argue that: *'Policy-makers and practitioners should take note that tackling youth unemployment from a resilience-based approach, which takes into consideration all aspects of the young person's life, can increase the likelihood of change. Such an approach also emphasises the importance of working at an individual and social level to tackle youth unemployment.'*

Which countries perform best and why?
Greater attention is given to the wider social level when comparing differences in country performance in the second part of this book. Why do countries have such different levels of performance and what helps reduce youth unemployment?

Contributors show how using different measures of youth unemployment rates, ratios or NEET rates highlight specific policy problems requiring different policy instruments (O'Reilly et al. 2015; O'Reilly et al. *forthcoming*). There have been significant achievements in preventing early school dropouts and increasing the number of young people in higher education, but country differences persist (Hadjivassiliou 2017).

Countries with lower rates of youth unemployment have more stable and well-integrated vocational education and apprenticeships supporting smoother School-to-Work (STW) transitions. Policy-makers have sought to improve these opportunities across Europe as an attractive alternative to general upper-secondary and tertiary education. But they often face the problem that they are seen as of lower status, or employers have limited interest in providing these in significant numbers (Grotti et al. *forthcoming*).

All EU countries have sought to reform their vocational and higher education systems. In many cases this has also been stimulated by EU policies like the Youth Guarantee (Hadjivassiliou et al. *forthcoming*). However, the success of these reforms is still largely influenced by institutional patterns of governance, a topic that is taken up in the third section of the book.

What can we learn about policy innovation?
The contributors to this section point to the relative lack of research on the barriers and triggers for policy learning and transfer to address the problems young people face. These obstacles and facilitators exist at the local, regional, national and supranational level. Understanding how governance mechanisms affect knowledge, learning and transfer is essential to making a significant change to traditional practices, especially where they have not been successful. It also allows us to identify how local and regional networks of policy actors, are, 'despite all odds', developing innovative programmes.

The researchers find that there is a lot of exchange of information between policy-makers at different levels, with identifiable 'policy entrepreneurs' promoting learning and transfer. They distinguish between countries that facilitate innovation and a diffusion of ideas at different levels, especially at the local and regional level, and those exhibiting considerable inertia (Petmesidou, González Menéndez and Hadjivassiliou 2017). These authors argue that *'EU level strategies, such as the Youth Guarantee and the European Alliance for Apprenticeships, recently opened up windows of opportunity for policy entrepreneurs.'*

The Dutch case presents various examples of innovation where a 'multiple helix' governance structure in different regions addresses issues of skills bottlenecks in regional labour markets. Van der Meer et al. (2017) argue that this *'innovative approach represents a shift from the classical modality of governance—which is project-oriented, subsidy-based, and coupled to financial incentives—to a network-based collaborative and more proactive and preventive approach that is conducive to innovative practices.'*

However, the low level of business sector engagement and the structure of micro-firms for example in Spain or Greece mean that some organisations have less capacity to access financial support for training and see this as too costly an activity (Petmesidou and González Menéndez 2016).

The polarisation of the employment structure with a decline of 'middle-rung jobs' and a splintering of pathways between those in professional, technical and managerial jobs alongside those in more elementary jobs such as construction, market sales and tourism, have left a significant gap in the labour market (Grotti et al. *forthcoming*). This is a trend observed across a number of highly developed economies. However, it is a trend exacerbated by the consequences of the recent economic crisis and has helped drive investment in higher education, a topic that is taken up in the fourth section of the book.

Skills and education mismatch

Educational reforms aimed at addressing low levels of educational attainment in the past have seen an increase in student participation rates. However, these changes can also create new sets of problems in terms of how educational and structural reforms are synchronised to absorb this better educated labour force. McGuinness et al. (*forthcoming*) argue that overeducation can be a result of an over supply of graduates relative to the capacity of the economy to absorb them; it can be an imbalance in educational attainment and the skills required by employers; or it can be due to asymmetric information or variations in individual preferences. This requires greater attention being given to understanding how an increase in the supply of qualified labour can be absorbed by future employer demand.

The contributions in this section underline how educational attainment remains key to determining many life chances. Educational choices are central to the nature, duration and quality of the school-to-work transitions. The authors concentrate on higher educational attainment, which is a key factor in increasing the likelihood of moving from unemployment into employment but also carries the risk of mismatch between qualifications and skills required in the job.

Across many EU states the expansion of higher or third-level education creates the potential risk of mismatch and over-education. Indeed over-education rates appear to be converging upwards overtime, although there is no overall increase and country differences persist (McGuinness et al. *forthcoming*). Trends in over-education have followed a cyclical pattern during the great recession reflecting the decline in available job opportunities in a downturn.

One of the unintended consequences of the increase in higher education participation has been an increase in working students. To work while studying may be a necessity for students from more modest backgrounds. But it also provides employers with a higher educated workforce. However, concerns that such working students may crowd out less-educated workers seeking regular work seem to be unfounded. Overall, Beblavý et al. (2017) find that working during their studies can be beneficial in providing young people with some initial exposure and work experience. While McGuinness et al. (*forthcoming*) find that the intervention of private employment agencies can increase risks of mismatch.

The research suggests that mismatch can be avoided where students have higher vocational components to their programmes, more project-based work and placements. However, national specificities in patterns of mismatch and over-education mean that policy makers should pay attention to one-size-fits-all policy measures. A key policy recommendation from the research findings discussed here point to the need for policies that promote greater links between employers and educational institutions as well as investment in career support services in universities and similar institutions (McGuinness et al. *forthcoming*).

Migration and mobility

Labour mobility has been a central tenet of the European project, and the recent period of youth unemployment has seen increased levels of youth migration. For young people these opportunities for mobility expand horizons for both education and employment. The contributions to this section of the book underline how expansion of the Union towards the east and the impact of the Great Recession shaped both the flows and available opportunities for young people.

While much is written about the migration into the EU, intra-EU mobility represents a non-negligible trend and one which shifts over time as old destinations, for example France as a traditional destination for young Spaniards have been complemented by young people moving to the UK, Germany and Ireland (Akgüç and Beblavý 2017).

Young migrants are characterised by being overqualified as they face challenges in terms of integration and recognition of their qualifications. However they are also a heterogeneous group as the "four stories" presented by Hyggen et al. illustrate. The research presented here tends to show that intra-EU youth migrants from northern and Western EU states are better integrated than those from the south and east (Leschke et al. 2017). The mixed experiences of migrants are also underlined by the interaction of migrant status and gender, reinforcing disadvantages that some young women face.

The policy conclusions of the contributions in this section point to the need for wider implementation of measures and tools to help avoid discrimination and promote integration (Mýtna Kureková and Ortlieb 2017). This includes greater use of gender mainstreaming and qualification recognition across borders and a role of labour market intermediaries in facilitating pan-European migration of young people.

Family matters

Family legacies remain a strong predictor of success on the labour market, the type of educational opportunities available and the probabilities of avoiding the worst of the consequences of the Great Recession. Family resources can provide protection for young people and also create divisions and polarisation between households and amongst different groups of young people.

Family support takes the form of advice, guidance and aspiration-building as well as resources to support risky transitions. The research here finds that working and worklessness are transmitted between generations. Young people growing up in working households fair better than those coming from workless households in avoiding unemployment or inactivity (Berloffa et al. 2017a; Zuccotti and O'Reilly *forthcoming*). Further, working brothers and sisters also help expand networks of working peers and opportunities for work (Filandri et al. *forthcoming*). In line with other contributions to this volume, the research presented in this section underlines the importance of gender differences, and how working mothers transmit important values in terms of attachment to the labour market especially for their daughters (Smith and Shanahan 2017a).

Yet social divisions and inter-family differences reinforce divisions for the next generation (Mariani and Gábos 2017; Filandri and Nazio 2017; Filandri et al. *forthcoming*). This intergenerational transmission of inequality has been the subject of previous research and while the contributions here underline these inequalities (for example in relation to access to higher education) they also point to the supportive role that families play in terms of coping with the impact of the Great Recession. For example, families provide a home in which to delay the transition to an independent household, or even to return to in times of crisis (Gökşen et al. 2017).

The long-term implications of these family legacies mean that policies are required to avoid the transmission of disadvantages between generations while permitting the on-going transmission of support and work-orientated values. Such policies need, therefore, to concentrate on those households without the resources to provide the support in terms of values, aspirations, advice and security for insecure transitions. The benefits of more gender-equal opportunities on the labour market also offer the possibility of addressing inter-family inequalities (Nazio and Gábos 2017).

Flexible working and precariousness

Young people are particularly at risk of the negative consequences of flexible working and precariousness on the labour market. As new entrants to the labour market, young people are frequently in a position of "outsiders". With limited employment histories they may be excluded from certain forms of income security measures for those without work. As a result young people are often caught in the tension between measures to promote flexibility and security, as they experience increasing insecurity on the labour market. Also, recent measures to increase flexibility have had a disproportionate impact upon the young.

The shifting patterns of participation on the labour market and the plethora of new forms of employment contracts in the shape of zero hour contracts or bogus self-employment mean that traditional dichotomous measures of being in work or without work are being questioned (Eamets et al. 2017). The conditions associated with youth self-employment, in terms of lower income and longer working hours, tend to be inferior to those in dependent employment, and for the young entrepreneurs, or those in ambiguous 'self-employment' contracts these are major challenges to the regulation of work and benefits.

Indeed the rise of precarious transitions calls for new measures that take into account young people's trajectories over time. It is not just the entry into work that is important but the need to capture the precariousness of this work that may extend into early careers, up to five years or more after leaving education (Berloffa et al. 2017b). Further, our analysis goes beyond the legal regulation of precarious employment to take account of experiences of subjective insecurity and its negative consequences on young people's wellbeing.

Both old and new measures of precariousness underline how gender gaps open up early in working careers and that young women and different ethnic groups are often at a disadvantage; although the nature of this disadvantage varies both by gender and ethnicity (Zuccotti and O'Reilly *forthcoming*). Gender gaps in unemployment rates appear to be closing, but this is largely due to young men experiencing higher rates of unemployment; young women are more prone to being NEETs and are more likely to be at a disadvantage in achieving employment-secure and income-secure trajectories during the school-to-work transition (Berloffa et al. 2017b).

The analysis of policies over the period before, during and after the Great Recession underlines how the plight of young people was largely ignored until the full force of the crisis had materialised into high youth unemployment rates (Smith and Villa 2017). Overall, policies have tended to follow trends of wider priorities rather than being well adapted to the needs of young people. It is therefore important to have a considered reflection on how new policies that promote self-employment (Ortlieb et al. 2017), or how Active Labour Market Policies (Hansen and Leschke 2017) and those that propose a universal basic income (Smith and Shanahan 2017b) will affect youth trajectories in the future in relation to the qualifications young people are obtaining and the types of employment they can secure.

Inspirational music and film

Finally, the last section of the book closes with a small selection of some inspirational music and films that capture youth transitions to employment and adulthood. These are tunes we have listened to, or referred to, as we have been conducting the research for this book. Some of these hark back to the 1980s and earlier, when some of us we were in our youth; some of these are much more recent reflecting the perennial problems facing young people in their transitions to adulthood. Some of these songs and films deal with very serious issues related to youth homelessness, crime, early pregnancy, prejudice and failed aspirations, alongside more light-hearted comic reflections on the challenges young people face and how they overcome them.

The final word

The idea to present our research here in this format was inspired by the Compas Anthology on Migration (**http://compasanthology.co.uk**). We hope, like the authors of that anthology, that this format will allow our work to reach a broader audience of readers who may come to it for different reasons and go away with some unexpected discoveries. For those interested in following up in more detail, many of the summary findings presented here can be read in full as working papers available on the project website (**www.style-research.eu/publications/working-papers**) and as chapters in the forthcoming book *Youth Labor in Transition* (Oxford University Press: New York).

Finally, through these multi-media platforms we will have met the European Commission's expected impact from the project: first, to advance the knowledge base that underpins the formulation and implementation of relevant policies in Europe with the aim of enhancing the employment of young people and their transition to economic and social independence. And, second, of equal importance, to have engaged with relevant communities, stakeholders and practitioners in the research with a view to supporting employment policies in Europe that impact upon the lives of young Europeans.

References

Akgüç, Mehtap, and Miroslav Beblavý. 2017. 'Changing patterns of migration in Europe' In *Youth Employment*, edited by Jacqueline O'Reilly, Clémentine Moyart, Tiziana Nazio and Mark Smith. Brighton: CROME.

Beblavý, Miroslav, Brian Fabo, Lucia Mýtna Kureková and Zuzana Žilinčíková. 2017. 'Are student workers crowding out low-skilled youth? In *Youth Employment*, edited by Jacqueline O'Reilly, Clémentine Moyart, Tiziana Nazio and Mark Smith. Brighton: CROME.

Berloffa, Gabriella, Eleonora Matteazzi and Paola Villa. 2017a. 'Workless partents, workless children?' In *Youth Employment*, edited by Jacqueline O'Reilly, Clémentine Moyart, Tiziana Nazio and Mark Smith. Brighton: CROME.

Berloffa, Gabriella, Eleonora Matteazzi, Alina Şandor and Paola Villa. 2017b. 'The quality of young Europeans' employment: A dynamic perspective' In *Youth Employment*, edited by Jacqueline O'Reilly, Clémentine Moyart, Tiziana Nazio and Mark Smith. Brighton: CROME.

Eamets, Raul, Katrin Humal, Miroslav Beblavý, Ilaria Maselli, Kariappa Bheemaiah, Mark Smith, Mairéad Finn and Janine Leschke. 2017. 'Introduction: Balancing flexibility and security for young people during the crisis' In *Youth Employment*, edited by Jacqueline O'Reilly, Clémentine Moyart, Tiziana Nazio and Mark Smith. Brighton: CROME.

Filandri, Marianna, and Tiziana Nazio. 2017. 'The luck is in the family: Continued financial support after leaving the nest.' In *Youth Employment*, edited by Jacqueline O'Reilly, Clémentine Moyart, Tiziana Nazio and Mark Smith. Brighton: CROME.

Filandri, Marianna, Tiziana Nazio and Jacqueline O'Reilly. *Forthcoming*. 'Youth Transitions and Job Quality: How Long Should They Wait and What Difference Does the Family Make?' In *Youth Labor in Transition*, edited by Jacqueline O'Reilly, Janine Leschke, Renate Ortlieb, Martin Seeleib-Kaiser, and Paola Villa. New York: Oxford University Press.

Gökşen, Fatoş, Deniz Yükseker, Alpay Filiztekin, İbrahim Öker, Sinem Kuz, Fernanda Mazzotta and Lavinia Parisi. 2017. 'Leaving and returning to the parental home during the economic crisis' In *Youth Employment*, edited by Jacqueline O'Reilly, Clémentine Moyart, Tiziana Nazio and Mark Smith. Brighton: CROME.

Grotti, Raffaele, Helen Russell and Jacqueline O'Reilly. *Forthcoming*. 'Where Do Young People Work?' In *Youth Labor in Transition*, edited by Jacqueline O'Reilly, Janine Leschke, Renate Ortlieb, Martin Seeleib-Kaiser and Paola Villa. New York: Oxford University Press.

Hadjivassiliou, Kari P. 2017. 'Introduction to comparing country performance' In *Youth Employment*, edited by Jacqueline O'Reilly, Clémentine Moyart, Tiziana Nazio and Mark Smith. Brighton: CROME.

Hadjivassiliou, Kari P., Arianna Tassinari, Werner Eichhorst and Florian Wozny. *Forthcoming*. 'How does the performance of school-to-work transition regimes in the European Union vary?' In *Youth Labor in Transition*, edited by Jacqueline O'Reilly, Janine Leschke, Renate Ortlieb, Martin Seeleib-Kaiser and Paola Villa. New York: Oxford University Press.

Hansen, Magnus Paulsen, and Janine Leschke. 2017. 'The strange non-death of ALMPs' In *Youth Employment*, edited by Jacqueline O'Reilly, Clémentine Moyart, Tiziana Nazio and Mark Smith. Brighton: CROME.

Hart, Angie, Niall O'Higgins, Martin Seeleib-Kaiser and Endre Sik. 2017. 'Emerging policy lessons from research on youth attitudes and values' In *Youth Employment*, edited by Jacqueline O'Reilly, Clémentine Moyart, Tiziana Nazio and Mark Smith. Brighton: CROME.

Leschke, Janine, Martin Seeleib-Kaiser and Thees Spreckelsen. 2017. 'What happens to young people moving to Germany, Norway and the UK to find work?' In *Youth Employment*, edited by Jacqueline O'Reilly, Clémentine Moyart, Tiziana Nazio and Mark Smith. Brighton: CROME.

Mariani, Elena, and András Gábos. 2017. 'When do you start your own family?' In *Youth Employment*, edited by Jacqueline O'Reilly, Clémentine Moyart, Tiziana Nazio and Mark Smith. Brighton: CROME.

McGuinness, Seamus, Adele Bergin and Adele Whelan. *Forthcoming*. 'Overeducation in Europe: Is there Scope for a Common Policy Approach?' In *Youth Labor in Transition*, edited by Jacqueline O'Reilly, Janine Leschke, Renate Ortlieb, Martin Seeleib-Kaiser and Paola Villa. New York: Oxford University Press.

Mýtna Kureková, Lucia and Renate Ortlieb. 2017. Emerging policy lessons for youth migration' In *Youth Employment*, edited by Jacqueline O'Reilly, Clémentine Moyart, Tiziana Nazio and Mark Smith. Brighton: CROME.

Nazio, Tiziana, and András Gábos. 2017. Policy themes on family matters' In *Youth Employment*, edited by Jacqueline O'Reilly, Clémentine Moyart, Tiziana Nazio and Mark Smith. Brighton: CROME.

O'Reilly, Jacqueline, Janine Leschke, Renate Ortlieb, Martin Seeleib-Kaiser and Paola Villa. *Forthcoming*. 'Comparing the Problems of Youth Labor Market Transitions in Europe: Joblessness, insecurity, institutions, and inequality' In *Youth Labor in Transition*, edited by Jacqueline O'Reilly, Janine Leschke, Renate Ortlieb, Martin Seeleib-Kaiser and Paola Villa. New York: Oxford University Press.

O'Reilly, Jacqueline, Werner Eichhorst, András Gábos, Kari Hadjivassiliou, David Lain, Janine Leschke, Seamus McGuinness, Lucia Mýtna Kureková, Tiziana Nazio, Renate Ortlieb, Helen Russell and Paola Villa. 2015. 'Five Characteristics of Youth Unemployment in Europe: Flexibility, Education, Migration, Family Legacies, and EU Policy'. *SAGE* Open 5 (1): 1–19. ***http://journals.sagepub.com/doi/abs/10.1177/2158244015574962***

Ortlieb, Renate, Maura Sheehan and Jaan Masso. 2017. 'Is self-employment a solution to young people's employment problems? In *Youth Employment*, edited by Jacqueline O'Reilly, Clémentine Moyart, Tiziana Nazio and Mark Smith. Brighton: CROME.

Petmesidou, Maria, and María González Menéndez. 2016. *Policy Learning and Innovation Processes.* STYLE Working Paper WP4.2 Policy learning and innovation processes drawing on EU and national policy frameworks on youth – Synthesis Report. Available at www.style-research.eu/publications/working-papers

Petmesidou, Maria, María González Menéndez and Kari P. Hadjivassiliou. 2017. 'What have we learnt about policy innovation and learning? In *Youth Employment*, edited by Jacqueline O'Reilly, Clémentine Moyart, Tiziana Nazio and Mark Smith. Brighton: CROME.

Smith, Mark, and Genevieve Shanahan. 2017a. 'What a difference a mum makes' In *Youth Employment*, edited by Jacqueline O'Reilly, Clémentine Moyart, Tiziana Nazio and Mark Smith. Brighton: CROME.

Smith, Mark, and Genevieve Shanahan. 2017b. 'Do young people want Universal Basic Income?' In *Youth Employment*, edited by Jacqueline O'Reilly, Clémentine Moyart, Tiziana Nazio and Mark Smith. Brighton: CROME.

Smith, Mark, and Paola Villa. 2017. 'Flexicurity policies to integrate youth before and after the crisis' In *Youth Employment*, edited by Jacqueline O'Reilly, Clémentine Moyart, Tiziana Nazio and Mark Smith. Brighton: CROME.

Van der Meer, Marc, Ruud Muffels and Sonja Bekker. 2017. 'Learning from the Dutch case: innovating youth (un)employment policies in Amsterdam, Eindhoven and Tilburg' In *Youth Employment*, edited by Jacqueline O'Reilly, Clémentine Moyart, Tiziana Nazio and Mark Smith. Brighton: CROME.

Wallace, Claire, and René Bendit. 2009. "Youth Policies in Europe: Towards a Classification of Different Tendencies in Youth Policies in the European Union." *Perspectives on European Politics and Society* 10 (3): 441–58. doi: 10.1080/15705850903105868.

Zuccotti, Carolina V., and Jacqueline O'Reilly. *Forthcoming*. 'Do Scarring Effects Vary by Ethnicity and Gender?' In *Youth Labor in Transition*, edited by Jacqueline O'Reilly, Janine Leschke, Renate Ortlieb, Martin Seeleib-Kaiser and Paola Villa. New York: Oxford University Press.

Young people's attitudes and values

Fortitude
SINK OR
SWIM

Introduction: Young people's attitudes and values

Jacqueline O'Reilly and **Clémentine Moyart**

Much of the analysis of youth labour markets and youth transition from education to employment takes little account of the attitudes and aspirations of young people themselves.

This part of the book is a deliberately eclectic selection of contributions that includes pieces written by a diverse range of young people who have been involved in the project as advisors or co-researchers. The desire behind this choice was to provide a platform where young people could give voice to their own perspectives. Other contributions in this part draw on the academic research conducted for the project. Here, researchers were particularly interested in examining young people's experiences, attitudes and aspirations.

We employed a diverse range of methodological approaches to examine beliefs and attitudes of young people towards work, families, politics and society. This includes testimonials, quantitative and qualitative analysis, experiments, in-depth interviews and participative approaches.

We sought to understand how values towards work, the impact of youth unemployment, poor quality employment and outsiderness with respect to social capital and political participation, as well as aspirations of vulnerable young people in foster care, shaped the perspectives of different groups of young people aged from 16-34.

Policy is often discussed as something that happens to others. This part of the book touches on young people's own aspirations, providing a platform for how their voices are expressed through different channels.

Do you have an invisible cape?

Sharon Dodua Otoo

The first time I moved to Berlin was in the mid-1990s. The wall had just come down and I could smell freedom in the streets of Mitte. It was an exciting, confusing time. Although I had been raised in the streets of East London (so to speak), my parents had been very strict and I was obedient (mostly). Consequentially, I did well academically and was a fairly well-trained future housewife, but only managed to go to my first concert or have my first kiss while I was a fresher at university. I didn't smoke (I still don't), I was a poor drinker, I was politically unengaged and – honestly – I was kind of boring. But the capital city of the reunited Germany was smaller than London, far more reasonably priced and full of optimism. I was simultaneously hyper-visible (not many people around who looked like me) and hyper-invisible (few people took the necessary time to see beyond their learned stereotypes). It was during my year abroad in Berlin that I first started serious study of a West-African language (Twi) and when I first learnt what it meant to identify politically as a Black person (deliberately written with a capital B). I also had my first serious love relationships here. I returned to London after twelve months, exhilarated, single and pregnant. A little over twenty years and four sons later, I won one of the most prestigious literary prizes in the German-speaking world in summer 2016. I now live in Berlin again and am currently working full time as a fiction author, with a book contract and speaking engagements in the USA, the UK, Germany, Switzerland and Austria. Having spent decades doing the work I love for free, I suddenly found recognition where I was least expecting it: among the traditionally educated German middle-class intellectuals.

I am loath to view this as the happy end though. It would be easy to see my literary success as something I had achieved only through my own hard work and talent. It would be possible, but probably irresponsible, for me to claim that anyone can do what I have done, if only they persevered long enough and pursued their dreams hard enough. I remember not too long ago being the kind of person who would avoid stories of people who had won an amazing prize, married a beautiful partner, landed an incredible film role and / or dazzled their employers into giving them a fantastic promotion. These were the kinds of things which made me feel inadequate, untalented, unloved and hopeless: I would have hated contemporary me. A while ago I read an article (Alam 2015) on jealousy, and have since been able to make sense of those feelings and give them a place. In a capitalist society, so argues the author, we are conditioned to think even of love, appreciation and recognition as being scarce and finite commodities. Anyone who is able to get some is envied by the rest of us – even if it is recognition for an achievement outside our own area of expertise.

So now that I am that shiny person in the dazzling story, being asked to write a short article about my work, I feel moved to mention the rigorous training in critical thinking I have received as a member of the African Diaspora in Germany, specifically as an active member of the Initiative of Black People in Germany (*Initiative Schwarze Menschen in Deutschland*) as well as its sister organisation ADEFRA Black Women in Germany (*Schwarze Frauen in Deutschland*). I should also mention my parents here, who were both born in humble circumstances in Accra, Ghana. My mother for example has told me the story of how she, as a small child, always dreamed that her children would one day go to school in white socks and shiny black shoes. I hated those knee-length socks with some kind of passion, but I do know about, and am grateful for, her sacrifices. It would also be fitting to mention my children, my siblings, my closest friends and my political allies at this point, all of whom have encouraged me to keep going, even when they did not necessarily understand exactly what I was doing or why, and may have secretly been hoping that I would just stop being so restless one day.

Yes, it is true that it took a lot of hard work for me to become this successful, and that not all of that work was done by me. And yet, I feel there is still an element of the story missing. This has to do with the construction of the story itself: the quite western and individualistic notion that we start somewhere, and we continue to progress until we reach a pinnacle of achievement at the end, somewhere else. It is a comforting story for the so-called winners. But for those of us who very rarely receive external recognition, this model sucks. And to be honest, when I first arrived in Berlin a little over twenty years ago, and during the years I spent raising my children alone, studying, struggling with debt, falling in and out of love, working jobs I hated, I was arguably risking more, learning more and living more than I am now. What, then, if we were encouraged to see ourselves not as empty vessels to be filled, but as full and complete individuals in our own right? What if our contributions to the communities we live in were not measured in terms of the amount of money we make or the number of external accolades we collect, but in our ability to practise mindfulness and self-care? What if we lived each day as if we were wearing invisible capes? Would that change anything? I would like to think so. I do think so.

References

Alam, Jordan. 2015. *'Jealous of Your Friends? Me, Too: Social Media, Scarcity and the Capitalism of Jealousy'. BGD.* ***http://www.bgdblog.org/2015/04/jealous-me-too-social-media-scarcity-and-the-capitalism-of-jealousy-2/****.*

Mawakha, Nzitu. 2013. *Daima. Images of Women of Colour in Germany.* Series: Witnessed, Edition 3. Münster: Edition Assemblage. ISBN 978-3-942885-31-7.

Otoo, Sharon Dodua. 2012. *the things i am thinking while smiling politely. Novella.* Münster: Edition Assemblage. ISBN 978-3-942885-22-5.

Otoo, Sharon Dodua. 2013. 'Correct me if I am (politically) wrong – "Echte" Kunst, Elitarismus und weiße Wahnvorstellungen der Erhabenheit'. In 'Critical Correctness', *Bildpunkt. Zeitschrift der IG Bildende Kunst (Wien)* 28 (Spring). ***http://micmovement.com/2013/04/correct-me-if-i-am-politically-wrong-real-art-elitism-and-white-delusions-of-grandeur/****.*

Editor of the book series Witnessed: Micossé-Aikins, Sandrine, and Sharon Dodua Otoo, eds. 2012. *The Little Book of Big Visions. How to Be an Artist and Revolutionize the World.* Series: Witnessed, Edition 1. Münster: Edition Assemblage. ISBN 978-3-942885-31-7.

Who do young people trust and why?

Niall O'Higgins and **Marco Stimolo**

Trust and trustworthiness between individuals permit mutually beneficial interactions in the face of the inevitable incompleteness of information and contracts. The existence of such social capital also provides the foundation of individuals' trust in institutions. It allows societies to overcome the inefficient outcomes associated with individual opportunism and myopic selfishness, boosting economic efficiency and economic growth. Being employed, being jobless, or having a temporary contract ... Does this affect young people's attitudes to trust and trustworthiness? And does it make any difference if you know the labour market status of the other person?

Indeed it does, on both counts. Those who have managed to find good jobs, along with those who choose not to participate in the labour market or education, are more trusting than students, while the unemployed and above all those who find themselves in precarious employment are the least trusting of all. Young people – whether employed or not – also showed strong signs of solidarity with those who did not have jobs.

Methodology

The questions were investigated using trust game experiments involving young people from three different European countries: Hungary (Budapest), Italy (Naples) and the UK (Oxford). Young workers, students and NEETS were brought into the laboratory, anonymously paired, and then asked to make decisions with immediate financial consequences both for themselves and for an anonymous counterpart about whom they initially knew only that they were also young.

Young people (aged 18-29) were drawn from outside the usual university background. This was one of several innovative aspects of the experiment as it is relatively unusual to undertake experiments on the general population rather than university students.

Trust games

In the trust game, the core element underlying the analysis, participants were divided into two groups: senders and receivers. Senders were given a sum of money and asked to decide how much of it to send to an anonymous partner (receiver). The receiver would receive any monies sent by the sender multiplied by three. S/he would then decide whether to reciprocate by sending back some or all of the money received from the sender. All these aspects of the game were common knowledge and, in a second round of the trust game, information was also provided on the labour market status of the counterpart.

The point is that decisions concerning the amount of money to send or send back were not motivated by knowledge of the personal characteristics of the partner, apart from – in the second round – their labour market status, but rather depended on the trust and reciprocity, in other words the social capital, of the participants.

A dictator game and a lottery choice

We also implemented a dictator game and individual decision problems such as a lottery choice in order to control for other motivational factors, including unconditional preferences (i.e., altruism and inequity aversion) and attitudes towards risk that might affect young people's behaviour in the experiment. Moreover, we further combined the behavioural information derived from the experiment with survey-based data to enrich our understanding of the role of attitudes.

The central twofold purpose was:

1. to explore whether behavioural trust and trustworthiness are systematically affected by subjects' socio-economic characteristics; and,

2. to test the extent to which behaviour is affected by knowledge of counterparts' labour market situation. Perhaps young workers would display solidarity towards their unemployed colleagues, for example.

Our findings

Diversity of NEETS

The experiment produced various interesting results, as well as suggesting a number of possible avenues for further investigation. We found, in the first place, statistically significant differences in behaviour – of both senders and receivers – across countries and across labour market states. Econometric analysis allowed us to qualify this basic observation, and in particular demonstrated the importance of distinguishing amongst different types of NEETs.

Consequences of precarious employment

A second major finding is the relevance of precariousness in employment in its deleterious effects on behavioural trust. Concerns have regularly been voiced in recent years about the negative effects of the increasing prevalence of temporary employment forms on young people's early labour market experiences; the results presented here appear to strongly support these concerns. Precarious employment appears to be at least as damaging to behavioural trust as unemployment, adding further support to those who would question the ever-increasing flexibilisation of youth labour markets.

The results of the analysis are consistent with, but also enlarge upon, existing findings in the behavioural economics literature. There are, for example, similarities in our results to those of Fehr et al. (2003) who found a negative impact of unemployment on behavioural trust amongst working-age adults in Germany. Unfortunately, the equally deleterious consequences of precarious forms of employment for social capital also emerge from our experimental analysis. This suggests that the rapid spread of such non-standard employment amongst young people in Europe today – and the predictability of the continuation of this upward trend – may also have consequences for long-term economic and social harmony.

References

Fehr, E., Urs Fischbacher, Bernhard von Rosenbladt, Jürgen Schupp and Gert Wagner. 2003. *A Nation-Wide Laboratory: Examining Trust and Trustworthiness by Integrating Behavioural Experiments into Representative Survey.* DIW Discussion Paper 319. Berlin: Deutsches Institut für Wirtschaftsforschung.

O'Higgins, Niall, and Marco Stimolo. 2015. *Youth Unemployment and Social Capital: An Experimental Approach.* STYLE Working Paper WP9.2 Youth unemployment and social capital: An experimental approach.

O'Higgins, Niall. 2017. *Rising to the youth employment challenge: New evidence on key policy issues.* ILO: Geneva.

Are young people's work values changing?

Gábor Hajdu and **Endre Sik**

Are younger people less work oriented than older generations? Are they more sceptical about achieving a successful career and sustainable salary? If the answers to these questions are yes, then we might expect young people to be less responsive to EU and national policies aimed at integrating them in the labour market.

We set out to explore the difference in attitudes between different age cohorts in Europe. We used the term birth cohort because the concept of generation is too loosely defined; it can vary significantly over time and by country as well as being affected by differences in technology, politics and policy.

Using a simple but straightforward definition of work values borrowed from Smola-Sutton (2002) we sought to find out regarding different age cohorts:

- How central work is as a part of their life and identity?
- Would they work even if there was no financial pressure to do so?
- And, how important are different extrinsic and intrinsic aspects of work: comparing having a 'good income', 'security' and 'flexibility' with having 'interesting work' and a job that is 'useful for society'.

We did not find significant gaps between the birth cohorts regarding centrality of work, employment commitment, or extrinsic or intrinsic work values in evaluating a job.

The methodology and data

The basic problem in analysing generations stems from the fact that age, period and birth cohort are linearly interdependent; their effects cannot be simultaneously estimated using standard regression models. A possible solution to this identification problem is to use a hierarchical age-period-cohort (HAPC) regression model.

Our analysis is based on the pooled data of the World Values Survey/European Values Study (WVS/EVS), the International Social Survey Programme (ISSP) and the European Social Survey (ESS) between 1980 and 2010 (N = ca. 160 000).

To control for the changing composition along the basic socio-economic characteristics of subsequent generations in our multivariate models, we use the following control variables: gender, education, marital status, labour force status and type of settlement. Additionally, every model contains country-fixed effects to control for time-invariant country characteristics.

Main findings

Centrality of work

We found that the centrality of work is higher in the middle-age groups than among the younger or older ones. The interpretation of this inverted U-shape by age is rather straightforward: younger people are not yet, and older people are no longer, involved in income-generating activities. We also found a decreasing linear trend of the centrality of work by period. This fits well into the theory stating that post-modern values have become more important nowadays than modern values (including the ethos of hard work).

Our results suggest that work is less central for the birth cohort born between 1940 and 1959 compared to those cohorts born earlier or later; however, these differences are very small. This result may be interpreted as a rather weak generational effect. For those who entered the education system and the labour market in the 1960s and 1970s, intrinsic values became more important than the extrinsic aspects of life. However, this change was reversed rather quickly, and those who entered the labour market after the mid-1970s became increasingly extrinsically oriented in their attitudes to work.

Comparing EU15 and post-socialist countries, we found that the general trend of the centrality of work was similar in these two groups; however, in the post-socialist countries, the age and cohort differences were larger than in the EU15 countries. Cohort differences in the post-socialist countries might be explained by a tendency on the part of the younger cohorts to disentangle from state socialist doctrines and/or to have a growing fear of unemployment and/or impoverishment.

Employment commitment

There is no relevant period and cohort effect on employment commitment, but this does decrease with age. Age differences are in accordance with both the labour market career and the life-course concept of working capacity: younger people are more motivated and are in better physical condition than older people.

Conclusions

Our research findings indicate that generational differences in attitudes to work are a myth, even though these are often referred to in public debates and used in political discourses. The most important conclusion from our results from a policy point view is that our 'search for gaps' was futile; that is, we were unable to identify any relevant gap in attitudes between different age cohorts. Kowske et al. (2010) quite rightly summarised their findings by suggesting that instead of generational differences we should speak about 'generational similarities'.

Our results imply that in contemporary Europe all generations follow a similar age trend; in other words, as the younger ones become older, their work values change similarly.

Policy-wise, the most important conclusion is that although birth cohort does not have a strong impact on work values, we detect differences in work values by age and period as well as between EU15 and post-socialist countries. For example,

- The slow but steady decrease in the centrality of work by period suggests that, in the long run, work may lose its dominant position as the source of identity;

- Employment policies are especially important for the youngest cohorts, where the level of commitment to employment is the highest.

References

Hajdu, Gábor, and Endre Sik. 2015. *Searching for Gaps: Are Work Values of the Younger Generations Changing?* STYLE Working Paper WP9.1 Searching for gaps: are work values of the younger generations changing?

Hajdu, Gábor, and Endre Sik. *Forthcoming.* 'Are the Work Values of the Younger Generations Changing?' *In Youth Labor in Transition*, edited by Jacqueline O'Reilly, Janine Leschke, Renate Ortlieb, Martin Seeleib-Kaiser and Paola Villa. New York: Oxford University Press.

Kowske, Brenda J., Rena Rasch and Jack Wiley. 2010. 'Millennials' (Lack of) Attitude Problem: An Empirical Examination of Generational Effects on Work Attitudes'. *Journal of Business and Psychology* 25 (2): 265–79. doi:10.1007/s10869-010-9171-8.

Smola, Karen Wey, and Charlotte D. Sutton. 2002. 'Generational Differences: Revisiting Generational Work Values for the New Millennium'. *Journal of Organizational Behavior* 23 (4): 363–82. doi:10.1002/job.147.

'One Step Forward': Resilient strategies supporting the aspirations of vulnerable young people in foster care

Young people partners:
Ross, **Jaymi**, **Sunneka**, **Amy**, **Matt**, **Sitara**, **Raija**, **Rosa**, **Katy**, **Chloe**, **Lorna**, **Laura**, **Sam**, **Katarina** and **Lefteris** *(some of these are real names, others are pseudonyms depending on the preferences of the young people involved)*

Academic authors:
Angie Hart, **Claire Stubbs**, **Stefanos Plexousakis**, **Maria Georgiadi** and **Elias Kourkoutas**

Young people with mental health difficulties are much more likely to have difficulty finding any form of employment. Young people who have grown up in foster care experience multiple disadvantages. Within the STYLE project, we established a collaborative research project between Greece and the UK to examine these issues. It aimed to understand the work aspirations of a group of vulnerable young people in care and the barriers they face in terms of youth employment.

The task within the project was to support young people in foster care using a qualitative participative approach to identify resilience strategies to help other young people in care. The main outcome from the collaboration resulted in co-producing an open-access resource book called One Step Forward, which is of value to the young people involved in the task in each country. We wanted to explore with the young people the questions 'What are the work aspirations of vulnerable young people in care? And what barriers do they face in finding work?'

What we did

Adopting a Youth Participatory Action Research approach (YPAR), the goal was to build the capacity of fifteen young people in Greece and England, enabling them to identify the issues they faced in relation to getting a job and to consider helpful strategies to overcome these problems. They acted as young researchers seeking to further understand the nature of the issues, and were supported in developing a resource that would be useful to other young people, foster carers and practitioners. The young people themselves developed highly illustrated resources.

(The resources are available to download from: ***http://issuu.com/boingboingresilience/docs/one_step_forward_-_resilience/1*** (UK edition) ***http://issuu.com/boingboingresilience/docs/one_step_forward_-_resilience_-_gre/1*** (Greek edition).

The concept of resilience

The resource begins by helping everyone to understand the concept of resilience and the benefits of adopting a resilience approach. The resource helps people understand resilience from a Boingboing perspective which includes a strong inequalities angle (Hart et al., 2016). The approach is brought to life through interactive activities that carers, young people and professionals can use in support of promoting resilience.

Through their work, the young people shared stories and role models that had been significant in supporting their own resilience. There are also examples from the political activist Malcolm X and the actress Jennifer Lawrence. These stories are used for the benefit of other young people.

How we used the resource to involve young people

The resource details the young people's pathways through foster care and the resilient moves that have been important in their lives in overcoming barriers to success.

In Greece

Following on from the completion of this task, members of the project team have used the resource in numerous training and conference presentations. The book was also exhibited in an art, play therapy and theatre studio in Greece. Parents and practitioners were invited to participate in experiential activities from the book.

In a second phase, children were asked to draw on a specific theme called the 'Forest of Good and Evil'. Those drawings were presented in an exhibition in the Cultural Centre of Rethymno, Crete, with large success. The Greek section of Play Therapy International has highlighted the *One Step Forward* book as a valuable resource for their membership.

In the UK

In the UK context, the use of the *One Step Forward* book has inspired the project team to develop further resources through the Boingboing social enterprise (*www.boingboing.org.uk*) with grants from the Arts and Humanities Research Council in the UK.

Academics, practitioners and young people have worked in partnership to produce games and other activities relating to resilience.
(***http://www.boingboing.org.uk/utopia-fair-somerset-house-blog/***).

These have all supported vulnerable young people in developing useful skills and in building their own resilience.

Three young people with complex needs who were previously unemployed have gained employment with the social enterprise Boingboing to develop and market these resources.

Most recently, a funding bid to set up Boingboing Blackpool has been successful. With support from the Big Lottery Fund in England as part of Boingboing Blackpool, further resources and training packages will be developed based on the resource produced in this task and on other resources that were subsequently innovated.

A UK-based philanthropist has also pledged a donation to the cause that will enable further marketing of the tools. The *One Step Forward* book produced in this project has acted as valuable springboard for the development of further co-produced outputs with vulnerable young people.

It has also already led to the actual employment of young people with complex needs and looks set to be a springboard for the development of even more social enterprise opportunities for young people with complex needs as well as further research into how to make this happen.

Reference

Hart, Angie, Claire Stubbs, Stefanos Plexousakis, Maria Georgiadi and Elias Kourkoutas. 2015. *Aspirations of Vulnerable Young People in Foster Care.* STYLE Working Paper WP9.3 Aspirations of vulnerable youth in foster care. STYLE Working Paper WP9.3 Aspirations of vulnerable youth in foster care

Hart, Angie, Derek Blincow and Helen Thomas. 2007. *Resilient Therapy: Working with Children and Families.* London: Brunner Routledge.

Hart, Angie, Emily Gagnon, Suna Eryigit-Madzwamuse, Josh Cameron, Kay Aranda, Anne Rathbone and Becky Heaver. 2016. Uniting resilience research and practice with a health inequalities approach. *SAGE* Open, 6(4), 1-15. doi:10.1177/2158244016682477

What matters to young mums?

Emma Mckay and **Emma Feasey**

Throughout the late 1990s and 2000s and fuelled by the Labour government's desire to reduce the teenage pregnancy rate, a lot of research was published about teenage pregnancy and motherhood. Since policy has changed direction, young motherhood has become less popular as a research topic and a quick review of the literature showed us that much of the research about young mothers, their lives and their entry into work and education was out of date.

The Young Women's Trust

In 2016, the Young Women's Trust decided to take a new look at young motherhood. We wanted to expand the topic beyond conversations about teenage pregnancy and include young women who have babies up to the age of 25. We also wanted to focus on the views and experiences of young mothers themselves. Our report *What matters to young mums?* is the result of that work.

Young Women's Trust is a charity supporting women aged 16-30 in England and Wales who live on low or no pay. We advocate for fair financial futures for young women, with fairly paid, good quality work at the core of that vision. Consequently, *What matters to young mums?* identifies the barriers to young mothers working and makes recommendations about how to remove them. Isolation, expensive or inflexible childcare, low pay and a lack of part-time or flexible work have combined to discourage mothers from working. Young women also have little confidence in the support to find work provided by the social security system.

A review of academic and policy literature published between 2010 and 2015 led us to conclude that there was plenty written about teenage parents but little about mothers aged 20-25. We also found there were fewer publications about the personal experiences of teenage or young mothers themselves. Consequently, we went on to conduct six focus groups with mothers under 25, to let them speak for themselves.

Participatory Research

We visited existing groups of mothers in spaces they were comfortable with, to make it easier for them to participate in the research. These included a communal kitchen in a mother and baby unit and a children's centre attached to a local library. We also adapted the structure of the session to suit each group and create an informal, open atmosphere – for example, we ate a meal prepared by the mothers before beginning one discussion. The groups often took place in noisy settings with children clamouring for attention. Therefore, the researchers kept the group engaged through a range of participation techniques using colourful props. We used methods including brainstorming (alone and collectively), pair discussions, whole group discussions and voting. This kept the session varied and catered for different 'learning styles' within the group (Honey and Mumford 1982).

Following the focus groups, we designed and commissioned a survey for a sample of over 300 young mothers using the polling agency Survation (the tables are available on their website.) This enabled us to generalise from some of the themes that emerged in the groups, such as their views on the high cost of childcare. We also asked some questions that we didn't think mothers would have answered in the groups, around their loneliness and about poverty.

As a charity, Young Women's Trust is committed to young women's participation in the work we do to support them, from guiding our campaigns and services to writing and speaking out about the issues that matter to them. Accordingly, mothers who took part in the research were encouraged to stay in touch with the charity and all the opportunities it could offer them. For example, one of the focus group participants wrote the foreword to the final report through a WhatsApp conversation with one of the researchers.

Main findings: *What matters to young mums?*

This was only a short project – the fieldwork was completed in four months – but it led to some clear conclusions about young mothers and their relationship with the world of work.

The costs of childcare

Young mothers mostly preferred to leave their children with relatives, but in general formal childcare was considered to be good for their children's development. However, formal childcare is expensive. Furthermore, mothers usually had prospects of low-paid work because of their youth or because they were starting out in their careers. Mothers agreed that if they were to work, childcare costs would total more than their earnings or only just allow them to break even. Missing out on their children growing up for no financial return made work a less attractive prospect; the mothers also conveyed a sense that whether they chose to work or stay at home, they would be making a sacrifice.

The pressure to a 'good mother'

Other research has highlighted that young mothers are under pressure to prove they are good mothers. This may be prompted by their awareness of stereotypes about feckless single teenage mothers; it is also shored up by their families' and communities' expectations (Ellis-Sloan 2012; Maguire and Mckay 2016). The cost of childcare and prospects of low-paid work may combine with societal stigma to push them towards mothering at the expense of working. Improving access to free childcare could help change this. For example, extending the 15 hours of free childcare policy so that it is available year round would encourage young mothers to work, while widening access to Care to Learn support would make retraining more affordable. Raising pay would also increase mothers' incomes, for example through extending the National Living Wage to under-25s.

Their social life

In addition, becoming a mother disrupts young women's social connections. They see their friends less and become lonelier, with 26% leaving the house once a week or less. At the same time, out-of-work mothers of young children have either negative or sporadic interactions with Jobcentre Plus. Our research suggests that this has the potential to keep mothers further from the labour market. One-to-one support or mentorship to develop mothers' relationships outside their family units might ease their move back into education or employment.

Their working conditions

Finally, we found that employers' attitudes and conditions for working were integral in helping young mothers to work. Mothers reported experiencing discrimination, some of it illegal: for instance, 39% had been questioned in a job interview about how being a mother affected their ability to work. Mothers also said it was important for them that more jobs were advertised with flexible or part-time hours.

This article is based on *What matters to young mums?* published by Young Women's Trust in March 2017.

References

Ellis-Sloan, Kyla. 2012. *'Becoming a Teenage Mother in the UK'.* PhD Thesis, University of Brighton.

Honey, Peter, and Alan Mumford. 1982. *Manual of Learning Styles.* London: Peter Honey.

Maguire, Sue, and Emma McKay. 2016. *Young, Female and Forgotten?* London: Young Women's Trust.

Are young people outsiders and does it matter?

Alessandro Arrigoni and **Emanuele Ferragina**

A lot of young Europeans struggle to find a job in a market that does not guarantee stable forms of employment. How does the experience of insecure labour market trajectories affect their social and political participation, or their sense of social exclusion and alienation from mainstream politics?

What is YLMO?

Youth Labour Market Outsiderness (YLMO) is a concept that allows us to go beyond conventional measures such as unemployment. This is because it also includes those who are inactive (NEETs) as well as those in part-time or temporary jobs that do not allow them to be financially independent.

We examined how the characteristics and composition of youth outsiders vary across Europe, and how this has changed during the economic crisis. Finally, we explored the consequences of YLMO for social and political participation and how different institutions mediate this behaviour.

Methodology

The study built on a mixed-method (qualitative and quantitative) approach. The quantitative analysis was conducted employing data from the EU-SILC data set for 30 European countries at two points in time – 2006 and 2012, in order to provide insights on pre- and post-crisis levels of YLMO.

In addition, we conducted more than one hundred semi-structured individual and group interviews with young outsiders and experts in five countries (Austria, Germany, Italy, Spain and the UK). These five case studies were selected with the objective of maximising institutional variation concerning education-to-employment transition, labour markets and welfare systems.

Main findings

Our research shows that YLMO is a significant phenomenon across Europe. In countries like Slovenia, which was less affected by the crisis, around a quarter of 15-29 years-olds were YLMO; in Mediterranean countries, like Italy and Spain, nearly half the young people were in this category.

Being YLMO is also a long-standing structural phenomenon: the economic crisis overall did not 'create' youth outsiderness, rather worsened already existing patterns.

Institutional arrangements can significantly impact on the prevalence of YLMO and the support available for young outsiders. Finally, our analysis confirms that there is a negative relation between being young and an outsider and participation in formal political activities. There are three aspects of this research that we consider particularly significant:

Levels of YLMO varies between countries

First, the level of YLMO varies significantly between countries. Looking at our five case studies, we observe that Italy and Spain have the highest proportions of YLMO with relatively larger proportions of young people in unemployment or inactivity. The UK has an intermediate level of YLMO, with relatively large proportions of inactivity or part-time employment. Instead, Austria and Germany have comparatively lower levels of outsiderness, with relatively high levels of part-time employment.

YLMO networks vary

Second, the effects of these cross-national differences are reinforced by national institutional constellations. For example, in Austria and Germany, low levels of youth outsiderness are associated with a relatively dense network of youth-related institutions and strong coordination among them.

In Southern European countries, the high level of youth outsiderness and the lack of strong formal institutions is only partially compensated by family networks.

In the UK, the labour market works as an effective mechanism of integration for a large proportion of young people in their transition from education to work. State institutions and policies tend to focus on disadvantaged young people, while families play a less prominent role.

Young people are involved, but not in formal channels

The low participation we observe in formal political activities does not mean young people are not at all involved in politics. Young people perceived formal mainstream politics as distant, difficult to understand and unresponsive to young people's needs. The message for traditional political parties and institutions is loud and clear: they need to engage with this constituency of young people.

However, young people are responsive to anti-establishment movements and parties willing to challenge the status quo. It is therefore not surprising that movements and parties like the Five Stars Movement in Italy, Podemos in Spain or Corbyn's brand of the Labour Party in the UK are attracting many young people, including labour market outsiders.

Using heterodox platforms and targeting specific policies, there are significant attempts to get young people's voices heard through conventional channels by proposing to expand and/or universalize social assistance, improve public health care services or ditch university fees (in the UK).

Consequences

A significant part of the young European population can be considered YLMO. Although the composition of this group is different across countries and the harshness of youth conditions is dependent upon the ability of institutions to protect and support them, our analysis of their numerical strength and personal perceptions indicates that they are a central social group, potentially able to influence and define the future of our societies. As recent upheavals in the political life of certain European countries seem to suggest, these young people can become an engine for social change.

References

Arrigoni, Alessandro, Bastian Betthaeuser, Elaine Chase, Emanuele Ferragina, Martin Seeleib-Kaiser and Thees Spreckelsen. 2016. *Young People as Outsiders: Prevalence, composition and participation.* STYLE Working Paper WP9.4 Youth as Outsiders: Prevalence, composition and participation.

Emmenegger, Patrick, Silja Häusermann, Bruno Palier, and Martin Seeleib-Kaiser. 2012. *The Age of Dualization. The Changing Face of Inequality in Deindustrializing Societies.* New York: Oxford University Press.

Ferragina, Emanuele, and Alessandro Arrigoni. 2014. *La Maggioranza Invisibile.* Milan: BUR-Rizzoli.

Ferragina, Emanuele, Joseph Feyertag and Martin Seeleib-Kaiser. 2016. 'Outsiderness and Participation in Liberal and Coodinated Market Economies', PArtecipazione e COnflitto, *The Open Journal of Sociological Studies* 9 (3): 986-1014.

The STYLE SQUAD @ European Parliament: European Youth Event (EYE)

Clémentine Moyart and **Jacqueline O'Reilly**

The European Youth Event (EYE) is an opportunity for young Europeans to make their voices heard. The second time this event took place – in the European Parliament in Strasbourg on 20-21 May 2016 – a group of young people participating in the STYLE project took part. The next event will take place in June 2018.

In May 2016, 7,500 young people aged 16-30 made their way to Strasbourg, France, to raise their voices and come together to debate, discuss and mobilise. A report of the EYE 2016 is available online, while EYE participants had the opportunity to present the most concrete ideas produced by young people to a number of parliamentary committees and to receive feedback from Members of the European Parliament.

Innovative experience of political participation

As part of the EYE, the European Youth Forum organises the YO!Fest – Youth Opinion Festival (EYE 2016) – a political youth-led festival taking place in front of the European Parliament. This festival aims at bringing young people closer to political institutions and giving them a space for dialogue. Thanks to its combination of high-level political debates, interactive workshops, education activities, simulation games, live music and artistic performances, YO!Fest creates a unique, fun and innovative experience of participation in political life for young people.

Young people's recommendations

Many groups of young people took part in this experience; the STYLE SQUAD of young advisors to the project were there – making it loud! The STYLE SQUAD came from Poland, Spain and the UK. During the event, they exchanged ideas and perspectives on youth-related issues, developed innovative solutions to crucial questions for the future and met with European decision-makers and speakers with a wide range of professional experience.

Let's youth up politics

When 72% of 16/18-24 year-olds do not vote but more than 50% of 65+ year-olds do (EES 2014), young people's interests are less and less a priority for political institutions – and this cannot be justified by a 'disengagement' of young people from politics. There are some common misconceptions regarding young people's so-called 'disengaged' relationship with politics, and it is time to recognise the need to look beyond elections and electoral turnout. The emergence of individualised, immediate and non-representative styles of politics – associated with protests,

petitions and social movements – presents challenges to traditional politics but also many opportunities (EYF 2015). We need to find ways to bring young people's issues into the political arena and to adapt political institutions to the political imagination of young people – these are two objectives of the EYE event!

Join the EYE 2018!

The third EYE will take place on 1-2 June 2018 with the motto of the event being 'the plan is to fan this spark into a flame'. Young people who want to take part need to register on the website of the European Parliament (**#EYE2018**) between October and December 2017. Let's show again next year that there is an interest among young people in the politics of organising, mobilising and contesting power from the outside.

References

EES. 2014. European Parliament Election Study 2014. **http://europeanelectionstudies.net/european-election-studies/ees-2014-study**.

EYE. 2016. **http://www.yofest.eu/wp-content/uploads/2017/01/report_2016_LOW.pdf**.

EYF. 2015. Young People and Democratic Life in Europe, European Youth Forum, 2015. **https://www.youthup.eu/app/uploads/2015/11/YFJ_YoungPeopleAndDemocraticLifeInEurope_B1_web-9e4bd8be22.pdf**.

#EYE2018 **http://www.europarl.europa.eu/european-youth-event/en/take-part!.html**

Boingboing Beyond Borders: Testimony from the EYE

Simon Duncan

So there I was: slightly disoriented, a little sweaty, and surrounded by thousands of other young people. All of us were listening to a performance of Lukas Graham's *7 Years*. I know what you're thinking, and the answer is no. I wasn't at a concert or in a stuffy nightclub somewhere in London. Instead, I was in Strasbourg, France, enjoying the opening ceremony of the European Youth Event (EYE) 2016.

Just to explain, the EYE is a two-day event held every two years at the European Parliament. Here, young people from all over Europe between the ages of 16 and 30 can voice their opinions and influence policy on issues affecting Europe, ranging from animal welfare to youth unemployment. Boingboing, the social enterprise I work for, was there on the invitation of the Style Project headed by the immensely talented Professor Jackie O'Reilly and Dr Margherita Bussi. Before I say anything else, thank you so much to both of you for organising such a marvellous trip. You really made sure the travel was smooth and were brilliant travel companions throughout our time on foreign soil. We shall have to do it again soon; if you'll let us Boingboingers gate-crash your trips again!

In coming to this event, all of the Boingboingers were excited to see whether we could bring some of our Resilience Magic to Europe. This was especially important after we re-enacted the plot of *Planes, Trains and Automobiles* to get to Strasbourg in the first place. May I say on behalf of the whole team that I think everyone showed amazing resilience through the travelling process. A special mention goes to Anne Rathbone, Boingboinger and PhD Student, who had returned from holiday only the day before! Whoops, I've digressed.

Over 7,500 young people attended the EYE. It was inspiring and challenging in equal measure. On the one hand, it was really heartening to see so many young people, like myself, who wanted to make a positive difference to Europe by discussing and finding solutions to issues that affect them. In this way, the EYE organisers really sought to embody their slogan of 'together we can make a change'. On the other hand, trying to get through the crowds and queues to the workshop sessions was quite stressful. This was particularly important for those of us who suffer anxiety stemming from enclosed spaces. It was a bit tricky for me as well, but given that I'm a wheelchair user I was able to use the fast track and avoid the queues. I just wish that security staff had been far more understanding with those of us who have hidden needs, like learning disabilities or mental health challenges. Anyway, nobody ever said that getting into

European politics was easy. I just didn't expect it to be this tricky. Luckily for me and fellow Boingboinger Lisa Buttery, our very own Professor Angie Hart and Margherita Bussi were our saviours. They convinced security to let us through with humour and a few quick French words. They truly were multilingual superheroes. It reminded me that 'Having a Laugh' is a key part of being resilient.

The next challenge began when we entered the main workshop building; the LOW building. It's a labyrinth of different rooms that don't necessarily go in numerical order. Again, I like to think that the building was built to be a representation of European politics – full of unexpected twists and turns, but a great opportunity for cross-cultural bonding. I struggled to find my workshop room and ran into a girl from Estonia in a similar situation to me. As we searched in vain for our respective workshops, we spoke about all manner of things. So, I guess the EYE really did achieve its aim of bringing people from different communities together!

Having succeeded in making it to a workshop on young entrepreneurs and business ideas, Lisa and I were quick to pitch the 'Boingboing way' of promoting tools, services and equality-based practices to help the most disadvantaged children and young people to be more resilient. We made the point that this ethos and practice should be embedded in all European organisations. Personally, I think this idea went over quite well with the rest of the workshop participants. We also talked about making it easier for office staff to work from home to allow for more family time.

One place I didn't expect to go was to a question and answer session on Animal Rights and Welfare in Europe. Lisa is a huge supporter of animal welfare, so I was along for the ride. I'm sure everyone could tell I wasn't supposed to be there as I tried to stealthily hide my leather wheelchair gloves in my bag and lean forward to block the view of my leather shoes. I don't think I have a future in covert operations, but it was worth a try to avoid a diplomatic incident. Still, it was interesting to learn something new.

I had a few personal highlights during the EYE. The first was attending a session about getting Employment with a Chronic Condition. During the session, I was able to tell everyone about the difficulties I faced trying to get into full-time employment after university, before joining Boingboing. This was incredibly rejuvenating for me. In talking about my own experiences, I was able to heal some of the emotional pain that remained from that year of constant job rejection. So a resilient move for me then! Also, talking about my experience helped to start discussion around potential ways that people with chronic conditions or disabilities can find employment successfully. It was equally empowering to be with people who truly understand the adversity you've experienced. Knowing you're not alone is an extremely effective motivator.

My second highlight was sitting in the Hemicycle, which is the place where the European Parliament debate and make rulings. While there, Lisa and I sat listening to Samantha Cristoforetti, an Italian astronaut, speak about space travel and future fuel sources. It was thrilling to know that even though I wasn't debating policy, I was directly in the seat of power.

My third highlight is not my own, it belongs to Katie Scott-Wilds. She's another Boingboinger who is part of Anne Rathbone's Arts Connect Group. This is a collective of young people/adults on the autistic spectrum and/or with learning disabilities who designed the Sun and Clouds game of 'Designing Resilience' fame, to enable others to learn about resilience and the adversity that learning-disabled people face. Through the magic of a smartphone I saw her confidently ask a question in front of an audience of over 500 people. Seeing the video brought an immediate smile to my face. Well done Katie for living the Arts Connect slogan: 'See ability, not disability!' Regardless of the challenges we face, we should all have the confidence to speak about the issues that affect us, so that we can directly effect change in the world around us.

All in all, I had a wonderful time in Strasbourg at the EYE 2016. I feel privileged to have gotten the opportunity to attend and would like to thank our collaborators from the Style Project once again. I'm sure I've made some friends for life.

It was with a heavy heart that I left sunny Strasbourg for rainy old England. I do hope we all get invited to the next EYE! This is not au revoir, Strasbourg, merely à bientôt.

Signing off, with my spirit in Strasbourg.

Getting involved in politics

Edward Badu

I grew up in Tottenham in North London, a neighbourhood where deprivation played a massive part in one's upbringing. I was fortunate enough to have come from a very good and stable upbringing, as my parents were extremely supportive. Having studied at a Catholic School I received a good education as well as gaining values and responsibilities which were vital to my development.

Despite all this, there were always hurdles I felt I had to jump due to the area I grew up in. But what really struck me was that we were probably one of the lucky ones, as there were people in the community who were having to jump bigger hurdles, from low household incomes to overcrowding, poor living conditions and lack of decent care for the elderly. In some cases, a few found themselves in trouble with the police and authorities. This hindrance meant they were always at a disadvantage at school and when it came to employment prospects. Because they weren't equipped with the correct skills, training and guidance, which limited their employment options or their ability to perform at work.

For this reason, getting involved in politics gave me the opportunity to influence and act on issues that directly affected me and my community. I believed getting involved in public life was the only way I was going to bring about the change I wanted to see in our community. My involvement with Citizens UK allowed me to be that voice for many young people from North London, Tottenham and the wider community, expressing and highlighting the issues we faced growing up. I was invited to meetings with Al Gore, David Cameron and Prince Charles, which was a true honour and an excellent experience. I was invited to be part of the Commission investigating the London Riots in 2011 because of the various involvements I have had in the past with North London Citizens. This was one of the reasons I was invited to join the local advisory board of the STYLE project.

My involvement in the inquiry allowed me to really understand what was causing this divide and hostility in my community. We narrowed it down to four main priorities which needed to be tackled. Firstly, powerlessness, as many (especially young people) felt they didn't have a stake in their community and were normally let down by local communities or the establishment. Secondly, we also found that there was a breakdown of trust and respect between the police and community. Thirdly, the reputation and condition of Tottenham – many people identified the cause of the riots as due to the aesthetics of Tottenham. Lastly, the lack of opportunities available, and the need for better education, and more vocational training for young people.

What I found interesting with the STYLE Project was being able to learn more about unemployment in different states and comparing the reasons behind why young people were not in employment. There were similarities with the causes of unemployment, for example particular ethnicities and groups were either more or less likely to be employed, which I saw frequently in my work, and I was able to discuss this when Jackie O'Reilly and Carolina Zuccotti presented their research findings at one of the meetings I attended.

However, what I saw that differed was the emphasis around apprenticeships and how beneficial they were in terms of preparing young people for work. What also struck me and was a point I never considered when looking at this matter was the attention on job security and how that played a part, as what you saw in some countries was that it was harder to dismiss an employee, which was taken into account when looking at youth employment. I also really enjoyed participating in the trip to Strasbourg.

Working with the STYLE SQUAD: A Spanish perspective

Fermín López

The recovery of the Spanish economy has been evident for some time now. In fact, according to official statistics, GDP annual growth has been positive since 2014 and employment has also started to increase since 2015. However, as a young Spaniard in his final formative stage, I perceive the situation differently. Many friends that have finished their university degrees are caught in a trap of precarious and low-quality employment. Others, especially those who have not continued with their education and training, accept jobs that last only hours or a few days, in the best cases.

Official statistics give over-optimistic politicians a clear advantage, since employment rates do not reflect the quality of jobs. However, the serious problem of youth employment in Spain is the lack of jobs for the less well qualified and, despite the improvement of the economy, the situation has not changed for young people. The weak performance of the Spanish labour market for young people has already been documented extensively by other significant studies from a multidimensional and longitudinal perspective (Hadjivassiliou et al. 2015; Grotti et al. *forthcoming*; Hadjivassiliou et al. *forthcoming*).

Table 1: *Employment rates in Spain and other EU countries by education and age in 2016*

	ISCED 0-2				ISCED 3-4				ISCED 5-8		
	16-19	20-24	25-29	20-64	16-19	20-24	25-29	20-64	20-24	25-29	20-64
Spain	4.5	36.9	54.6	52.7	5.7	22.4	60.9	61.8	45.7	70.6	78.3
EU27	11.6	44.5	54.5	53.9	30.7	49.9	74.0	71.7	60.8	80.8	83.7
Sweden	20.4	41.2	55.5	61.4	65.6	68.4	82.4	82.5	64.8	82.9	88.3
Italy	1.5	32.6	49.6	50.6	12.0	31.2	56.8	65.5	24.1	54.6	78.5
UK	20.9	54.3	63.7	61.9	42.8	66.9	81.3	77.7	78.4	87.9	85.1
Germany	21.5	55.7	54.0	59.0	51.2	64.4	80.2	79.0	71.9	84.7	87.9

Source: Eurostat, EU-LFS.

These facts lead to highly relevant questions, which have been part of my research and to which I would like to respond here from my personal point of view. Since I started my university studies, I have always had a special interest in sociology, labour economics and public policy analysis. In these academic fields, I have found the motivation and support necessary to expand and deepen my knowledge on the situation of young people in the labour market. The following questions and their answers arise from a body of research that I have been revising since I joined the Department of Sociology of the University of Oviedo in 2016. In addition to these short questions, I would also like to share my experience within the STYLE project and how this has helped me to discover new perspectives on the issue of youth employment.

Are the low youth employment rates associated with the crisis or are they structural traits of the Spanish labour market?

Figure 1 shows the evolution of employment by age groups and education level for the second quarters of different years from 2000 to 2016. It can be seen that the employment of Spanish young people was already low before the economic crisis. In spite of this, it is also true that those with a low education level aged between 20 and 29 years had high employment rates, even higher than other young people with more education. This can be explained by the high level of early school dropouts registered before the crisis (Hadjivassiliou et al. *forthcoming*). Many young people abandoned their studies to seek employment in the services and building sector (Grotti et al. *forthcoming*).

Figure 1: *Youth employment evolution in Spain* (2000-2016)

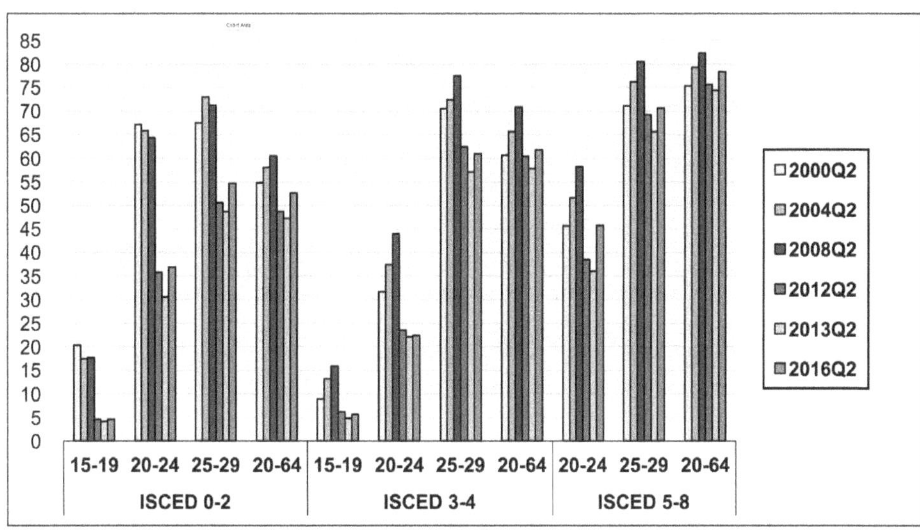

Source: Eurostat, EU-LFS.

Which young people have been more affected by the economic recession in Spain?

Although the inclusion of young people in the labour market was already low before the crisis, the employment reduction has significantly affected those between 15 and 24 years with low education levels (see Figure 1 above). Besides that, it has been reported by other studies that women, immigrants and children from low socio-economic backgrounds have been particularly hit by the economic downturn (Moreno Mínguez 2015).

Why is youth employment especially low in Spain?

Some authors have already pointed out the long-term nature of low youth employment rates. Garrido et al. (2016) disaggregate the evolution of employment rates by different population cohorts and argue that what really fails is the youth labour integration model as a whole. This integration model has been discussed broadly in comparative research. Following an institutional approach, there are two main reasons that can explain the low labour market participation of young Spanish people.

On the one hand, the disconnection between the educational system and employability has caused an increase in long-term youth unemployment and NEET rates. Many students left their training during the expansionary phase of the previous economic cycle and others did not invest enough training time to be able to get a job afterwards. This, in addition to the lack of effective and targeted active labour market policies, is one of the main reasons for the exclusion of less qualified young workers from labour participation.

On the other hand, the Spanish contractual framework has fostered a pattern of 'biographical' dualism. What this means is that the formal rule and primary channel of young people to reach stable employment is through fixed-term employment contracts. Unlike labour segmentation in other countries, working conditions that involve temporality in Spain are much more correlated with biographical and working age. This temporality pattern, besides being involuntary, reduces future labour opportunities and blocks employees' professional development (Dolado et al. 2013).

My experience with STYLE: What I have learned

My interest in the previous questions and the support of my Professor María González Menéndez gave me the opportunity to accompany the STYLE research network during their visit to the European Parliament in the European Youth Event (EYE). I participated in different workshops and presentations discussing how we can tackle youth unemployment.

One of the main concerns expressed in the different thematic sessions was the implementation of the Youth Guarantee. Young people coming from across Europe agreed in identifying a set of potential improvements to this policy. The most important were those related to training and the funding of the policy. Too often education authorities are not involved or don´t form part of the development of the policy. As a result, firms don't consider training initiatives a priority and focus on hiring young people at lower wages than older age groups.

There is a serious problem with training in policies like Youth Guarantee. What happens is that money is not spent on policies that are highlighted in the original plans and, sometimes, companies only implement training initiatives in order to get special bonuses or deductions for hiring young people. In order to avoid these types of problems, performance and impact assessments are necessary. These need to be conducted by organisations that do not have a vested interest in benefitting from the policy incentives.

Despite the unquestionable benefits of the workshop discussions, I would like to stress that probably the greatest lesson I have learnt was the spirit of the EYE event and the attitude of the STYLE 'squad'. During those days, I shared impressions and perceptions with other young people who face youth unemployment in their countries from different perspectives and with different social concerns. I also became part of a diverse group of people that included teachers, students, practitioners of social organisations and others, some with disabilities.

Having had the opportunity to meet all those people has helped me to realize that many times society gives us a wrong view of social problems and how to cope with them. It is normally assumed that some issues require complex and difficult solutions. But what I really think is that great solutions do not come from very sophisticated schemes. Great solutions arise when different and diverse people come together and talk about their own problems and think about what they, and the rest of society, can do to improve the situation.

References

Dolado, Juan, Florentino Felgueroso, Marcel Jansen, Andrés Fuentes and Anita Wölf. 2013. *Youth Labour Market Performance in Spain and its Determinants – A M-level Perspective.* OECD Economics Department Working Paper 1039. Paris: OECD.

Garrido, Luis, Rodolfo Gutiérrez and Ana Guillén. 2016. 'Biographical dualism: Youth Employment and Poverty Patterns in Spain'. In *Child Poverty, Youth (Un) Employment, and Social Inclusion*, edited by Maria Petmesidou, Enrique Delamonica, Christos Papatheodorou and Aldrie Henry-Lee. Stuttgart: Ibidem.

Grotti, Raffaele, Helen Russell, and Jacqueline O'Reilly. *Forthcoming.* 'Where Do Young People Work?' In *Youth Labor in Transition*, edited by Jacqueline O'Reilly, Janine Leschke, Renate Ortlieb, Martin Seeleib-Kaiser and Paola Villa. New York: Oxford University Press.

Hadjivassiliou, Kari P., Arianna Tassinari, Werner Eichhorst and Florian Wozny. *Forthcoming.* 'How Does the Performance of School-To-Work Transition Regimes in the European Union Vary?' In *Youth Labor in Transition*, edited by Jacqueline O'Reilly, Janine Leschke, Renate Ortlieb, Martin Seeleib-Kaiser and Paola Villa. New York: Oxford University Press.

Hadjivassiliou, Kari, Laura Kirchner Sala and Stefan Speckesser. 2015. *Key Indicators and Drivers of Youth Unemployment.* STYLE Working Paper WP3.1 Indicators and Drivers of Youth Unemployment.

Moreno Mínguez, Almudena. 2015. 'La empleabilidad de los jóvenes en España: Explicando el elevado desempleo juvenil durante la recesión económica'. *Revista Internacional de Investigación en Ciencias Sociales* 11 (1): 3-20.

Youth voice at the ballot box and in the economy: Lost or unheard?

Mark Smith and **Genevieve Shanahan**

The rise of nationalism across the European Union and in the United States has led to much discussion about its impact on global trade, the future of trading blocks and the changing nature of politics. One common factor among these developments has been that young people's voice appears to have been largely ignored. France seems to be different in that the new president had vocal youth support. However, if youth are visible on the stage alongside candidates, does that mean their voice will be heard after the election?

Old and new lenses on the past

One characteristic of the rise of populism across the EU and the US is a romanticisation of a past time when a country was 'great' and times were somehow 'better'. This nostalgic view of the past is something held largely by older voters, while younger voters have only ever known more precarious times. Indeed it could be said that those young people who entered the labour market during the economic and financial crisis were truly in the wrong place at the wrong time.

With the UK's EU referendum, it was older voters who helped swing the vote towards leaving the EU: 60% of voters over 65 voted leave, while just 27% of those under 25 did. If we factor in the lower participation (and registration) of young people, the missing voice of young people becomes even starker (O'Reilly 2016).

Paying the price of nationalism

Young people have much to lose from a more insular perspective of nationalisation and a desire to turn back time. Open borders and the promotion of a spirit of inter-nation cooperation have created a youth cohort that has seen the benefits of European integration. Admittedly, these young people are among the more privileged in each country, but their concerns around the end of student mobility and loss of European identity are very real. While the consequences for youth in Britain are now becoming obvious, these risks are present across Europe with the rise of nationalism.

Young people's weak position amid these emerging political trends can be replicated in terms of their representation in key political decisions. Research confirms that young people were among the hardest hit by the economic crisis, experiencing rapid rises in unemployment and declining employment opportunities. Yet we also see that the policies enacted to address the crisis were not necessarily in their interests or were weakly implemented. Young people are on the wrong side of an intergenerational divide that threatens to deepen inequalities across age groups as well as inequalities between households and families.

Can young people engage politically?

Election turnout has long been lowest amongst youth, and this trend seemed to be on the rise. In the 2014 European elections, only 28% of under-25s voted. Furthermore, Europeans' membership in political parties has been declining.

Yet elections are not the only means of political engagement. Research has shown that protests are especially popular amongst those aged under 34. Likewise, Nuit Debout, similar to the Occupy Movement elsewhere in the world, has offered an alternative form of political engagement – a space for public discussion and cooperation without traditional hierarchies.

Investigations of young people's use of social media as a form of political engagement highlight the potential for these platforms to encourage critical engagement by increasing their ability to share and discuss politically relevant information.

Online engagement, offline influence?

Yet while alternative forms of engagement are invigorating, they may be difficult to translate into political power and influence. Although there is some evidence to suggest that online political engagement is correlated with offline participation, as long as young people fail to turn out for elections, politicians have fewer incentives to cater to their interests, fuelling a cycle of disaffection.

France is perhaps different in this respect. The foregrounding of young supporters and politicians by the Front National appealed to a neglected demographic: polls ahead of the first round of the presidential election showed that 39% of 18- to 24-year-olds intended to vote for Le Pen. Other parties made efforts to build their youth share. The same polls showed Macron, the subsequent election winner, to be the second most popular candidate among young people, perhaps in part attributable to the Youth with Macron group's online engagement strategies.

There are also attempts to mobilise young people without an explicit agenda. In the run-up to the French presidential election, Voxe.org attempted to capitalize on and develop the link between online and offline engagement with the #Hello2017 initiative. Their website offered attractive, video-heavy explainers of parties, candidates and policies with debates taken into the 'real world' at cafés and bars.

This seduction of youth is a trend emerging in other elections as well: in the UK, the Green Party and the Labour Party were foregrounding youth interests. It seems young people are now motivated to have their voices heard in post-Brexit politics – over 100,000 under-25s registered in the three days following the announcement of the snap General Election in the UK in 2017. The power of social media can also be seen in an earlier spike in online voter registration, attributed to a UK-wide Facebook reminder.

The extent to which these youth engagement initiatives deliver a higher youth turnout and a true voice for young people's concerns will be seen in the short term in the election results but then only in the medium term as we observe the extent to which policies are put into place. Whatever the outcomes, the rise of precariousness and disaffection means that building a political voice for young people has never been more important, both in Europe and elsewhere in the world.

Music as a platform: Grime cuts through

Stuart Hedley

In June 2015, I attended the Wild Life festival in Shoreham-by-Sea, in the UK. I, and everyone over 25 there, went to see the Wu-Tang Clan. Wu-Tang was the iconic breakthrough New York underground hip hop supergroup of the 1990s. However, everyone under 25 was there to see somebody else. The act on before Wu Tang were a couple of London Grime MCs, Skepta and JME, from the Boy Better Know collective, acts that I (and my fellow over-25s) had vaguely heard of but always had down as minor UK rappers warming things up for the main event.

An hour before Wu Tang were due to start, a London MC (I later identified as Skepta) began acapella rapping over the main stage sound system, and suddenly thousands of under-25s came running from all over the festival site, leaving the other stages quiet. The kids packed to the front and then started to form circled off areas within the crowd where they could throw themselves about. Siblings JME and Skepta and their Boy Better Know stablemates ran the show, with energy and crowd participation, directing the big screen cameras to zone in on balaclava wearing youths in the mob. This was my introduction to British Grime. They opened with Skeptas' 2014 hit *ThatsNotMe* and proceeded to blow the place apart for an hour. I was 35 and didn't understand it, but the kids were going crazy and that's exactly when I knew it was good, really good.

Going back 20 years, urban electronic music emanating from London estates has given a creative output for young people to represent their views in their own way. The Wild Life experience echoed my own teenage awakenings to jungle and drum and bass in the mid-90s. However, back then and until recently I and the artists themselves relied on mainstream media and mostly major record labels to get the word out beyond their local London scenes. Artists such as Goldie in the 1990s (my major teenage reference point), Dizzee Rascal (2003) and Tinie Tempah (2011) could only champion the sound and genre they represented via Mercury prizes, conventional press and required endorsement from major record labels. The 'majors' were the essential channels for the work to thrive and reach a wider audience via traditional distribution networks.

In the past five years, new media platforms have matured to a point that allows Grime artists to set up their own labels and media outlets independently of mainstream record labels and mainstream media support. Mirroring the evolution of vloggers, established new media platforms such as YouTube, Instagram, Twitter and Spotify enable Grime artists and scene supporters to get their music and message out to audiences beyond their local London base and across the globe. From its humble beginnings in West London, self-made, under-30, media millionaire Jamal Edwards' SBTV YouTube channel that initially specialised in Grime music has rocketed in global success and value. New media also permits getting work out in a far more rapid fashion than ever before and, most importantly, the artists and protagonists within the scene are running it.

Penetrating the USA has always been a target for the majority of UK musicians, which traditionally required the support of a major label for access, whereas the Grime scene has shown this is no longer the case. In his 2015 BRIT awards performance, American hip hop superstar Kanye West invited UK Grime artists including Skepta, JME and Stormzy (prior to any record deal) to join him on stage. Skepta, JME and their fellow artists were visible to the US hip hop elite without major label involvement. Skepta and JME's successful 2014 *ThatsNotMe* track and accompanying YouTube video (shot for a budget of £80) put their work onto the global stage and at present has more than 3 million views. US hip hop and RnB superstar Drake performed with the Boy Better Know collective in 2016 and has been rumoured to be in negotiations to be on the roster for a forthcoming Boy Better Know international record label.

The Grime MCs have also managed to broaden their influence beyond music. They have had an impact on their own terms at a political, social and cultural level. Artists including JME, Stormzy and Novelist have all urged their twitter followers to register to vote and back Jeremy Corbyn in the 2017 UK general election. The recent #Grime4Corbyn campaign offered people the opportunity to win tickets to a secret Grime concert if they registered to vote, notably not telling people how to vote, merely to just do so.

References

Wu-Tang Clan. 1993. *Enter the Wu-Tang* (36 Chambers). Loud Records, RCA, BMG.

Goldie. 1995. *Timeless.* Metalheadz, FFRR.

Dizzee Rascal. 2003. *Boy In Da Corner.* XL Recordings.

Wiley. 2008. *See Clear Now.* Asylum Records, Warner Music UK Ltd.

Tinie Tempah. 2010. *Disc-Overy.* Parlophone, Disturbing London Records.

JME. 2015. *Integrity.* Boy Better Know.

Skepta. 2016. *Konnichiwa.* Boy Better Know.

Drake. 2017. *More Life. A Playlist by October Firm.* Cash Money Records.

Duggins, Alexi. 2017. #grime4Corbyn – why British MCs are uniting behind the Labor leader. *The Guardian*, 17th May 2017. ***https://www.theguardian.com/politics/2017/may/17/grime4corbyn-why-british-mcs-are-uniting-behind-the-labour-leader***

How can trade unions in Europe reconnect with young workers?

Kurt Vandaele

Many trade unions are in trouble today. The percentage of employees paying a union fee has almost universally declined across Europe in recent decades. Moreover, what is left of the unions' membership base is generally 'greying'; Figure 1 shows that today many members are in their mid-40s to early 50s. Among the different categories of under-represented groups in unions, young people are considered to be the most 'problematic' in this regard. What could unions do to reconnect with them? To answer this question, I focus on three areas of motivation for union membership.

Figure 1: *Median age of union members in 2014 in Europe and change compared to 2004*

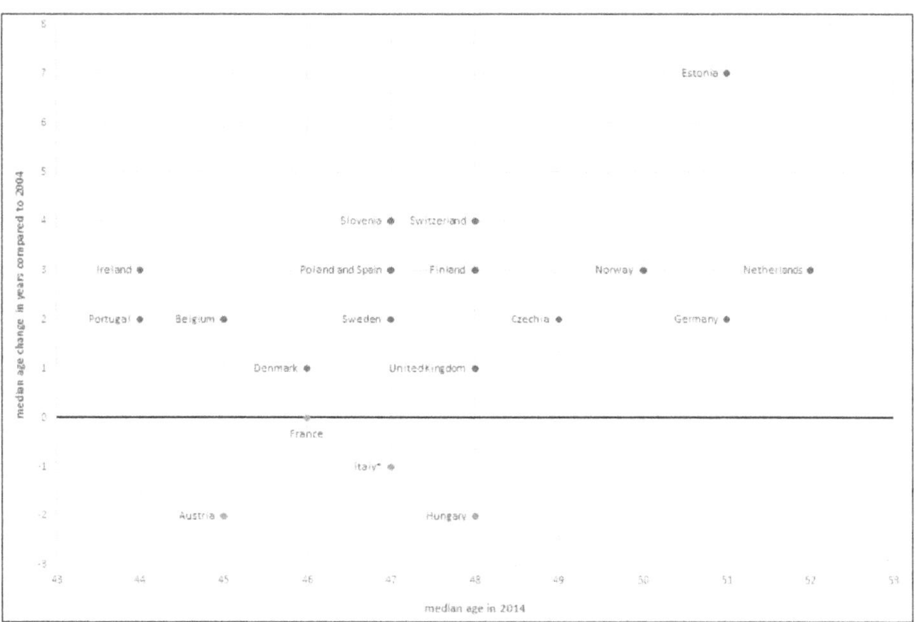

Source: European Social Survey. The original survey question refers to membership of a union or *similar organisation.* *Italy: 2012 data.

There is no such thing as widespread anti-unionism

The **first motive** relates to union membership as a social custom. The presence of parents, relatives and friends who support unionisation increases the likelihood of a young person developing a favourable attitude towards unions. But the transmission of such attitudes has become (much) weaker. In countries where unions have been in decline, union-friendly social networks are clearly shrinking. I argue that this provides an alternative explanation for the low rate of youth unionisation to that of media representations and political discourses, which are wrong to focus on intergenerational shifts in attitudes towards unions.

Despite claims to the contrary, virulent anti-unionism is not the problem. Certainly, tensions between young activists and unions exist. But these should be put in context: often they can be linked to inadequate union strategies, as has been the case in several south European countries since the Great Recession. All too often, however, unions tend to believe narratives that emphasise generational stereotypes, which risks excusing a lack of self-reflection on their part.

Young people's attitudes towards unions are in fact (critically) supportive – even in the US. However, for most of these young people, there is a big question mark over the role of unions. The dwindling presence of union-friendly social networks has made unions unfamiliar to youth prior to their labour market entrance. Unions across Europe have seen this lack of deeper union knowledge as a chance to inform young people about the work of unions and about social rights. But once young people make the transition from school to the labour market, it is crucial that they also find a union in their workplace, which is not always a possibility.

Labour market experiences need to be a priority focus

The **second motive** for union membership concerns instrumental factors. Favourable institutional frameworks, by lowering the costs of organising or servicing workers, can have a strong influence here. Figure 2 demonstrates the effect of such frameworks. In the Nordic countries and Belgium, which recorded high youth unionisation in both 2004 and 2014, unions are institutionally strongly integrated in young people's school-to-work transitions, allowing them to gauge the benefits of membership first-hand.

The graph also reveals that a high youth unionisation rate leads to a high adult unionisation rate. Early unionisation is therefore key. As the window of opportunity becomes smaller the older workers get, unions must demonstrate their relevance in the school-to-work transition of young people. The difficulty of this lies in the fact that young people are more likely to be employed in those workplaces and economic sectors where favourable frameworks for unions are weak or lacking. The hostility of employers to union membership and a fear of victimisation among young people further contributes to a low rate of youth unionisation.

Today's school-to-work transitions are plagued by precariousness, and the quality of youth jobs has deteriorated, with a rise in part-time and temporary work since the Great Recession. Therefore, union strategies around precarious work are of fundamental importance. Unions should reflect upon how they could develop organising strategies focused on a life-cycle approach instead of only a job-centred one. A good start for engaging young people would be to map what proportion of them are exposed to unionism and to analyse their experiences at work. If necessary, unions should also address their own current statutes and representation structures, as these might act as obstacles to union membership for those workers frequently changing employment status..

Figure 2: *Unionisation rates among youth and adults in Europe, 2004 and 2014*

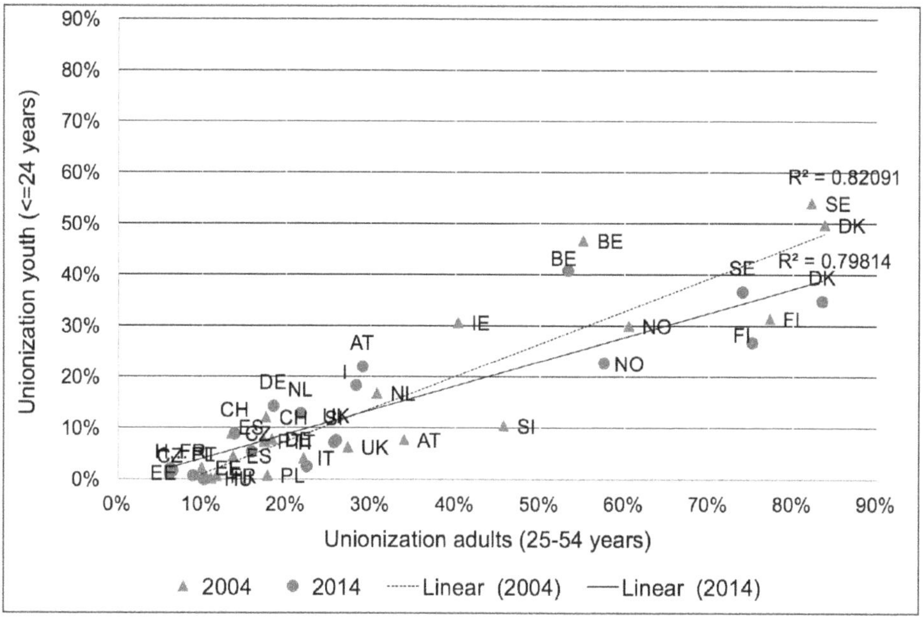

Source: See Figure 1.

Decisive union action is needed

The above point leads us to the third motive for union membership, which concerns ideological convictions. By promoting the principle of solidarity, unions could help to revive and strengthen the weakened traditional and instrumental motives for membership.

A good example of this approach is the successful Dutch 'Young & United' campaign, which achieved the partial abolishment of the youth minimum wage. In many ways, this campaign differed from union campaigns that use advertising channels highlighting the historical achievements of the labour movement. Instead of only a top-down approach, the campaign gave room to youth-led activism by escalating direct action, giving young people the confidence that their own contribution could make a difference to achieving a better regulation of the labour market. The campaign engaged them based on like-by-like recruitment, but did not address these young people as an age-defined group. Instead, by focusing on the youth minimum wage, a collective identity was forged based on a salient workplace issue that matters to them today. Making heavy use of social media, this issue-based campaign seemed effective at tapping into youth networks by using a language, visuals and messages that appealed to young people; it presented a different public image of trade unions.

Many unions still have a lot to learn about communication policies for engaging young people, whose preference for social media is based on the opportunities it offers for participation. A vast shift in resource allocation is needed to overcome the widening representation gap and to turn small-scale, local initiatives into large-scale organising efforts, especially in those growing occupations and sectors where young workers are employed and need unions the most. If the difficulties in organising young people are not addressed, other or new organisations might emerge or gain further prominence for representing them, particularly in specific segments of the labour market like the 'gig economy'.

Unions' organisational structures and predominant (decision-making) culture appear unattractive and unfavourable for youth participation in union democracy and action. Unions should be more responsive to and knowledgeable about the aspirations, interests and needs of young people. One way of achieving this would be to experiment with participatory democracy and informal engagement around such issues as precariousness. Fostering alliance-building between unions and relevant youth organisations, like student organisations, is another way to gain a better understanding of youth issues, including those outside the workplace. Today's age-based union structures for youth, if and where they are in place, are insufficient for instigating a more transformative change in union strategies and practices. Training and education via mentoring and union leadership development programmes could do even more to empower young unionists. Finally, a greater involvement of young people in union life and activities should form an essential part of a broad strategic vision on the future of unions.

There is no intergenerational shift that is dooming youth unionisation to failure. Therefore, unions should not resign themselves to such a fate, but rather recognise that there is still room for manoeuvre; and, it must be stressed, the sooner the better.

References

Vandaele, Kurt. *Forthcoming*. 'How Can Trade Unions in Europe Connect with Young Workers?' In *Youth Labor in Transition*, edited by Jacqueline O'Reilly, Janine Leschke, Renate Ortlieb, Martin Seeleib-Kaiser and Paola Villa. New York: Oxford University Press.

Getting your message across: How can a press agency help?

Natalie Sarkic-Todd and **Irene Marchi**

EURACTIV, the pan-European media network specialised in EU policies, is the dissemination partner of the STYLE Project. The aim of EURACTIV's participation was to raise the profile of the project in EU policy-making circles and to present the outcomes of the STYLE Project's research to relevant policy stakeholders, hence ensuring the uptake of the Project's results in EU policies.

Throughout the implementation of the Project, EURACTIV ensured editorial coverage of youth (un)employment with articles, interviews, opinion pieces and videos published in English on its main website, euractiv.com. The Social Europe & Jobs section acted as the policy hub for project-related coverage, collecting all relevant editorial content for an easier consultation and a continuous flow of information.

The logo of the STYLE Project was clearly visible and listed as one of the section's sponsors. The logo directed readers to the STYLE website with a view to making them learn more about the Project. A dedicated RSS feed also linked the EURACTIV Social Europe & Jobs section content to the Project website.

Stories were translated into French and German and published on euractiv.fr and euractiv.de, respectively, reaching a wider number of readers in their local language. More than 150 editorial items were published in French and German.

During the implementation of the Project, EURACTIV published more than 400 editorial items in English on euractiv.com, resulting in more than 800,000 page views (of which approximately 350,000 are unique visitors) and hence raising awareness of youth (un)employment policy among stakeholders.

Policy-makers from the EU institutions and national governments represent approximately 23% of readers on EURACTIV. It is therefore estimated that approximately 80,000 of these policy-makers have been informed of youth (un) employment policy through EURACTIV, proving the impact created by the Project's dissemination activities.

The top 15 countries of origin of the readers are: US, Belgium, UK, France, Germany, Italy, the Netherlands, Spain, Romania, Australia, Canada, Portugal, Denmark, Poland and Ireland. Other countries of origin of the readers include countries in which the EURACTIV Network is present and others participating in the STYLE

Project, including Greece, Bulgaria, the Czech Republic, Estonia, Lithuania, Turkey, Switzerland, Norway.

Special coverage was ensured through two ad-hoc publications on euractiv.com: a Linksdossier and a Special Report.

A Linksdossier is a comprehensive editorial overview that presents the main issues and stakeholders' positions in the policy debate – the Linksdossier *Fighting youth unemployment: an EU priority* was published in July 2014 (attracting more than 6,000 page views, more than 4,000 of which are unique page views).

A Special Report is an in-depth publication comprising five articles published over the period of one week to raise the visibility of a specific policy issue – the Special Report *Youth unemployment* was published in September 2015 (attracting more than 12,000 page views, more than 9,000 of which are unique page views).

Of the topics covered by EURACTIV in the Social Europe & Jobs section and related to the Project, the most read articles were related to:

- **Youth guarantee** See Youth Employment Initiative under threat in 2016 (05/11/2016) Thyssen: Our fight against youth unemployment is beginning to bear fruit (22/01/2016) Pushing the Youth Employment Initiative into overdrive (10/03/2015)

- **Over-education** See Don't just take first job offer, new graduates warned (19/01/2016) Youth leader: 'We need to stop internships replacing real jobs' (18/03/2016)

- **Unemployment** See Addressing youth unemployment through human rights (13/05/2016) Youth unemployment: Addressing the skills gap (01/04/2015) Study: Countries with faster school-to-work transitions have lower unemployment (18/08/2014)

- **Migration** See Immigration helps push German employment to record high (04/01/2016) Germany debates new immigration law amid skills shortage (17/04/2015)

- **Social impact** See Young Europeans continue to find it difficult to fly the nest (28/11/2016) Youth organisations have role to play in tackling violent radicalisation (20/05/2016) Commission seeks to reach disenfranchised youth (25/03/2015)

- **Investment in education and skills** See EU eSkills campaigns reduce gap in the labour market (18/11/2016) Giving youth the skills to innovate and lead Europe in the 21st century (19/05/2016) Education expert: Linking schools with businesses is win-win (02/06/2015) Can Juncker's investment plan live up to the promise it offers young people? (20/04/2016) ILO: EU investment plan could create 2.1 million jobs (29/01/2015)

- **Gender issues** See Promoting gender equality in the construction sector (11/03/2016) MEPs' last attempt to save maternity leave extension (16/03/2015)

Editorial items concerning the effects of Brexit and of new technologies and job models (e.g., Uber) on employment in Europe also attracted the attention of the readers. For example, see How the gig economy is changing employment (28/11/2016) Brexit could cost Britain £100 billion and one million jobs, CBI says (21/03/2016) Good jobs – threatened by the Internet (15/02/2016)

EURACTIV also organised a final policy conference in Brussels in September 2017. The conference presented the Project's results to policy stakeholders and researchers, creating a constructive debate with institutional representatives. More than 500 stakeholders received the invitation, including MEPs, European Commission officials, representatives from the industry and association level, NGOs, think tanks and universities. Approximately 50 participants attended the final event.

For a first-hand account of EURACTIV's role in the STYLE Project and to discover how editorial coverage helped raise the profile of the Project among policy-makers, see the video interview with Natalie Sarkic-Todd, EURACTIV European Network and Projects Director.

References

EurActiv LinksDossier. 2014. *Fighting youth unemployment: an EU priority.* ***http://www.euractiv.com/section/social-europe-jobs/linksdossier/fighting-youth-unemployment-an-eu-priority/***

EurActiv Special Report. 2016. *Youth Unemployment.* ***http://www.euractiv.com/section/social-europe-jobs/special_report/youth-unemployment/***

Emerging policy lessons from research on youth attitudes and values

Angie Hart, **Niall O'Higgins**, **Martin Seeleib-Kaiser** and **Endre Sik**

Drawing on some of the research findings from the project, we identified four key areas to inform policy debates.

Generational differences: A myth

First, the generational differences in relation to work attitudes often referred to in public debates and in political discourses are myths. 'Millennials' are not 'procrastinating'; their attitude to work cannot explain youth unemployment today. Young people today give as much importance to work as other generations at the same age. The value of work differs for everyone throughout the life cycle. Therefore, EU or national policies should not fail because of generation-specific cultural deviations. In other words, if we accept the findings of the literature that work values have a significant impact on values in general, then the stable nature of work values generation by generation provides policy-makers with firm ground to act. However, we detected differences in work values by age and period, as well as between two groups of European countries, so we should be aware that generational stability does not mean full-scale similarity.

The high level of commitment to employment in the youngest cohorts suggests that employment-generating policies can be important for helping the young enter into the labour market.

Youth unemployment: An insufficient focus

Second, focusing solely on the dimension of unemployment is insufficient for analysing labour market conditions and their impact on young people in Europe. Youth labour market outsiderness is an expression of unemployment, but also of precarious employment, and it has consequences for social and political participation. The implication is that the increasing diffusion and promotion of flexible employment is likely to have long-term negative consequences for young people's labour market attachment. The negative effects of precariousness in employment will affect young people's social capital. This provides a further reason for doubting the efficacy of temporary forms of employment as a means to promote the long-term stable employment of youngsters.

Institutions matter

Third, the economic crisis did not 'create' youth outsiderness, rather exacerbated already existing patterns. Institutional arrangements can significantly impact on the prevalence of young labour market outsiders and the support available for them.

The deleterious effects on social capital of specific unemployment and unstable employment are of more concern in some countries and contexts than others – interventions need to be targeted to suit local circumstances. Future (EU) youth policy initiatives should have a stronger element of institutional capacity building in order to facilitate their effectiveness in countries with comparatively weak institutions in the domain of school-to-work transitions and youth policy in general. For example, in Austria and Germany, low levels of youth outsiderness are associated with a relatively dense network of youth-related institutions and strong coordination among them.

Co-production of research: Implications for policy and practice

Fourth, including young people and those with complex needs as co-researchers should be encouraged because it can lead to research that more readily reflects the realities of young people's lives. Policy-makers and practitioners should take note that tackling youth unemployment from a resilience-based approach, which takes into consideration all aspects of the young person's life, can increase the likelihood of change. Such an approach also emphasises the importance of working at an individual and social level to tackle youth unemployment, rather than solely focusing on the individual.

Co-produced resources, such as the *One Step Forward* book, can be valuable tools for use in training practitioners (for example, social workers, teachers, psychologists, therapists and nurses), as well as foster carers and young people themselves.

Good practice example:

In Greece, the *One Step Forward* book was used in the training of over 200 support teachers (up to 2016). This was part of their vocational training and professional development run by the Greek Ministry of Education's special education training programme.

Many support teachers work with students from foster care and they desperately need resources to help them with these relationships.

They have also used the Resilience Framework included in the resource as it contained useful ideas and basic guidelines for supporting those students.

These are new resources for the Greek context where support from central government is scarce.

The teachers involved evaluated the use of the book in training these teachers very positively and many suggested that it be used in the training of other professional groups working with young people.

Resources

The resources are available to download from: ***http://issuu.com/boingboingresilience/docs/one_step_forward_-_resilience/1*** (UK edition) ***http://issuu.com/boingboingresilience/docs/one_step_forward_-_resilience_-_gre/1*** (Greek edition).

Which countries perform best and why?

Introduction to comparing country performance

Kari Hadjivassiliou

Young people have been particularly hard hit across the EU by the long-term effects of the Great Recession. This has resulted in:

1. A dramatic rise in youth unemployment;
2. Lengthier, unstable, and non-linear school-to-work (STW) transitions;
3. A deterioration in the quality of jobs for youth with greater precariousness;
4. An increased discouragement and labour market detachment; and
5. Greater labour market vulnerability of disadvantaged youth such as the low skilled, migrants and the disabled.

While recession-related economic deterioration and subsequent job-poor recovery account for such developments, these are also rooted in persistent structural deficiencies such as poorly performing education and training systems, segmented labour markets and low Public Employment Services (PES) capacity to address the problem.

Although the labour market situation of young people has started to improve in a number of countries since the Great Recession of 2007/8, youth unemployment still remains very high across Europe. In January 2016, the EU28 youth unemployment rate (15-24 years) was 19.7%. There is, however, a large divergence between countries in Europe, with rates ranging from 7.1% in Germany to 45% in Spain.

Youth unemployment rates
High youth unemployment rates reflect young people's difficulties in securing employment, or the inefficiency of the labour market. However, high youth unemployment rates do not mean that the total number of unemployed young people aged 15-24 is large, since many in this age group are in full-time education and are, therefore, neither working nor looking for a job. This can make meaningful comparisons between countries difficult (O'Reilly et al. *Forthcoming* a). Some analysts prefer discussing youth unemployment ratios, which measure youth unemployment over the total youth population including students. (O'Reilly et al. 2015).

'The *unemployment rate* is the proportion of youth actively looking for a job as a percentage of all those in the same age group who are either employed or unemployed; students are excluded from this measure. The unemployment ratio includes students as part of the total population against which youth unemployment is calculated. Because they are measured against a wider population, unemployment ratios are lower than unemployment rates. Ratios provide an indicator of the proportion of youth looking for a job vis-à-vis the relative share of youth in education. The NEET rate is the percentage of the youth population not in education or training among all young people in the same age group, including those who are working or studying, or both; it can be interpreted as a measure that reflects the fragility of STW transitions in a particular country.' (O'Reilly et al. *Forthcoming* a)

Youth unemployment ratios

The unemployment ratio, however, does not reveal if young people are not working or studying (economically inactive) because they are in education or because they are discouraged, that is, they have given up on even trying to get a job. This is why the NEET rates of young people aged 15-24 (those who are *not in employment, education or training*) are often a preferred measure for cross-country comparisons. NEET rates range from 15.6% in Spain to 4.7% in the Netherlands in 2015 (Hadjivassiliou et al. 2016).

Effective institutions

Germany and the Netherlands have established the most effective institutions to achieve a high integration of 15-19 year-olds in education and employment. High performance is consistent over time, showing that institutional effectiveness is robust at different stages of the economic cycle. However, Germany also suffered from high rates of youth unemployment in the early 2000s before the crisis hit the rest of Europe. This was in part due to the consequences of the reunification of Germany and difficult economic circumstances at that time. As a result, the picture in Germany and the Netherlands is slightly less positive for 20-24 year-olds. Nevertheless, both Germany and the Netherlands are amongst the highest performing countries in the EU for making sure their young people are in employment.

Austria and Denmark also achieve good youth labour market and employment outcomes. For 20-24 year-olds, performance is highest in Austria and has, since 2004, improved for 15-19 year-olds. This coincided with the extension of jobsearch instruments, the introduction of youth guarantees (YGs) and the extension of active labour market policies (ALMPs) for young people in Austria (Hadjivassiliou at al. 2015).

Work experience, vocational education and apprenticeships

Independent of educational attainment, work experience can be seen as one important pillar for sustainable school-to-work (STW) transitions in every country. Whereas countries like Germany, the Netherlands or Sweden achieve this by means of well-established schemes where school or study and work are combined, countries like France and the UK try to facilitate STW transitions by lowering labour costs through subsidies or low employment protection.

Overall, although with some notable exceptions (such as Germany and the Netherlands), vocational education and training (VET) is frequently perceived as being associated with jobs of lower status and quality than those resulting from a general/academic education; fewer students voluntarily choose the VET track. Crucially, there has been a convergence in policy across the EU, in that VET is now being promoted as a high-quality route to achieving improved labour market outcomes for young people (Hadjivassiliou et al. 2016).

Social partner cooperation

The provision of apprenticeships reflects the extent, type and nature of social partners' involvement in providing pathways into work for young people; in other words, how well employers, training providers and unions work together.

This involvement varies considerably between member states of the European Union and VET programmes. The role of social partners is clearly prescribed in highly regulated VET/apprenticeship systems with a corporatist form of governance such as Germany and Sweden. This results in very strong and active social partner involvement. In contrast, in market-led systems such as the UK, social partner involvement is rather weak and uneven. Likewise, social partner involvement in school-based VET systems tends to be less extensive than in work-based VET systems.

Given the importance of educational attainment in determining a young person's employment chances, there has been a major policy push (at both the EU and national levels) to both prevent early school leaving (ESL) and reduce educational underachievement. Indeed, reducing the ESL rate below 10% by 2020 is one of the headline targets of the Europe 2020 strategy. Despite this policy focus, in many member states – albeit with clear and considerable country variations – a large number of young people do unfortunately drop out of school and need help in re-engaging with the world of education. For example, of the countries studied as part of our research, Poland, Sweden, the Netherlands, France and Germany have already achieved the Europe 2020 target of ESL rates below 10%, as opposed to Spain, which has one of the highest ESL rates in the EU; and the UK, which has a relatively high but declining ESL rate.

Policy implications

Improving the situation of many millions of young Europeans who are failing to find gainful employment and, more generally, are suffering from deprivation and social exclusion, has been identified as a clear priority for both national (EU member states) and EU-wide initiatives (Eichhorst et al. 2015; Hadjivassiliou et al. 2016). EU and national policies have, in recent years, intensified support for young people, with a much greater focus on enhanced VET and youth-related active labour market policies (ALMPs).

Well-integrated VET systems with strong employer involvement

Well-integrated VET systems with strong employer involvement and clear labour market connections and supportive ALMPs have emerged as important institutional characteristics that have historically enabled comparatively better performance in countries like Germany, the Netherlands and Sweden.

There is currently a major policy drive across the EU regarding Youth Guarantees – YG/ALMP interventions for young people at risk of disengagement – which have been found to be effective policy instruments in the Scandinavian countries and Austria.

Integrating or centralising support for young people

Integrating or centralising support for young people by ensuring effective cooperation between relevant administrative bodies and other stakeholders can be another important pillar in fostering smooth STW transitions because it prevents young people from getting lost between different policy domains and avoids service fragmentation.

Closely linked to this is the need for partnership/multi-agency working to offer an integrated service to youth at risk, notably at the local level. Such partnerships are more effective if they include a wide range of relevant actors, notably PES, education, social services and health services, employers, NGOs and youth organisations. However, such partnerships will not necessarily be set up spontaneously, and a national drive, combined with appropriate resourcing, may be required. That said, this should also allow for flexibility at the local level.

Early vocational guidance

Early vocational guidance in combination with early jobsearch assistance and further support is another promising approach in improving STW transitions, especially for more disadvantaged young people (Eichhorst et al. 2015). Given the specific characteristics of youth at risk/NEETs who have multiple and varied needs, the design and delivery of programmes and policies should be informed by the involvement of all relevant stakeholders, ranging from social and health services to education and training providers, including schools, PES, employers, local authorities and third-sector organisations, including NGOs and youth organisations, etc.

Targeted policy interventions

Given the high diversity of the NEET population, each NEET-related sub-group requires targeted policy interventions tailored to their specific (and quite varied) needs. However, in general, in view of the major adverse impact of low educational attainment on a young person's likelihood of becoming NEET, it is generally accepted that preventative measures in relation to early school leaving and/or remedial measures aimed at re-integrating youth at risk are needed. Such measures should be so designed as to motivate, at an early stage, youth at risk of disengagement by focusing more on practical, vocational or work-related provision, either school-based or in alternative settings. That said, the provision of the required level of basic and soft skills, together with the development of confidence and self-esteem, should be an integral part of such interventions.

Reducing early school leaving

In general, prevention and early intervention are critical. For example, for those at risk of early school leaving or who have dropped out of school because of alienation from the more traditional (academic) teaching methods and formats, the provision of more vocation-oriented training options and/or alternative learning environments has also proved an effective way of either preventing their early school leaving or re-integrating them in education. Moreover, since the greater risk of dropping out occurs at key transition stages, notably between lower and upper secondary education, early intervention at these key transition stages is also critical.

Outreach

However, given the fact that a significant proportion of youth at risk is not registered, for example with PES, there is an urgent need for proper outreach and tracking-down approaches in order to identify such young people and include them in mainstream provision. To this end, the involvement of NGOs and youth organisations with specialist knowledge and skills in how best to engage with hard-to-reach young people is critical, although there are also good-practice examples where such outreach activities are conducted effectively by state actors. Second-chance education/'bridging' programmes have also proved effective in preparing vulnerable young people for entry to mainstream education.

Vulnerable young people

Similarly, systems for diagnosing vulnerable young people's specific needs and circumstances and putting in place a comprehensive range of person-centred services and interventions are essential for effectively addressing their complex and multiple needs. Indeed, the focus of interventions should be person-centred and have enough flexibility and variety so as to cater for different pathways toward STW transition, taking into account the different profiles and needs of youth at risk.

For the hardest to reach and most disaffected youth, this may mean that, as a first step towards their active engagement, much more emphasis should be put on their motivation and the development of their self-confidence and self-esteem. To this end, personalised counselling, mentoring and on-going support is critical, with the mentor not only helping the young person navigate the various and, many times, complicated administrative systems, but also guiding and offering him/her support throughout the intervention. Indeed, mentoring and on-going support has proved to be very effective for youth at risk.

Effective case management

Linked to this is the need for effective case management that again has been shown to be essential for such youth. Individual action planning together with personalised help and support throughout the young person's journey, and follow-up well after the end of the intervention, contribute to more sustainable outcomes. Here ensuring that there is sufficient PES capacity and resources is critical, especially in relation to properly servicing youth at risk, who require much more intensive and personalised attention.

Labour demand

Despite EU funding, reforms are, in most cases, being introduced against a backdrop of tight public finances, austerity and spending cuts, which undermines their effective implementation. Moreover, a general lack in labour demand will soon show the limitations of ALMPs or VET systems if these are used on their own as a means for addressing youth unemployment. This is because incentive mechanisms for employers and potential employees, like those included in ALMPs, are quite unsuitable under difficult macroeconomic conditions. Against a fragile economic recovery in many member states, the scope for providing training places (such as apprenticeships and jobs) to young people may be limited. Furthermore, Hadjivassiliou et al. (2015) show that simply reducing labour costs by increased flexibility does not improve the STW transition per se.

In our research into the STW transition systems in eight countries, we identified favourable policy changes that could improve STW transitions, such as the greater policy focus on VET and the wider implementation of the YG with a distinct focus on NEETs. However, strong labour demand shocks can only partly be tackled by employment and education policy at least in the short run.

The Youth Guarantee

Although the YG framework serves as a strong basis for effective interventions, it is not clear that it provides the extended timeline and flexibility required for reaching out to those youth at risk who are farthest from the labour market and need a longer-term integration process. Here, the effort of identifying and engaging them as well as addressing their multiple and complex needs and stabilising their social and employment situation is a labour-intensive and time-consuming process. This should be reflected in the way the YG is resourced, implemented and monitored across the EU.

References

Hadjivassiliou, Kari, Laura Kirchner Sala and Stefan Speckesser. 2015. *Key Indicators and Drivers of Youth Unemployment.* STYLE Working Paper WP3.1 Indicators and Drivers of Youth Unemployment

Gonzalez Carreras, Francisco, Laura Kirchner Sala and Stefan Speckesser. 2015. *The Effectiveness of Policies to Combat Youth Unemployment.* STYLE Working Paper WP3.2 Policies to combat Youth Unemployment

Eichhorst, Werner, Kari Hadjivassiliou and Florian Wozny, eds. 2015. *Policy Performance and Evaluation: Qualitative Country Case Studies.* STYLE Working Paper WP3.3 Policy Performance and Evaluation – Synthesis Report

Hadjivassiliou, Kari, Catherine Rickard, Sam Swift, Werner Eichhorst and Florian Wozny. 2016. *Comparative Overview.* STYLE Working Paper WP3.4

O'Reilly, Jacqueline, Werner Eichhorst, András Gábos, Kari Hadjivassiliou, David Lain, Janine Leschke, Seamus McGuinness, Lucia Mýtna Kureková, Tiziana Nazio, Renate Ortlieb, Helen Russell and Paola Villa. 2015. 'Five Characteristics of Youth Unemployment in Europe: Flexibility, Education, Migration, Family Legacies, and EU Policy'. *SAGE Open* 5 (1): 1–19. ***http://journals.sagepub.com/doi/abs/10.1177/2158244015574962***

Hadjivassiliou, Kari P., Arianna Tassinari, Werner Eichhorst and Florian Wozny. *Forthcoming*. 'How Does the Performance of School-To-Work Transition Regimes in the European Union Vary?' In *Youth Labor in Transition*, edited by Jacqueline O'Reilly, Janine Leschke, Renate Ortlieb, Martin Seeleib-Kaiser and Paola Villa. New York: Oxford University Press.

O'Reilly, Jacqueline, Janine Leschke, Renate Ortlieb, Martin Seeleib-Kaiser, and Paola Villa. *Forthcoming*. 'Integrating Perspectives on *Youth Labor in Transition*: Economic Production, Social Reproduction and Policy Learning'. In *Youth Labor in Transition*, edited by Jacqueline O'Reilly, Janine Leschke, Renate Ortlieb, Martin Seeleib-Kaiser and Paola Villa. New York: Oxford University Press.

O'Reilly, Jacqueline, Janine Leschke, Renate Ortlieb, Martin Seeleib-Kaiser and Paola Villa. *Forthcoming* a. "Comparing the Problems of Youth Labor Market Transitions in Europe: Joblessness, insecurity, institutions, and inequality" in Jacqueline O'Reilly, Janine Leschke, Renate Ortlieb, Martin Seeleib-Kaiser, and Paola Villa (eds.) *Youth Labour in Transition* (New York: Oxford University Press).

What drives youth unemployment?

Kari Hadjivassiliou, **Laura Kirchner Sala** and **Stefan Speckesser**

The Great Recession of the late 2000s and ensuing economic recovery hit young people in the EU disproportionately hard, although with significant country variations. However, even before this major crisis, the performance of youth labour markets across the EU was highly varied and closely linked to the different institutional configurations at member state level.

Labour market performance: A single index measure
Here, we examine labour market performance affecting young people in the light of recent policies in Europe, drawing on an analysis of EU Labour Force Survey (EU-LFS) data in the period 2004-2012. Indeed, crucial to our analysis presented here has been a consistent availability of EU-LFS data, so that a time series of the EU before, during and after the recession can be constructed for the key age groups of young people: 15-19 and 20-24 year-olds.

Our aim was to develop a single index measure of labour market performance that would combine nine variables of labour market inclusion, human capital formation, labour market segmentation and transitions out of education.

The index provides a way of comparing the relative performance of youth labour markets across member states. It seeks to measure each country's youth labour market performance (and achievement) on the basis of four key dimensions: (i) labour market inclusion; (ii) human capital formation; (iii) labour market segmentation; and (iv) school-to-work (STW) transitions, including transitions out of education and/or into NEET status.

Figure 1 below graphically presents the nine indicators used for this analysis that are, in turn, grouped in these key four dimensions of youth labour market performance. Crucially, these dimensions are closely related to strategic policy and programme objectives at both EU and member-state levels.

These aim to improve

a) inclusion in the labour market and
b) human capital accumulation while reducing
c) segmentation and
d) transitions from school to NEET status.

Figure 1: *Framework of Performance Indicators*

LM Inclusion	**Human capital formation**
• Employment rate • NEET rate • Long-term unemployment • Youth-to-adult unemployment ratios	• Education participation • Transitions from school-to-work with VET
Labour market segmentation	**School-to-work transition**
• Fixed-term employment outside VET • Involuntary part-time work	• Transition into NEET (+ unemployment) status

Source: Speckesser, S, (2015). D3.1 – Key Indicators and Drivers of Youth Unemployment, presentation at the STYLE Grenoble meeting, 5/3/2015

By adopting such an analytical framework and developing an index of multiple performance variables in order to assess country performance over time and across the EU, we sought to extend and enrich existing descriptive comparative studies of youth labour markets in two ways:

1. Based on consistent data and formulas for 27 EU member states and a time series of nine years, our analysis is less affected by measurement issues, as cross-country differences in the multi-dimensional nature of policy performance over time are likely to be constant, similar to a fixed effect. In addition, to address measurement issues we used Principal Component Analysis to create a second index aimed at capturing a latent concept of labour market performance not affected by institutional differences in outcome variables. For example, by doing so we sought to address the issue of possibly underestimating youth unemployment in countries with large-scale apprenticeship systems.

2. For individual countries, we describe how performance improved over time by indexing the starting value in 2004 to 1. This allows us to show whether a country's combined performance along the four key dimensions mentioned above improved over time.

This study does not follow the conventional conceptual framework of econometrics, which aims to obtain estimates of the quantitative magnitude of effects of institutional reform. In this case, one is, for example, interested in estimating how much macroeconomic outcomes – such as high employment levels or economic growth – would change if particular institutional arrangements were altered (Hadjivassiliou et al. 2015; Gonzalez Carreras et al. 2015; Hadjivassiliou et al. *forthcoming*). In contrast, here our focus is on the description of performance and measures associated with youth-related policy reform in particular countries. In doing so, we adopt an inductive rather than a theory-led approach to obtain high-level inference on how institutional change can affect complex outcomes, such as young people's transitions to the labour market that are, in turn, affected by a multiplicity of factors such as those examined here.

Nine indicators

To this end, as mentioned earlier, we first used the nine indicators (shown in Figure 1 above) to describe each country's performance across four dimensions: (i) labour market inclusion; (ii) human capital formation; (iii) labour market segmentation; and (iv) STW transitions.

For example, in terms of employment rates – a key indicator of labour market inclusion – Denmark, Norway, the Netherlands and the German-speaking countries are the best performers with their high and stable youth employment rates over time.

Likewise, in terms of STW transitions as measured by a young person's transition into NEET and unemployed status, the Netherlands and the German-speaking countries outperformed all the other member states over the entire period under study (2004-2012). These were closely followed by the Nordic countries, which also managed to reduce the proportion of young people becoming NEET/unemployed after leaving education.

Policy effectiveness

We have additionally created index measures for the analysis of policy effectiveness in the light of the strategic objectives set at EU and national levels. In doing so, we sought to address the multi-dimensional nature of policy performance since index measures are able to capture improvements in some dimensions, such as a reduction of long-term unemployment, while other dimensions of youth labour market performance remain unchanged.

In cross-country analyses such as the one presented here, using index measures to compare country performance can both reveal how much countries have improved in relation to the best performer or an absolute benchmark ('aggregate loss function') and also show whether differences in youth labour market performance narrowed or widened over time. On the basis of such index-based analysis we are, in turn, able to both examine a country's youth labour market performance over time and show whether policy performance has improved.

Composite indicators
To this end, two composite indicators were constructed summarising each country's performance over time and in relation to the two groups of young people under study (i.e., those aged 15-19 and those aged 20-24). Overall, on the basis of the composite indicators, Denmark, Germany and the Netherlands are the best performers in terms of youth labour markets. This is, broadly, in line with the strong body of evidence that consistently shows that countries with effective dual (work-based/apprenticeships) or school-based VET systems are characterised by successful STW transitions.

A third part of our analysis involved using the composite indices to compare change in a country's youth labour market performance over time. This showed that Austria, Belgium, Poland and the Nordic countries improved in relation to countries with the best youth labour market performance between 2004 and 2012. However, the gap between Southern European countries and the top performers has widened, reflecting both structural factors such as the weak links between education and the labour market, in the former, as well as the fact that they were hit disproportionately hard by the Great Recession and associated Eurozone crisis.

A fourth part of our analysis comprised the estimation of probit models using EU-LFS micro-data to identify the potential drivers of and barriers to STW transitions and how these have changed over the last ten years. The probit models show that, in terms of individual characteristics, the main barriers to effective STW transition include the following: (i) being young; (ii) being female; (iii) having low levels of educational attainment (and no or low qualifications); and (iv) having an immigration background/ foreign nationality. On the other hand, higher levels of qualifications and parental qualifications definitely improve transitions from education to employment.

NEETs
Again, our findings are in line with the existing evidence base according to which the level of educational attainment is a key determinant of young people's likelihood of being unemployed and/or NEET. For example, as the seminal work of Eurofound (2012) has shown, young people with low educational attainment (ISCED 0-2) are 300% more likely to be NEET than better qualified youth, while those with an immigration background are 70% more likely to become NEET.

STW transitions are becoming relatively more segmented
In general, we assumed that where the barriers to youth labour market integration have increased over time (i.e., between 2004 and 2012), STW transitions are becoming relatively more segmented in relation to people's existing qualifications, gender, nationality or the effects of parental education on youth transitions.

In contrast, where barriers have decreased, then STW transitions have been relatively less segmented. Indeed, our analysis also showed that, over time, the significant barriers of gender, age, foreign nationality and education levels to successful STW transitions decreased in most EU countries. Not surprisingly, consistent with our earlier labour market performance assessment, the individual barriers to STW transitions decreased most in countries with improving youth labour market conditions. That said, as is always the case with EU-wide comparative analysis, the emerging picture is more nuanced. For example, in some countries, such as Austria, Belgium and France, young people with low educational attainment levels now have more difficulties than before the Great Recession.

Moreover, we found no clear picture on how an overall deteriorating economic situation affected the individual transitions and labour market performance of a particular country. For example, in Portugal and Spain, where the youth labour market deteriorated dramatically as a result of the Great Recession and its aftermath, the impact of individual characteristics such as gender became less important altogether.

Gender differences

However, such 'fading gender differences' cannot be interpreted as progress for young women in terms of achieving better labour market outcomes; rather, the recession had a stronger negative effect on young men's STW transitions. For example, the collapse of the construction sector in Spain, which historically employed a large share of young men, resulted in a 72% fall in youth employment between 2008 and 2011. In other countries, drivers and barriers to STW transitions have remained broadly unchanged.

Parental education

Finally, parental education was also found to significantly affect young people's STW transitions. Young people whose parents have low educational attainment (ISCED 0-2) are up to 150% more likely to be NEET compare to those whose parents have a secondary level of education, and are up to 200% more likely to be NEET than those whose parents are tertiary education graduates (Eurofound 2012).

Growing inequality in young people's transitions

This, in turn, suggests growing inequality in young people's transitions originating from family circumstances in the form of parental level of educational attainment. Indeed, this could be a further issue for policy action in addition to improving the labour market situation for young people more generally.

Overall, the use of our composite indicators has exposed a latent concept of youth labour market outcomes. This, we argue, provides a more useful tool for monitoring policy progress and for evaluating and interpreting the outcomes for high-level policy decision-making in relation to STW transitions.

Moreover, the analysis of aggregate indicators needs to be complemented by an analysis of micro-data on individual drivers of and barriers to successful transitions so as to improve the targeting of policy to specific groups and decrease inequality.

References

Eurofound. 2012. *NEETs – Young People not in Employment, Education or Training: Characteristics, Costs and Policy Responses in Europe*, 21.10.2012, http://www.eurofound.europa.eu/sites/default/files/ef_publication/field_ef_document/ef1254en.pdf

Gonzalez Carreras, Francisco, Laura Kirchner Sala and Stefan Speckesser. 2015. *The Effectiveness of Policies to Combat Youth Unemployment. STYLE Working Paper WP3.2 Policies to combat Youth Unemployment*

Hadjivassiliou, Kari, Laura Kirchner Sala and Stefan Speckesser. 2015. *Key Indicators and Drivers of Youth Unemployment.* STYLE Working Paper WP3.1 Indicators and Drivers of Youth Unemployment

Hadjivassiliou, Kari P., Arianna Tassinari, Werner Eichhorst and Florian Wozny. *Forthcoming.* 'How does the performance of school-to-work transition regimes in the European Union vary?' In *Youth Labor in Transition*, edited by Jacqueline O'Reilly, Janine Leschke, Renate Ortlieb, Martin Seeleib-Kaiser and Paola Villa. New York: Oxford University Press.

What policies are effective in combatting youth unemployment?

Francisco J. Gonzalez Carreras, Laura Kirchner Sala and **Stefan Speckesser**

The Great Recession and scarring effects

The Great Recession of the late 2000s and the ensuing rather anaemic economic recovery – or rather stabilisation in most member states – has hit young people all over the EU disproportionately hard, though with clear variations between countries (and, in some cases, regions). Against a backdrop of very high youth unemployment and, in some cases, dramatically and persistently high NEET rates (and their well-documented long-term 'scarring' effects), as well as precariousness in employment, the EU has made the need to improve the labour market prospects and employment chances of young people one of its key priorities.

Policies to combat a 'lost generation': The Youth Guarantee

In the face of a dramatic rise in youth unemployment, especially during and after the Great Recession, and the risk of a 'lost generation' of young Europeans, EU institutions such as the European Commission, together with national governments, have put the promotion of youth employment at the top of the political agenda. Often following European Commission recommendations, many member states have embarked upon ambitious reform programmes—such as the introduction of the Youth Guarantee (YG), structural reforms of vocational education and training (VET) and activation policies—which have the potential to significantly alter the way in which STW transitions are structured.

Our research goals

We set out to:

- provide quantitative estimates of the impact of specific active labour market policies (ALMPs) and associated programmes on youth unemployment;
- conduct a causal analysis on the impact of specific youth-related labour market and education and training policies on youth labour market outcomes; and
- carry out a cost–benefit analysis on the welfare implications of the different policy options available in order to improve the situation of young people in the labour market.

In order to assess the performance of youth labour markets and the effectiveness of implemented policies, our analysis covered the EU27 and Turkey. Macroeconomic as well as microeconomic indicators were analysed in order to explain structural, cyclical and individual factors affecting STW transitions. Furthermore, a single index measure of youth labour market performance was developed to simplify the evaluation of the multi-dimensional nature of factors influencing STW transitions. At the same time, we conducted a comprehensive literature review of the existing evidence on the effectiveness of ALMPs, both in general and in relation to young people, as well as in terms of their impact at macroeconomic level (e.g., aggregate employment/unemployment, functioning of the labour market/Beveridge curve).

Research questions

Our review highlighted the fact that there is little or no evidence concerning (i) the quantitative impact of improved policy interventions in the form of ALMPs in relation to young people and (ii) the long-term/future social benefits of increased public spending at present.

Our research aims to contribute to the debate, first, by estimating the quantitative impact of ALMP and other institutional features on youth unemployment and, second, by discussing costs and benefits of different policy options that would, ideally, lead to better informed and more evidence-based policy-making in relation to young people's labour market entry.

Our research methods

Our analysis provides quantitative estimates of the impact of ALMPs on youth unemployment in Europe based on a macroeconomic panel data set of youth unemployment, ALMP and education policy variables, and further country-specific characteristics of labour market institutions and the broader demographic and macroeconomic environment for all EU member states.

Using Blundell, Bond and Windmeijer's (2000) GMM estimator for dynamic panel data models, we estimated the impact of different ALMP options on youth unemployment ratios. This is a more reliable indicator than the youth unemployment rate because it reflects the proportion of unemployed youth in relation to the total youth population (employed, unemployed and inactive, including those in full-time education).

Active Labour Market Programmes

In terms of the different ALMP options examined, we adopted the typical classification used by both the EU and the OECD. This includes

1. provision of public employment services (PES), such as jobsearch assistance;
2. training programmes for unemployed people, including those that offer subsidies for trainees who attend courses, including VET or apprenticeships, and for companies that take on people who combine work with relevant training;
3. subsidies for regular employment in the private sector in the form of wage subsidies or tax reductions; and

4. direct job creation such as public works programmes and support to agencies or local authorities for hiring unemployed (young) people. Because of methodological and data limitations, for our quantitative estimates on the impact of ALMPs on youth unemployment we restricted our analysis to using participation in ALMP as the relevant policy variable.

Vocational Education and Training: Apprenticeships
In addition to ALMPs, VET, including apprenticeships, is considered key to lowering youth unemployment and facilitating youth STW transitions. Policy-makers across Europe have been attempting to improve VET in order to provide an attractive alternative to general upper-secondary and tertiary education and in order to better meet the skill requirements of the labour market. Since VET plays an increasingly crucial role in the policy response to youth unemployment, in particular in the longer term, we have also used participation in VET as a percentage of the total population of the age range 15-24 to analyse the impact of vocational education policy on the youth unemployment ratio.

Our results
Overall, our results show that participation in vocational education at ISCED-3 level and in some ALMPs and associated programmes has significant effects on aggregate youth unemployment, while ALMP-related training programmes do not show a significant impact.

Based on models without a lagged policy variable, our estimates show that significant reductions of youth unemployment ratios could be achieved by increasing VET. Specifically, the youth unemployment ratio (15-24 year-olds) would decrease by 0.25 percentage points if participation stocks in vocational education (as a percentage of all 15-24 year-olds) increased by one percentage point. Introducing a lag does not change this finding by much.

The picture is different for the variables estimating the impact of ALMP on young peoples' unemployment ratios. For example, the increase in participation in employment incentive programmes (relative to youth unemployment) by one percentage point reduces youth unemployment by 0.7 percentage points.

Likewise, youth unemployment ratios would decrease by about 0.4 percentage points if participation in job-creation schemes (stocks as a percentage of youth unemployment) increased by one percentage point. On the other hand, increasing the participation in ALMP-related labour market training was found to increase youth unemployment. Table 1 summarises the findings of our analysis.

Table 1: *Impact of participation in ALMPs as % of unemployment (15-24 average annual stocks) on unemployment ratios*

	Coef.	**Robust SE**	**z**	**P>|z|**
ALMP part. as % of UE (under 25)				
a) Employment incentive programmes	**-0.0075**	**0.0036**	**-2.0600**	**0.0400**
b) Job creation schemes	**-0.0399**	**0.0199**	**-2.0100**	**0.0440**
c) Labour market service	-0.0002	0.0042	-0.0600	0.9560
d) Labour maket training	0.0012	0.0051	0.2300	0.8150
e) Business start ups	-0.1154	0.1160	-0.9900	0.3200
L3 vocational education (all)				
% of 15-24 year olds	**-0.0249**	**0.0079**	**-3.1600**	**0.0020**

Source: Speckesser, S, (2015). D3.1 – *Key Indicators and Drivers of Youth Unemployment*, presentation at the STYLE Grenoble meeting, 5/3/2015

Note: Marginal effect percentage point change in observed unemployment ratio (UE as a percentage of the 15-24 year-old population); significant estimates are in bold.

ALMPS and NEETs

We have also contextualised our analysis with an evidence base on the impact of ALMPs on youth unemployment. We have related our findings to available estimates of individual and social benefits of reducing youth unemployment and the number of NEETs.

This literature found that being NEET at a young age is likely to result in lower earnings over the life course, poorer health and higher probability of committing crime, for which various studies – mainly from the UK – have provided estimations of these costs in monetary terms.

Cost-Benefit Analysis

A full Cost-Benefit Analysis relating to the increase in VET and ALMP as a value measure of social benefits could not be undertaken as part of our research because the evidence base on the benefits of reducing youth unemployment (and the cost of NEETs) is limited to only very few countries.

However, we have produced estimates that can be used for some policy reform modelling by parameterising a model of the incremental costs of policy reform; for example, extending employment incentive programmes to temporarily improve young people's position in the job matching process. The resulting value parameters are shown in Table 2 below. This allows us to gain an understanding of the costs associated with increasing the use of policy interventions relating to ALMPs and VET in order to reduce youth unemployment.

Table 2: *Impact of spending (in €1,000 per UE) and VET participation on unemployment ratios*

	Impact on 15-19 youth unemployment ratio				Impact on 20-24 youth unemployment ratio			
	COEF.	**Std. Err**	**z**	**P>|z|**	**COEF.**	**Std. Err**	**z**	**P>|z|**
Employment incentive programmes	-0.017	0.096	-0.18	0.856	0.034	0.208	0.16	0.869
Job creation schemes	**-0.164**	**0.072**	**-2.28**	**0.023**	-0.201	0.105	-1.91	0.056
Labour market service	**0.196**	**0.072**	**2.14**	**0.032**	**0.281**	**0.091**	**3.09**	**0.002**
Labour market training	-0.077	0.105	-0.74	0.46	-0.062	0.155	-0.4	0.69
Business start ups	0.63	0.758	0.83	0.406	-0.777	1.657	-0.47	0.639
People in L3 vocational programmes	**-0.031**	**0.007**	**-4.81**	**0**	**-0.024**	**0.011**	**-2.27**	**0.023**

Source: Speckesser, S, (2015). D3.1 – *Key Indicators and Drivers of Youth Unemployment*, presentation at the STYLE Grenoble meeting, 5/3/2015

Conclusions

On the basis of our estimates presented in both Table 1 (impact of ALMPs and VET on youth unemployment ratios) and Table 2 (cost of policy reform), we can draw the following tentative conclusions:

- Increasing VET by one percentage point significantly reduces youth unemployment, but it would have to be a large-scale intervention for such an effect to take place since there are already many young people in vocational education. Moreover, such education and training has comparatively high costs per participant.

- Employment incentives are a more costly ALMP-related programme but, on average, fewer people are engaged. Extending this element, as part of the youth-related policy mix, would potentially be more costly per participant (in most countries); however, the overall spending to achieve a significant reduction in youth unemployment could be potentially lower.

- Job creation schemes are the most costly option, but there is also some evidence of higher impacts than other interventions. However, it should also be stressed here that, as our literature review highlighted, the evidence regarding the impact of such schemes in terms of sustainable employment and cost effectiveness is not very robust. As a result, this finding of our analysis should be interpreted with extreme caution.

- Overall, it seems that work experience (acquired as part of either job-creation schemes and/or employment incentives) reduces youth unemployment most and is most cost effective. On the other hand, training programmes as part of

> ALMPs do not reduce youth unemployment. As far as extending vocational education is concerned, its impact on reducing youth unemployment is positive; however, the magnitude of this impact is rather small.

The above discussion notwithstanding, we firmly believe that in order to understand the welfare implications of policy change, such estimates as those presented above would have to be further refined, for example considering differential impacts across countries; the choice of countries is also dependent on which suitable data would have to be made available.

We are fully aware that the findings of this aggregate analysis of the impact of ALMPs on youth unemployment should be interpreted with caution since we were severely constrained by the limited availability of relevant, consistent and comparative data across the EU. In that regard, we were indeed constrained by having to rely for our analysis on very rough measures of ALMP spending and participation. Following this analysis, we believe that there is an urgent need to set up a proper data collection and monitoring system across the EU which should, *inter alia*, include micro- and macro-economic data with coherent concepts of policy interventions (and indicators for policy effectiveness) for young people. Improved estimates of the long-term cost of youth unemployment (and the long-term economic benefit of reducing NEETs) to the European economy also need to be produced in order to allow for consistent research on the impact of policy and programmes (e.g., ALMPs). This will also contribute to better policy-making based on improved understanding of the social return on investment of policy aimed at reducing youth unemployment.

References

Gonzalez Carreras, Francisco, Laura Kirchner Sala and Stefan Speckesser. 2015. *'The Effectiveness of Policies to Combat Youth Unemployment'* STYLE Working Paper WP3.2 Policies to combat Youth Unemployment

Blundell, Richard, Stephen Bond and Frank Windmeijer. 2000. *Estimation in Dynamic Panel Data Models: Improving on the Performance of the Standard GMM Estimator.* IFS Working Paper 12. London: Institute for Fiscal Studies.

Comparing youth transition regimes in Europe

Werner Eichhorst, **Kari Hadjivassiliou** and **Florian Wozny**

Comparing countries

The purpose of our research here was to map out and compare dynamics, performance and effectiveness of youth labour markets in Europe in different institutional and policy settings, using qualitative and quantitative analyses. Our comparative framework and selection of country case studies was informed by Pohl and Walther's youth transition regime typology because we wished to capture, compare and contrast the existing diversity and variety of STW transitions not only between but also within regimes (Pohl and Walther 2005; 2007; Walther 2006). We therefore identified five main types of youth transition regimes:

Universalistic (SE), where the focus of STW transition policies is mainly on education in the broad sense of personal development as well as on supportive activation;

Liberal (UK), which focuses more on the young person's rapid labour market entry;

Employment-centred (DE, FR, NL), each of which, although belonging to this regime, has a different STW transition focus: mass (company-based) apprenticeships (dual training) in Germany, school-based STW transition in France and a mixed apprenticeship and school-based VET system in the Netherlands, which, in any case, combines elements of both the liberal and the universalistic system;

Subprotective/Mediterranean (ES, TR), which has traditionally had the weakest links between the worlds of education and work and quite protracted STW transitions; and

Post-socialist/Transitional (EE, PL), which has adopted a mix of liberal and/or employment-centred approaches.

An in-depth analysis was carried out for eight selected countries (DE, EE, ES, NL, PL, SE, TR, UK) by Eichhorst et al. (2015) and Hadjivassiliou et al. (*forthcoming*). This provided detailed information about the education system as well as institutions responsible for the STW transition. Local experts (comparable groups comprising policy-makers and policy-implementing organisations, social partners, academic experts, etc.) were asked to give their assessment of national systems of STW transitions and how these can be improved – or have been improved – by recent policy innovations, including the EU-wide introduction of the Youth Guarantee and a stronger policy focus on vocational education and training (VET), including apprenticeships (Eichhorst et al. 2015).

Why compare countries?

Establishing a comparative overview of different youth labour markets in Europe such as those represented by the eight countries studied here is valuable for several reasons. For example, the existing heterogeneity between educational systems in Europe is an opportunity for mutual learning. To this end, cross-sectional differences between countries or longitudinal developments within countries concerning how education structures and systems (together with educational attainment) have been improved by recent policy innovations can be used as best practice, especially with respect to STW transitions. In this regard, the governance structure is one major pillar because decision-making structures are decisive for understanding administrative capacities and limitations. Within Europe, there is substantial variation in governance structures, ranging from rather centralised decision-making processes in Poland and Estonia to decentralised processes, as in Germany or Sweden.

Educational legislation is centralised

In most European countries, education legislation is centralised. This ranges from high levels of centralisation, as in Turkey, where the basic structure of education is planned and operated by the state, to intermediate levels, as in Estonia or Spain, where planning takes place at the state/regional level and operation happens at the local level, and to low levels of centralisation, as in Germany or Sweden, where both planning and operating is realised at the state/regional and local level.

Schooling

The basic structure of schooling is similar in most European countries. Every country offers primary, secondary, vocational and tertiary education, with compulsory schooling components. Nevertheless, there are country-specific differences in the emphasis of each educational part. Whereas, for example, vocational education has traditionally been important in Germany and the Netherlands, the opposite is true in the case of the UK. Such factors explain differences in the levels of highest educational attainment and country-specific prioritisation of vocational as opposed to general education. In the case of Estonia, Germany and the Netherlands, high-school drop-out rates became an issue in tertiary or vocational education, while early school leaving (ESL) is especially an issue in the UK and Spain, which still has the highest ESL rate in Europe, albeit with significant differences across its 17 regions.

Education systems, shaped by the governance structure of each country, interact with various youth-related labour market policies. The latter are active labour market policies (ALMPs) that support young people in finding a job and/or, where appropriate, training or work experience placement, but additionally also legislation that hampers employment by increasing the costs of labour or decreasing incentives to work. Thus, country-specific employment protection, working-hour and minimum wage legislation, welfare benefits and labour taxation are of major importance when assessing education systems concerning school-to-work transitions.

Youth-related ALMPs

Youth-related ALMPs focus on the transition between education and the labour market, especially for disadvantaged youth. For example, it has been shown that individualised and intensive support such as personalised job/career counselling together with individualised action planning by PES facilitates STW transitions. However, if such policies are in place, they are often complex and fragmented, for example, as in Germany and the UK. This is related to the fact that ALMPs are often decentralised and not always implemented by adequately resourced PES in terms of either funding and/or staffing. For example, despite the dramatic increase of youth unemployment in Spain, public spending cuts and austerity measures have led to a recruitment freeze in the Spanish PES and thus affected its capacity to provide assistance to an increasing number of young jobseekers. Indeed, as the European Commission itself underlines, the PES capacity in many member states is still too weak to provide personalised and individualised counselling, or active labour market measures and interventions tailored to the various jobseeker profiles. Unfortunately, little effort has been undertaken in evaluating these policies.

Work experience

Independent of educational attainment, work experience can be seen as one important pillar for sustainable STW transitions in every country. Whereas countries like Germany, the Netherlands or Sweden achieve this by means of well-established schemes where school or study and work are combined, countries like France and the UK try to facilitate STW transitions by lowering labour costs through subsidies or low employment protection, respectively.

Employment protection legislation (EPL)

Employment protection legislation (EPL) is usually universal rather than youth specific, especially in the case of dismissal protection. Nevertheless, young people tend to be over-represented in certain forms of employment, such as fixed-term contracts and part-time or other atypical forms of employment. For example, Poland and Spain are among the EU countries with the highest rates of temporary employment among young people. At the other end of the spectrum, in Estonia and the UK, the use of temporary employment is among the lowest in the EU.

Such country variation reflects, *inter alia*, different labour market structures, STW transition patterns, EPL characteristics, the extent to which traineeships form part of the national education and training system, and youth-related policy measures. For example, the low EPL in Estonia and the UK – and associated greater labour market flexibility – has been regarded as a contributing factor to the low incidence of temporary employment in these countries.

Involving the social partners

Involving the social partners in decision-making processes could facilitate the efficiency and acceptance of youth-specific legislation that seeks to both promote greater labour market participation and safeguard the quality of employment of young people. Countries like Estonia, Germany, the Netherlands and Spain show how such social partner involvement can be achieved. The positive impact of social partner involvement is not only limited to legislation, but also to education programmes – adapted to better reflect employer requirements – or ALMPs.

Rigorous evaluation

Empirical evidence is essential for the rigorous evaluation of practices that improve STW transitions. However, it is necessary to point out that differences in youth labour market statistics between countries are at present partly driven by the recent crisis as opposed to solely reflecting the structure and effectiveness of STW transition in a particular member state. As such, the rather bleak picture that these statistics paint are, in many cases, the result of a lack in labour demand caused by both the Great Recession and the ensuing fiscal consolidation and austerity policies. For example, institutional factors are overshadowed by a lack of labour demand in Spain as the main factor explaining poor performance in youth transitions. Youth-related policies, however, focus (mostly) on the supply side of labour, like human capital formation, for example. Therefore, interpreting good labour market statistics as being the outcome of effective youth labour policy can be misleading.

The macroeconomic environment

Furthermore, the macroeconomic environment also drives the focus of policies, making skill mismatches a topic discussed more in countries like Germany or the Netherlands, while the distribution of jobs is of particular importance in a country like Spain. That said, institutions shape the youth labour market despite labour demand shocks, and analysing these institutional arrangements is important for enhancing one's understanding about their structure, functioning and effectiveness. This in-depth examination of youth-related institutional frameworks must recognise differentiation between heterogeneous groups of young people. These differences range from young people who passed through the education system and became directly employed afterwards without any assistance, to those who are (long-term) unemployed without any formal school-leaving qualification. Even within these extreme cases, as Eurofound's work on NEETs has highlighted, there are several and significant differences concerning family background, ethnicity, nationality or sex, for example.

References

Eichhorst, Werner, Kari Hadjivassiliou, and Florian Wozny, eds. 2015. *Policy Performance and Evaluation: Qualitative Country Case Studies.* STYLE Working Paper WP3.3 Policy Performance and Evaluation – Synthesis Report

Hadjivassiliou, Kari P., Arianna Tassinari, Werner Eichhorst and Florian Wozny. *Forthcoming.* 'How Does the Performance of School-To-Work Transition Regimes in the European Union Vary?' In *Youth Labor in Transition,* edited by Jacqueline O'Reilly, Janine Leschke, Renate Ortlieb, Martin Seeleib-Kaiser, and Paola Villa. New York: Oxford University Press.

Policy overview of school-to-work transitions

Kari Hadjivassiliou

Cyclical and structural factors

The dramatic rise of youth unemployment during the Great Recession and its aftermath can be largely attributed to *cyclical factors* such as the recession-related economic deterioration that typically affects young people more than older workers. However, there are also *structural factors* contributing to high youth unemployment, such as ineffective education and training systems with poor outcomes and ensuing skills mismatches; labour market segmentation; structural changes affecting youth labour markets (e.g., the hollowing-out of labour markets and skills polarisation); the patchy availability of quality work experience – which increasingly plays a crucial role in STW transitions; and the uneven PES capacity and effectiveness in providing tailored support to young people.

Policy action

In light of such structural determinants of high youth unemployment, it is not surprising that, following the Great Recession, considerable policy action has focused, across the EU, on reforming and redesigning various institutional arrangements that structure the process of STW transitions. Indeed, EU and national policies have in recent years intensified support for young people with, *inter alia*, a much greater focus on enhanced VET and youth-related ALMPs, notably the Youth Guarantee. For example, given the fact that VET/apprenticeships have proved effective in supporting smooth STW transitions, policy-makers across Europe have been attempting to improve VET in order to provide an attractive alternative to general upper-secondary and tertiary education and to better meet the skill requirements of the labour market.

VET/apprenticeships are critical

Overall, VET/apprenticeships still play a critical role in facilitating fast and smooth transitions, albeit to varying degrees and depending on the path-dependent institutional and cultural context. They have proved to be a key STW transition mechanism in the employment-centred cluster, notably Germany and the Netherlands, but less so in the subprotective (ES, TR) and liberal clusters (UK), while their take-up is decreasing in the universalistic cluster (SE). Not surprisingly, we found that VET participation was much higher than the EU average in the employment-centred regimes and much lower in the subprotective and the post-socialist clusters. These differences in the participation rates in VET across EU countries can be attributed in part to the differing perceptions of VET and its centrality in the STW transition process.

Policy convergence and societal differences

Crucially, there has been a convergence in policy across all clusters, in that apprenticeships are now being promoted as a high-quality route to achieving improved outcomes for young people in all clusters. However, the success of this policy shift is dependent on the specific structural and institutional frameworks that are in place to support this agenda, which varies greatly between clusters.

Dual (work-based/apprenticeships) or school-based VET systems, the strong involvement of all relevant stakeholders and a co-operative institutional framework ensure that the employment-centred regimes have a strong STW transition model. For example, Germany and the Netherlands, particularly, have below-average youth unemployment rates and STW transition duration. On the other hand, France is characterised by lengthier STW transitions and diverse labour market inclusion instruments, ranging from a variety of subsidised employment contracts to an array of VET placements, each with varying degrees of effectiveness.

The STW transitions under the UK's liberal regime are fast but unstable, with a focus on youth employability and the promotion of young people's economic independence as quickly as possible. Within the subprotective cluster, characterised by high youth unemployment, STW transitions are lengthier, unstable and complex. In Spain, for example, STW transitions are protracted and fragmented, while the prevalence of temporary, short-term employment contracts among young people reflects the fact that this type of employment has traditionally been a key (but controversial) STW transition instrument.

The Estonian STW transition model is focused more on a general education (school-based) pathway, while its work-based VET in the form of apprenticeships is relatively underdeveloped. In Poland, youth unemployment has been a key policy issue for the past decade, but Poland is also characterised by a high degree of labour market dualism, with the highest share of fixed-term contracts in the EU and a low (20%) transition rate from temporary to permanent employment. This has clear and negative implications for the STW transitions of Polish youth.

The Swedish model has historically been associated with a high-quality and effective education and training system, including VET, producing well-educated youth able to make fast and successful STW transitions. Similar to Germany and the Netherlands, it has been argued that these smooth STW transitions can be attributed to a high share (well above the EU average) of students combining work and study. However, as in other countries, these smooth STW transitions do not hold for all young people. Those who have not completed secondary education, or young migrants and refugees or those with disabilities, face particular barriers to labour market entry.

Employment Protection Legislation

The countries also varied in their EPL as well as the focus of their ALMPs. Differences in ALMPs between France, Germany and the Netherlands are driven by the highly different education systems and the general economic performance of these countries. Whereas dual vocational training is one important pillar of the German education system, it is less important in the Netherlands and even still less in France. Instead, wage subsidies as part of ALMPs play a crucial role in France and the Netherlands to facilitate the acquisition of work experience and/or a first job by young people. In the UK, ALMPs are not specifically targeted at young people, although there have been some flagship initiatives such as the Youth Contract as well as some youth-specific support targeted at disadvantaged youth, notably NEETs.

Likewise, although Swedish ALMPs are often aimed at all age groups, programmes like the Job Guarantee focus on young people. ALMPs in Spain often seek to improve young people's skills, both theoretical and practical, and/or provide them with work experience. In the post-socialist cluster (EE, PL), labour market policy is less differentiated compared to employment-centred countries like Germany. This is also true for ALMPs, where there is little focus on youth in both countries, although some recent projects/programmes do focus on the specific needs of young people. In both countries, ALMPs that are used to support the STW transition of young people include training and/or employment subsidies to increase the supply of work experience placements.

Youth transition regimes are in a state of flux

Our analysis has also highlighted that, especially as a result of the Great Recession of the late 2000s, some of the characteristics of each of Pohl and Walther's STW transition regimes are in a state of flux. For example, VET (and apprenticeships) are becoming more important STW transition mechanisms even in clusters such as the liberal (UK) and the subprotective (ES, TR). On the other hand, in the universalistic cluster, the quality and effectiveness of the Swedish education and training system (including VET, which in the past produced well-educated young people who could make fast and successful STW transitions) is currently under-performing, with obvious implications for these transitions. At the same time, VET take-up is falling. That said, it is still too early to assess whether such changes represent paradigmatic shifts in the key STW transitions mechanisms, especially in view of the path dependency and cultural and institutional specificity of STW transitions.

A requirement highlighted by our review is the need for Pohl and Walther's typology of STW transitions to be updated and further refined on the basis of the developments that have occurred during and after the recent crisis. These developments have led to an on-going reconfiguration of education and training systems, labour market policies and institutional arrangements which are pertinent to young people's successful entry to sustained employment. Linked to this is the need for further differentiation within the clusters themselves given the variation in institutional arrangements, which leads in turn to variation in the STW transition outcomes, as is, for example, the case of the employment-centred cluster (DE, FR, NL). The above discussion notwithstanding, our analysis did not really change the way STW transitions in each cluster have been traditionally regarded, especially in relation to their length, quality and sustainability.

References

Hadjivassiliou, Kari, Catherine Rickard, Sam Swift, Werner Eichhorst, and Florian Wozny. 2016. *Comparative Overview.* STYLE Working Paper WP3.4

Werner Eichhorst, Florian Wozny, Kari P. Hadjivassiliou. 2016. *Policy Synthesis and Integrative Report.* STYLE Working Paper WP3.5

Hadjivassiliou, Kari P., Arianna Tassinari, Werner Eichhorst and Florian Wozny. *Forthcoming.* 'How does the Performance of School-to-Work Transition Regimes in the European Union Vary?' In *Youth Labor in Transition*, edited by Jacqueline O'Reilly, Janine Leschke, Renate Ortlieb, Martin Seeleib-Kaiser and Paola Villa. New York: Oxford University Press.

O'Reilly, Jacqueline, Janine Leschke, Renate Ortlieb, Martin Seeleib-Kaiser and Paola Villa. *Forthcoming.* 'Integrating Perspectives on *Youth Labor in Transition*: economic production, social reproduction and policy learning'. In Youth Labor in Transition, edited by Jacqueline O'Reilly, Janine Leschke, Renate Ortlieb, Martin Seeleib-Kaiser and Paola Villa. New York: Oxford University Press.

O'Reilly, Jacqueline, Werner Eichhorst, András Gábos, Kari Hadjivassiliou, David Lain, Janine Leschke, Seamus McGuinness, Lucia Mýtna Kureková, Tiziana Nazio, Renate Ortlieb, Helen Russell and Paola Villa. 2015. 'Five Characteristics of Youth Unemployment in Europe: Flexibility, Education, Migration, Family Legacies, and EU Policy' SAGE Open 5 (1): 1–19. ***http://sgo.sagepub.com/content/5/1/2158244015574962***

Further reading on comparing school to work transitions in Europe

Country Reports

Eichhorst, Werner, Florian Wozny and Michael Cox. 2015. *Policy Performance and Evaluation: Germany.* STYLE Working Paper WP3.3 Performance Germany

Eamets, Raul and Katrin Humal. 2015. *Policy Performance and Evaluation: Estonia.* STYLE Working Paper WP3.3 Performance Estonia

González Menéndez, María, Javier Mato, Rodolfo Gutiérrez, Ana Guillén, Begoña Cueto and Aroa Tejero. 2015. *Policy Performance and Evaluation: Spain.* STYLE Working Paper WP3.3 Performance Spain

Bekker, Sonja, Marc van de Meer, Rudd Muffels and Ton Wilthagen. 2015. *Policy Performance and Evaluation: Netherlands.* STYLE Working Paper WP3.3 Performance Netherlands

Ślezak, Ewa and Bogumila Szopa. 2015. *Policy Performance and Evaluation: Poland.* STYLE Working Paper WP3.3 Performance Poland

Wadensjö, Eskil. 2015. *Policy Performance and Evaluation: Sweden.* STYLE Working Paper WP3.3 Performance Sweden

Gökşen, Fatos, Deniz Yükseker, Sinem Kuz and Ibrahim Öker. 2015. *Policy Performance and Evaluation: Turkey.* STYLE Working Paper WP3.3 Performance Turkey

Hadjivassiliou, Kari, Arianna Tassinari, Stefan Speckesser, Sam Swift and Christine Bertram. 2015. *Policy Performance and Evaluation: United Kingdom.* STYLE Working Paper WP3.3 Performance UK

Hadjivassiliou, Kari, Laura Kirchner Sala and Stefan Speckesser. 2015. *Key Indicators and Drivers of Youth Unemployment.* STYLE Working Paper WP3.1 Indicators and Drivers of Youth Unemployment

Gonzalez Carreras, Francisco, Laura Kirchner Sala and Stefan Speckesser. 2015. *The Effectiveness of Policies to Combat Youth Unemployment.* STYLE Working Paper WP3.2 Policies to combat Youth Unemployment

Eichhorst, Werner, Kari P. Hadjivassiliou and Florian Wozny, eds. 2015. *Policy Performance and Evaluation: Qualitative Country Case Studies.* STYLE Working Paper WP3.3 Policy Performance and Evaluation – Synthesis Report

Hadjivassiliou, Kari P., Catherine Rickard, Sam Swift, Werner Eichhorst and Florian Wozny. 2016. *Comparative Overview.* STYLE Working Paper WP3.4

Werner Eichhorst, Florian Wozny and Kari P Hadjivassiliou. 2016. *Policy Synthesis and Integrative Report.* STYLE Working Paper WP3.5

O'Reilly, Jacqueline, Werner Eichhorst, András Gábos, Kari Hadjivassiliou, David Lain, Janine Leschke, Seamus McGuinness, Lucia Mýtna Kureková, Tiziana Nazio, Renate Ortlieb, Helen Russell, and Paola Villa. 2015. 'Five Characteristics of Youth Unemployment in Europe: Flexibility, Education, Migration, Family Legacies, and EU Policy'. SAGE Open 5 (1): 1–19. ***http://journals.sagepub.com/doi/abs/10.1177/2158244015574962***

Hadjivassiliou, Kari P., Arianna Tassinari, Werner Eichhorst and Florian Wozny. *Forthcoming*. 'How does the Performance of School-to-Work Transition Regimes in the European Union Vary?' In *Youth Labor in Transition*, edited by Jacqueline O'Reilly, Janine Leschke, Renate Ortlieb, Martin Seeleib-Kaiser and Paola Villa. New York: Oxford University Press.

O'Reilly, Jacqueline, Janine Leschke, Renate Ortlieb, Martin Seeleib-Kaiser and Paola Villa. *Forthcoming*. 'Integrating Perspectives on Youth Labor in Transition: Economic Production, Social Reproduction and Policy Learning'. In *Youth Labor in Transition*, edited by Jacqueline O'Reilly, Janine Leschke, Renate Ortlieb, Martin Seeleib-Kaiser and Paola Villa. New York: Oxford University Press.

O'Reilly, Jacqueline, Janine Leschke, Renate Ortlieb, Martin Seeleib-Kaiser and Paola Villa, eds. *Forthcoming*. *Youth Labor in Transition*. New York: Oxford University Press.

What can we learn about policy innovation?

Introduction: What are the barriers to and triggers for policy innovation?

Maria Petmesidou and **María C. González Menéndez**

Research questions

There is a rich literature on policy learning, policy transfer and policy change, and youth transition regimes (Hall 1993; Dolowitz and Marsh 2000; Walther and Pohl 2005). However, there is no systematic comparative analysis of the possibilities for, and the barriers to, policy learning and transfer that focuses specifically on the problems related to youth unemployment, and how such learning and transfer works at various levels of interaction for local, regional, national and supranational stakeholders in the EU.

The salience of youth employment problems in many European countries has brought the need to develop effective measures of school-to-work (STW) transitions to the top of the EU agenda. It has generated EU initiatives for integrated policies addressing youth at risk and has accelerated mutual learning, policy transfer and experimentation within and across countries.

But how do European countries compare in terms of the institutional structures and processes that facilitate or hinder policy learning and innovation with respect to effective measures for sustained STW transitions?

How we carried out the research

We selected nine countries for our study on the basis of three criteria: to have joined the EU at different stages of enlargement (including Turkey as an accession country); to span the entire spectrum of STW and welfare regimes; and to represent cases of varying scale and severity of the youth problem.

Our analysis is based on information obtained through in-depth, semi-structured interviews that were carried out in the first half of 2015 in each of the countries studied with key stakeholders, academics and researchers. A template with a common set of questions (adapted for each country) was used as a guide. The available literature on each country was also scrutinised with the aim of unravelling the major planks of academic and public debate on facilitators or constraints of policy innovation.

Key findings: Diffusion and inertia

We found a significant distinction between countries with policy machineries that are conducive to coordinated sharing and diffusion of information and experience between different levels of administration and joint stakeholders' bodies, and those exhibiting considerable inertia as regards policy learning and experimentation.

Local/regional administrations and agencies are more likely to exchange knowledge on policy processes and tools between themselves and also to get involved in cross-country mutual policy learning.

Policy governance supporting regional and local partnerships and policy entrepreneurs

Experimentation with proactive youth employment measures, more importantly, is facilitated by a mode of policy governance that supports (regional/local) partnerships and networks of public services, professional bodies and education/training providers, employers, youth associations and other stakeholders. We found that policy entrepreneurs play a significant role in promoting policy learning and transfer.

Our analysis provides evidence of a clustering of the countries studied into two groups. Denmark, the Netherlands, the UK and, to some extent, France stand out as rather 'proactive' countries, though to varying extents and through different mechanisms. Belgium, Greece, Spain, Slovakia and Turkey show a higher inclination to path dependency or inertia.

However, in France and the UK, innovative policies do not seem to yield significant outcomes in dealing with the youth problem. This applies both to the efficiency dimension (given the fact that youth unemployment remains high in France), but most notably to the equity dimension, given that the NEETs rate and the risk of poverty and social exclusion among the young are considerable in both countries and gender disparities persist.

Conclusions: Multi-level governance structures and interactions

Our findings emphasise the importance of (a) the role played by overall governance structures in the dynamics of policy change and innovation, and (b) the major institutional aspects and interactions facilitating or hindering policy innovation.

Most of the countries studied exhibit a multi-level governance structure: regional/local administrations have competences over certain elements of policy relevant to youth transitions, while central government institutions play a significant role in strategic policy decisions and in the overall regulatory framework. However, the degree of administrative decentralisation cannot by itself explain the differences in policy experimentation and innovation among the countries studied.

Within the first group of countries, Denmark exemplifies systematic interaction and feedback among all levels of governance from the bottom upwards and vice versa, which is conducive to negotiated and evidence-informed innovation. In the Dutch case, multi-level plans to tackle youth unemployment and facilitate transitions are of significant importance in enhancing innovation and learning. In the more centralised

UK, market mechanisms, competition and choice are seen as key in driving policy innovation but, at the same time, the marketised logic of competition can act as an obstacle to sharing of best practice among multiple public and private providers.

In the second group of countries, piloting, programme evaluation and impact assessment are performed less systematically. It is also difficult to ascertain whether the acquired evidence feeds into policy design (e.g., in Belgium). In France, state dirigisme with policy centralisation implies that most innovations focus on an extensive array of market and non-market youth contracts.

Barriers to policy learning and innovation: Fragmentation

In all these countries, barriers to policy learning and innovation stem from fragmentation and overlapping of policy competences in the fields of education, training and employment for youth.

Policy innovation and knowledge diffusion are limited by highly centralised administration structures (Greece, Turkey) or excessive bureaucratisation (Greece). Coerced transfer has been the case in Greece under the bailout deals, while political interests overrule policy decisions to different extents in Turkey, Slovakia, Greece and Spain. Nonetheless, Slovakia and a number of regions in Spain stand out as examples of innovative initiatives.

Path shift in VET structures

Further, in Spain, Greece and Slovakia, a path shift is under way in VET structures via an attempt to strengthen the dual system and raise its public visibility and attractiveness for young people. Local entrepreneurs, drawing experience from across Europe, are playing a significant role in instigating reform.

Soft forms of learning

As for inter-linkages between national institutional contexts and international actors, soft forms of learning across countries and through supranational channels of knowledge transfer/adaptation are of relevance in all national cases. However, the influence is more decisive in initiating policy change in the second group of countries, particularly given that policy patterns of some Northwestern European countries are often adopted (and diffused) by EU institutions as 'best practices'.

Structural factors

Finally, a general trend at the macro level is pointed out in most of the country reports. Structural factors are tending to make STW transitions lengthier and more uncertain. At the same time, the progressive polarisation of the labour market, resulting in fewer intermediate jobs, significantly diminishes opportunities for progression beyond entry level for many young people.

References

Dolowitz, David, and David Marsh. 2000. 'Learning from Abroad: The Role of Policy Transfer in Contemporary Policy Making'. *Governance* 13 (1): 5-24.

Hall, Peter. 1993. 'Policy Paradigms, Social Learning, and the State: The Case of Economic Policymaking in Britain'. *Comparative Politics* 25 (3): 275-296.

Petmesidou, Maria, and María González Menéndez. Forthcoming. 'Policy Transfer and Innovation for Building Resilient Bridges to the Youth Labor Market'. In *Youth Labor in Transition*, edited by Jacqueline O'Reilly, Janine Leschke, Renate Ortlieb, Martin Seeleib-Kaiser and Paola Villa. New York: Oxford University Press.

Petmesidou, Maria, and María C. González Menéndez, eds. 2015. *Barriers to and Triggers of Innovation and Knowledge Transfer. STYLE Working Paper WP4.1 Barriers to and triggers of policy innovation and knowledge transfer*

Walther, Andreas, and Axel Pohl. 2005. *Thematic Study on Policies for Disadvantaged Youth in Europe.* Final report to the European Commission. Tübingen. *http://ec.europa.eu/employment_social/social_inclusion/docs/youth_study_en.pdf*

Country Reports

Bekker, Sonja, Marc van der Meer and Ruud Muffels. 2015. *Barriers to and Triggers for Innovation and Knowledge Transfer in the Netherlands.* STYLE-D4.1 Country Report Netherlands

Carstensen, Martin B., and Christian Lyhne Ibsen. 2015. *Barriers to and Triggers of Policy Innovation and Knowledge Transfer in Denmark.* STYLE-D4.1 Country Report Denmark

Gökşen, Fatoş, Deniz Yükseker, Sinem Kuz and Ibrahim Öker. 2015. *Barriers to and Triggers for Innovation and Knowledge Transfer in Turkey.* STYLE-D4.1 Country Report Turkey

González Menéndez, María, Ana Guillén, Begoña Cueto, Rodolfo Gutiérrez, Javier Mato and Aroa Tejero. 2015. *Barriers to and Triggers for Innovation and Knowledge Transfer in Spain.* STYLE-D4.1 Country Report Spain

Hadjivassiliou, Kari, Arianna Tassinari and Sam Swift. 2015. *Barriers to and Triggers for Innovation and Knowledge Transfer in the UK.* STYLE-D4.1 Country Report UK

Martellucci, Elisa, and Gabriele Marconi. 2015. *Barriers to and Triggers for Innovation and Knowledge Transfer in Belgium.* STYLE-D4.1 Country Report Belgium

Petmesidou, Maria, and Periklis Polyzoidis. 2015. *Barriers to and Triggers for Innovation and Knowledge Transfer in Greece.* STYLE-D4.1 Country Report Greece

Smith, Mark, Maria Laura Toraldo and Vincent Pasquier. 2015. *Barriers to and Triggers for Innovation and Knowledge Transfer in France.* STYLE-D4.1 Country Report France

Veselkova, Marcela. 2015. *Barriers to and Triggers of Policy Innovation and Knowledge Transfer in Slovakia.* STYLE-D4.1 Country Report Slovakia

Policy learning, networks and diffusion of policy ideas

Maria Petmesidou and **María C. González Menéndez**

Research questions

Major policy innovations in the form of the EU Youth Guarantee and apprenticeship-type VET schemes have been introduced across Europe to reduce youth unemployment. But how does this impact on policy governance? Do these policy schemes trigger significant institutional changes and actors' involvement in policy design and implementation? Does a 'bottom-up' push for cooperation at the local/regional level) trigger policy learning, transfer and experimentation? What mechanisms of change underlie the innovative schemes that we studied? Is there more or less intentional learning? What is the role of policy entrepreneurs? How does EU funding conditionality affect these changes?

Research methods

To address these questions and the processes that facilitate or hinder policy learning and innovation with respect to effective measures for sustained STW transitions, we carried out case studies in nine partner countries. We examined policies with an innovative potential that are at the forefront of EU priorities for improving STW transitions, such as the Youth Guarantee (YG) – or a similar scheme of 'holistic' intervention for reaching out to disadvantaged youth – and an apprenticeship-type VET scheme. We also searched for evidence of changes in VET that bring employers to the centre of policy design and delivery and how such innovations can promote multi-actor cross-learning. In autumn 2015 and early 2016, we conducted in-depth, semi-structured interviews in each country with key stakeholders, academics and researchers involved to varying degrees in the design, implementation and monitoring of the schemes we studied, using a common thematic template.

Key findings: The challenge of novel policies

We found significant differences between the nine countries around the extent to which policies aimed at young people fulfilled the Youth Guarantee. Where the YG is a novel policy (Greece, Slovakia, Spain), designing and delivering individually tailored services and coordinating the system at the national level posed a challenge. Nevertheless, in Spain, where existing local initiatives fitted the YG, this policy intervention formalised existing practice. In Slovakia, local collaborative trust-based relationships were enhanced by the EU YG initiative; it also triggered novel practices at the local level, drawing upon policy learning and transfer from other EU countries. Key practitioners at the local level played a central role in this respect.

Among the partner countries that have a youth guarantee in place, the 'Pact for a Youth-Unemployment-Free Zone' in the Mid-Brabant region in the Netherlands is an example from which policy practitioners can draw inspiration as to the governance and delivery of interventions for STW transitions.

Innovative interventions

The innovative interventions examined imply significant changes in terms of policy formulation, policy content and governance. In countries with a higher inclination to inertia (see previous entry), the EU initiative for a Youth Guarantee and the European Alliance for Apprenticeship have fostered more or less structured networks and multi-agent partnerships that are conducive to (small-scale) experimentation and innovation, in specific localities and or policy sectors. Examples are the 'National Project Community Centres' in Slovakia targeted at disadvantaged Roma youth, or the piloting of dual VET in the automotive and tourism sectors in Slovakia and Greece, respectively. This effect is clearly stronger in some regions/localities in Belgium and Spain. Yet a systematic transfer of knowledge to other levels of government is limited in all these countries. Particularly in Greece, Spain and Slovakia, change and innovation are closely conditioned by the aims of EU programmes incorporated into the funding conditionalities of the European Social Fund (ESF) and other EU financial instruments. These can change the domestic opportunity structure.

In France, EU influence played a significant role in the past in the establishment of the Second Chance schools. Still, these schools exemplify a significant innovation in VET governance and policy tools. They epitomize a local/regional network-type mobilisation of relevant actors and a shift from the mainstream qualification-based approach to the acquisition of competences in a flexible learning process following the student's progress.

Lessons drawn constitute major pathways of policy change and innovation in the other three countries with a more proactive inclination: In the UK, lessons are drawn (in a fragmented way) from previous domestic experience. In Denmark, policy learning takes place through a systematic interaction and feedback between different levels of government. And in the Netherlands, inspiration, emulation and adaptation of practices developed in other regions of the country constitute the main conduit of innovation diffusion. This is the case of the 'Pact for a Youth-Unemployment-Free Zone' in the Mid-Brabant region and of the VET innovative policies in Amsterdam – both inspired by a partnership-based development model in another region of the country. In the latter two cases, new policy tools include a youth monitor database linking schools, public employment offices and local agencies, and a partnership-based mode of policy governance. The VET initiative also embeds vocational training in an integrated system of service provision embracing health, housing, family conditions and labour market integration.

What do the case studies tell us about policy learning?

In a nutshell, in all countries (with the exception of Turkey), we find the commitment to the youth guarantee linked to attempts at strengthening the dual vocational training system, particularly by mobilising employers to play a more active role in it. The employer-driven initiative to set in motion a learning process on matching VET to the skill demands in Denmark, the coalition of stakeholders in the Amsterdam region for placing VET within an integrated system of service provision and adapting it to the skill demands of the 21st century, as well as the Apprenticeship Trailblazers in the UK are all significant examples of a shift in the design, delivery and knowledge content of VET systems. A similar tendency is also present in France (e.g., the Second Chance schools). In Greece, Slovakia and Spain, EU influence has been particularly crucial in creating 'windows of opportunity' for local policy entrepreneurs to experiment with novel practices that promote work-based learning. Nonetheless, these remain experiments of a limited range.

The case studies provide evidence of the significance of (more or less) systematic interaction, feedback and diffusion of policy knowledge between all levels of administration as a factor enabling policy learning and innovation. Equally important are partnership- and network-based initiatives at the regional level for policy experimentation (also see Verschraegen et al. 2011). Poor channels of sharing and diffusion of policy knowledge constitute major barriers to policy innovation. Over-centralised administrative structures, fragmentation/overlapping of competences and bureaucratic inertia are among the factors accounting for this.

References

Petmesidou, Maria, and María González Menéndez. 2016. *Policy Learning and Innovation Processes.* STYLE Working Paper WP4.2 Policy learning and innovation processes drawing on EU and national policy frameworks on youth – Synthesis Report

Verschraegen Gert, Bart Vanhercke and Rika Verpoorten. 2011. 'The European Social Fund and Domestic Activation Policies: Europeanization Mechanisms'. *Journal of European Social Policy* 21 (1): 55-72.

Acknowledgements

The research inputs of the partner institutions that participated in Work Package 4 of the STYLE project are greatly acknowledged. We truly appreciate the contributions by the following colleagues: Martin B. Carstensen and Christian Lyhne Ibsen (Copenhagen Business School); Kari Hadjivassiliou, Arianna Tassinari, Sam Swift and Anna Fohrbeck (Institute of Employment Studies, United Kingdom); Sonja Bekker, Marc van der Meer and Ruud Muffels (Tilburg University); Mark Smith, Maria Laura Tolado and Vincent Pasquier (Grenoble École de Management); Marcela Veselkova (Slovak Governance Institute); Elisa Martellucci, Gabriele Marconi and Karolien Lenaerts (Centre for European Policy Studies); and Fatoş Gökşen, Deniz Yükseker, Sinem Kuz and Ibrahim Öker (Koç University). Many thanks go also to our colleagues at Democritus University (Periklis Polyzoidis) and the University of Oviedo (Ana M. Guillén, Begoña Cueto, Rodolfo Gutiérrez, Javier Mato, and Aroa Tejero) for their valuable help.

Gender inequalities in the early labour market experience of young Europeans

Gabriella Berloffa, **Eleonora Matteazzi**, **Alina Şandor** and **Paola Villa**

Gender differences in youth labour markets exist across Europe, although with large variations between different countries. In 2015, almost one quarter (23%) of young women aged 20-34 in the EU28 were classified as NEETs (not in employment, education or training), while the corresponding share among young men was 8.1 percentage points lower, at 14.9%. The gender gap was larger among older individuals within this age group: the gender gap in NEET rates was only 1.7 percentage points for 20-24 year olds, but rose to nine points for those aged 25-29 and to 12.8 points for 30-34 year olds (Eurostat 2016).

Although gender differences in labour market outcomes – particularly wages and labour force participation – have been widely investigated, fewer studies have focused on early career patterns or the transition from school to work (see Plantenga, Remery and Samek 2013). It is crucial to understand whether these differences are mainly a result of women's participation decisions or whether they reflect difficulties that women face on the labour market. A new perspective on the employment outcomes of women and men can improve our knowledge of how gender inequalities emerge and evolve during the early labour market experiences of young Europeans.

A new dynamic approach to youth employment outcomes

Using data that follows individuals over a number of years (in this case, EU-SILC from 2006 to 2012), we can investigate the evolution of gender inequalities. We can identify two phases of young people's working life: first, their entry into the labour market and then a subsequent phase, around five years after leaving full-time education. For the first phase, we analyse gender differences in the type of monthly employment status trajectories that characterise the transition from school to the first relevant employment experience. For the second phase, we explore gender differences along various dimensions of employment quality, evaluated not at a single point in time but over an extended period. These dimensions of employment quality include employment security, income security, income success and a successful match between education and occupation.

Measuring the quality of school-to-work transitions and employment

We can consider the school-to-work trajectory to be the first three years after leaving full-time education and then identify successful trajectories on the basis of whether a young person gains an employment spell of at least six months (see Berloffa et al.

2017 for more details). Less successful trajectories are then those in which individuals experience a small number of long workless spells (spells of unemployment or inactivity) or a large number of short employment and workless spells. In fact, it is possible to identify six different types of school-to-work transitions:

1. Speedy: a relevant employment spell is achieved within six months after leaving full-time education.

2. Long-search: a relevant employment spell is achieved after more than six months of unemployment or inactivity.

3. In&out successful: various non-relevant employment spells, interspersed with short periods of unemployment or inactivity, end in a relevant employment spell.

4. In&out unsuccessful: various non-relevant employment spells, interspersed with short periods of unemployment or inactivity, do not end in a relevant employment spell.

5. Continuous unemployment and/or inactivity: only spells of unemployment or inactivity.

6. Return to education: a spell in education lasting at least six consecutive months is experienced at least six months after having left full-time education.

Three to four years after leaving education can be considered as the beginning of the second phase or the early-career period when a more nuanced definition of an individual's employment condition is required. This can be captured by four dimensions:

1. Employment security: having a secure job or being able to change it without going through a long period of unemployment or inactivity.

2. Income security: being able to rely on a stable and sufficiently high labour income so as to avoid the risk of poverty.

3. Economic success: attaining higher earnings than one's peers (with the same education level).

4. Education-occupation success: experiencing a good match between educational attainment and type of occupation.

Limited gender differences early in the school-to-work trajectory

Upon labour market entry, women's chances of rapidly entering into paid employment and avoiding long periods of unemployment/inactivity are similar to (or even better than) men's chances. However, in the transition from school to work, labour market policies and institutions, especially the employment protection legislation regarding regular contracts, seem to have some adverse effects on female labour outcomes (the probability of a speedy transition decreases from 69% to 62%, while that of being continuously unemployed/inactive increases from 11% to 21%).

Gender differences emerge in the early-career phase

In contrast with the pattern observed at labour market entry, gender gaps start to emerge in this early-career phase with men and women experiencing different employment pathways.

- Around five years after leaving education, women are clearly disadvantaged compared to men in terms of achieving employment security. Females' probability of being employment-secure is 48 percentage points lower than males' probability, while that of being continuously unemployed or inactive is 32 percentage points higher.

- Around five years after leaving education, females and males have the same likelihood of achieving income security. In fact, the gender gap in terms of income security is much smaller. Thus, women encounter many more difficulties than men in attaining a stable employment pathway, but when they have one they are considerably more likely to be income-secure.

- If we look at the probability of being successful, men's chances of achieving success are higher than those of women, both overall (20% vs. 5%) and conditional on having a stable pathway (28% vs. 22%). Moreover, policy variables seem not to be very effective for tackling the gender gap in terms of having a successful employment condition.

- Family formation adds other types of difficulties. Indeed, women in couples are not only less likely than men to have a stable employment pathway, but they are also less likely to achieve annual labour earnings above the poverty line, and to be successful in terms of both earnings levels and a good match between education and occupation.

What can policy-makers do about the gender gap?

We have seen that women's chances of accessing paid employment rapidly after leaving education are similar to, or even better than, men's. However, women's labour market conditions deteriorate over the following few years, especially if they are in a couple. Specifically, women are less likely to achieve employment security, income security and a successful employment condition around five years after having left education. However, those women who succeed in achieving a stable employment pathway are similarly or even more likely than men to earn wages above the poverty threshold. And yet women are always less likely to be successful, even when they manage to remain continuously employed.

From a policy perspective, our findings suggest that more stringent regulation of the use of temporary contracts plays a key role in improving women's performances in the labour market a few years after having left education. First, it increases young people's chances of being employment-secure and, second, it raises women's probability of being both income-secure and successful. These effects are mainly due to the increased likelihood of following a stable employment pathway that triggers a positive effect on women's earnings. As a result, stricter rules on the use of temporary contracts systematically and significantly reduce the gender gap in terms of employment security, income security and success.

References

Berloffa, Gabriella, Eleonora Matteazzi, Gabriele Mazzolini, Alina Şandor and Paola Villa. 2015. *Youth School-To-Work Transitions: From Entry Jobs to Career Employment.* STYLE Working Paper WP10.2 Youth School-To-Work Transitions: from Entry Jobs to Career Employment

Berloffa, Gabriella, Eleonora Matteazzi, Gabriele Mazzolini, Alina Şandor and Paola Villa. 2017. *The Quality of Employment in the Early Labour Market Experience of Young Europeans.* DEM Discussion Paper 05. Trento: University of Trento.

Berloffa, Gabriella, Eleonora Matteazzi, Gabriele Mazzolini, Alina Şandor and Paola Villa. Forthcoming. 'How Can Young People's Employment Quality be Assessed Dynamically?' In *Youth Labor in Transition*, edited by Jacqueline O'Reilly, Janine Leschke, Renate Ortlieb, Martin Seeleib-Kaiser and Paola Villa. New York: Oxford University Press.

Berloffa, Gabriella, Eleonora Matteazzi and Paola Villa. Forthcoming. 'The Worklessness Legacy: Do Working Mothers Make a Difference?' In *Youth Labor in Transition*, edited by Jacqueline O'Reilly, Janine Leschke, Renate Ortlieb, Martin Seeleib-Kaiser and Paola Villa. New York: Oxford University Press.

Eurostat. 2016. *Statistics on Young People neither in Employment nor in Education or Training.* ***http://ec.europa.eu/eurostat/statistics-explained/index.php/Statistics_on_young_people_neither_in_employment_nor_in_education_or_training***

Plantenga, Janneke, Chantal Remery and Manuela Samek. 2013. *Starting Fragile: Gender Differences in the Youth Labour Market.* Luxembourg, Publications Office of the European Union.

Policy-making and gender mainstreaming

Fatoş Gökşen, **Alpay Filiztekin**, **Mark Smith**, **Çetin Çelik** and **İbrahim Öker**

Gender differences in youth labour markets and school-to-work transitions are frequently underestimated and there is often an assumption that gender gaps only emerge around parenthood, so that younger generations are largely unaffected (Plantenga et al. 2013). However, the evidence presented here from this comparative research suggests that gender differences open up early in the life course and that the policy environment across European countries is not well adapted to these differences on the youth labour market.

Research methods

In order to illustrate the differences between young women and men on the labour market we can map vulnerability by gender across countries (Göksen et al. 2016). Vulnerability can be considered as individual risks to low quality, precarious or low-paid employment. However, gender differences are not the only factor shaping these risks and we can observe layers of risk whereby gender interacts with other risks factors such as country of birth and class. This is known as intersectionality (Verloo 2006). We then focus on the extent to which policies for young people recognise gender differences and adopt a gender mainstreaming approach (Gökşen et al. 2016).

We use a sample of countries in order to represent four types of regimes for school-to-work transitions – universalistic (Denmark and the Netherlands), liberal (the UK), employment-centred (France and Belgium) and subprotective (Spain, Greece and Turkey); where the data permits, we also include an analysis of Slovakia as an example of a post-socialist regime, but we are unable to provide a policy analysis for this country.

Furthermore, we benefit from specific, detailed inputs from national researchers in the case of five case-study countries covering four of the regimes – Denmark, Spain, France, Greece and the UK. Our analysis of the EU-SILC data demonstrates that gender gaps for young people exist across almost all measures of education and labour market statuses used to assess vulnerable outcomes. We also find strong evidence of the intersectionality of youth, gender and other forms of vulnerability linked to migrant status. The extent of these vulnerabilities varies across different school-to-work regimes but is nevertheless present.

Gender-blind policy environment

Our analysis of the policy environment towards young people shows that policy on youth labour markets is often gender blind and that there is limited evidence of consistent gender mainstreaming. Given the gender gaps identified in our mapping exercise, these policies could be more efficient if they recognised gender differences – for example school drop-out rates for boys, segregation of training opportunities for girls, and the interaction of gender and ethnicity in education choices. Although we find some evidence of good practice that recognises gender differences at the margins and indeed the intersectionality of youth, for gender and other forms of vulnerability more could be done.

Our Findings: Policy towards youth labour markets is often gender blind

We draw a number of conclusions from our work for future research in the area of school-to-work transitions.

- We suggest that researchers need to approach the youth labour market from a more consistently gender-sensitive perspective in order to understand the nuances and dynamics of emerging gender gaps.

- We suggest that greater consideration of the intersectionalities of gender with other demographic factors can help explain the segmentation of the youth labour market and improve understanding of the life-long repercussions for the risks of vulnerabilities.

- We suggest that in relation to vulnerabilities, researchers need measures and data that are sensitive to the impact of young people living in the parental home and to the risk that vulnerabilities are disguised by household-level data.

We also draw a number of conclusions from our work for future policy-making in the area of school-to-work transitions.

- We suggest that policy-makers adopt a more consistent gender mainstreaming approach in order to develop more efficient policies that reflect the realities of youth labour markets.

- We suggest that policy-makers adopt a more consistent gender mainstreaming approach in order to address emerging risks for vulnerabilities along gender lines.

- We suggest that policy-makers adopt a more consistent gender mainstreaming approach in order to capture the intersectionality of gender with other demographic characteristics.

References

Gökşen, Fatoş, Alpay Filiztekin, Mark Smith, Çetin Çelik, İbrahim Öker and Sinem Kuz. 2016. *Vulnerable Youth and Gender Mainstreaming.* STYLE Working Paper WP4.3 Vulnerable Youth & Gender in Europe

Plantenga, Janneke, Chantal Remery and Manuela Samek Lodovici. 2013. Starting Fragile. *Gender Differences in the Youth Labor Market.* Luxembourg: Office for Official Publications of the European Communities

Verloo, Mieke. 2006. 'Multiple Inequalities, Intersectionality and the European Union.' *European Journal of Women's Studies* 13 (3): pp. 211-228.

Ethnicity and gender differences of being employed in the UK: Policy implications

Carolina V. Zuccotti and **Jacqueline O'Reilly**

Scarring and ethnicity: An agenda

There is a substantive literature showing that the poor labor market integration of young people can have long-term negative impacts on their adult lives, for example by increasing the probability of subsequent periods of unemployment or by affecting their income (Gregg 2001). We also know that migrants and their children perform differently in the labor market than majoritarian populations. In particular, those coming from developing countries are often disadvantaged in terms of access to jobs (Heath and Cheung 2007). However, surprisingly little is known about how early job insecurity affects different ethnic groups in the labor market over time. Our study (Zuccotti and O'Reilly 2017) addresses this gap in the literature by examining the impact of the early labor market status of young individuals in the UK on their later labor market outcomes ten years later, focusing on how this varies across ethnic groups and by gender.

The study: Data, ethnic groups and methods

The research was based on the Office for National Statistics Longitudinal Study (ONS-LS), a data set linking census records for a 1% sample of the population of England and Wales across five successive censuses (1971, 1981, 1991, 2001 and 2011). We studied men and women who were aged between 16 and 29 in 2001 and followed them up in 2011, when they were between 26 and 39 years old. In particular, we looked at whether an early experience of being NEET (not in employment, education or training) affected their employment probabilities and occupational status ten years later. The analysis focused on White British and second-generation minority groups born in the UK; we also included individuals who arrived in the UK at a young age. The ethnic minority groups we studied were: Indian, Pakistani, Bangladeshi and Caribbean.

How scarring effects vary by ethnicity and gender

Our study shows that – on equality of education, social background and neighbourhood deprivation – those who were not in employment, education or training in 2001 have around 17 percentage points less chance of being employed in 2011 and around 10 percentage points less chance of being in a professional/managerial position compared to those who were employed in 2001.

However, the transmission of disadvantage occurs differently across ethnic groups and genders: some groups/genders perform better (and others worse) in terms of overcoming an initial disadvantaged situation. Scarring connected to a previous period of being NEET is less severe for Asian men: Indian, Pakistani and Bangladeshi men who were NEET in 2001 have a higher probability of being employed in 2011 than equivalent White British men. Pakistani and Caribbean women, on the contrary, experience a deeper scar connected to a previous period of being NEET than White British women.

Implications of our study: Who should be the target of policies?

Often, being an ethnic minority is equated with being disadvantaged, but our results show that this is not universally the case in the UK. The fact that some ethnic minorities are less penalised by previous unemployment or inactivity, compared to some of their White British counterparts is, in part, good news in terms of integration processes. Further research is needed to understand the mechanisms behind this finding. These could include parental aspirations, motivational factors, the role of networks at the neighbourhood and the university level (especially for Indians and Bangladeshis), the exploitation of resources such as internships and the type of university degrees chosen.

However, significant concerns remain regarding employment probabilities among young White British men, for whom scarring connected to having experienced a period of unemployment or inactivity is particularly high. At the same time, there is also an 'ethnic minority disadvantage' in the labour market for women: this could be connected not only to discrimination, but also to the cultural values of the different groups. More research is needed to explore the determinants behind these results.

In the context of a dramatic rise in youth unemployment since the 2008 crisis (O'Reilly et al. 2015), understanding how and why early labor market experiences differently affect later outcomes for different ethnic groups and genders can help develop more targeted policies. This is particularly relevant in countries where the number of ethnic minorities is considerable and increasing.

References

Gregg, Paul. 2001. 'The Impact of Youth Unemployment on Adult Unemployment in the NCDS'. *The Economic Journal* 111 (475): 626-653.

Heath, Anthony F., and Sin Y. Cheung. 2007. *Unequal Chances. Ethnic Minorities in Western Labour Markets.* New York: Oxford University Press.

O'Reilly, Jacqueline, Werner Eichhorst, András Gábos, Kari Hadjivassiliou, David Lain, Janine Leschke, Seamus McGuinness, Lucia Mýtna Kureková, Tiziana Nazio, Renate Ortlieb, Helen Russell and Paola Villa. 2015. 'Five Characteristics of Youth Unemployment in Europe: Flexibility, Education, Migration, Family Legacies, and EU Policy'. *SAGE Open* 5 (1): 1–19. doi: 10.1177/2158244015574962 ***http://sgo.sagepub.com/content/5/1/2158244015574962***

Zuccotti, Carolina V., and Jacqueline O'Reilly. Forthcoming. 'Do scarring effects vary by ethnicity and gender?' In *Youth Labor in Transition*, edited by Jacqueline O'Reilly, Janine Leschke, Renate Ortlieb, Martin Seeleib-Kaiser and Paola Villa. New York: Oxford University Press.

Acknowledgements
We are grateful for the detailed comments and suggestions by Martin Seeleib-Kaiser, Paola Villa and Eskil Wadensjö. Thank you also to the STYLE researchers who commented on this work during our meetings.

What works? Exploring a database inventory

Kari Hadjivassiliou

Building a database

To review the range of policies of effective youth employment measures we compiled a database/inventory for specific member states (Belgium, Denmark, France, Greece, Netherlands, Slovakia, Spain and UK). The database provides an overview of the main representative and/or most effective programmes that have been in operation in these member states in the period 2008 (pre-crisis) to 2016. Specifically, for each youth-related programme, the database summarises country-specific information in relation to:

- An overview of the programme, including its aims and objectives, target group(s) and main activities, i.e., what interventions it supports and how it is delivered on the ground.
- The main body responsible for the programme and other key actors involved;
- Sources and level(s) of funding;
- Quantitative data about its take-up and outcomes, particularly employment outcomes; and
- Overall evaluation of the programme, including its effectiveness and the extent to which it facilitates young people's school-to-work transitions; its main strengths and weaknesses; any innovative elements; as well as key lessons learnt (i.e., what works and for whom, and what does not work and why) that can be used as policy pointers.

In order to add validity and to enhance the thoroughness of the approach towards compiling the database, the partners involved in the project [CEPS (BE), CBS (DK), DUTH (EL), UNIOVI (ES), CCIG (FR), UVT (NL), SGI (SK) and IES (UK)] adopted a systematic approach both to identifying and analysing key documents:

Programme review

First, the scope of the country-level review was focused and provided an overview of the main representative programmes that have been in operation in a specific member state in the period 2008 (pre-crisis) to 2016.

An inclusive approach

Second, the partners adopted an inclusive approach as to the type of documents reviewed. To this end, their data search focused on main types of content from:

- Official national/regional data and policy documents, including the National Youth Guarantee Implementation Plans, National Youth Employment Plans, Programme Guidance and related documentation, including evaluation reports and related studies specific to the programme under review, etc.;
- Data, including administrative data, available from national statistical sources and monitoring systems on the take-up and cost of the implemented programmes, e.g., Public Employment Services (PES) for programmes that form part of ALMP, etc.; ESF-related data from ESF Managing Authorities, where applicable; relevant Ministries (e.g., Ministry of Employment/Labour, Ministry of Education, Ministry for Youth, etc.);
- Relevant databases, e.g., European Commission's Database of Labour Market Practices and European Employment Policy Observatory (EEPO); Eurostat's Labour Market Policy Database (LMP); ILO's Youth Employment Inventory; etc.;
- The European Commission's Mutual Learning Programme (MLP), including a number of relevant Peer Reviews;
- Key published material (e.g., books, academic journals, research articles, independent research, and evaluation studies and reports); and
- Survey data, including employer and beneficiary surveys.

Common data collection tool

Third, in order to collect information in a consistent and comparable way, the partners adopted a quasi-systematic approach to the country-level review by using a common data collection tool (in the form of an Excel proforma/template) that sought to elicit information in line with the key focus of the task. Such a standardised pro-forma/template facilitated the collection of comparable data on youth-related programmes in each selected member state and ensured consistency of information gathering across the partners.

Interviews

Fourth, in order to fill in data gaps, especially in relation to quantitative and evaluation data, including data on the programme's funding/budget, participation/take-up and outcomes in terms of positive employment and other outcomes for young people, the partners conducted, where possible, interviews (face-to-face or via telephone/Skype) with the most relevant informants who could provide such information.

Data sources

Fifth, given the fact that the database can be used as a useful repository/knowledge base in relation to youth-related programmes in the countries reviewed, it also includes key references and data sources used, including (where available) the relevant online links and programme websites.

In total, the database includes 48 youth-related programmes that cover a wide range of interventions, many of which have proved effective in facilitating school-to-work transitions, including those of youth at risk/NEETs. Using a classification developed by Eurofound (2012) in relation to young people's pathway to employment, these can be grouped in six broad categories (see Table below):

Type/Category of Programme/Measure	Range of Programmes/Measures
Youth Guarantee	• Early intervention; integrated approach; personalised and intensive support; individualised action planning; quality options; monitoring
Preventive measures for early school leaving (ESL)	• Diagnostic measures for early identification & intervention • Alternative learning environments • Information, advice and guidance (IAG) & support at key transition points, especially between lower- and upper-secondary education
Remedial measures for re-integrating early school-leavers	• Tracking and/or outreach services • Second-chance education programmes • Pre-vocational training, including basic and soft skills training • VET and work-related, practical training • Integrated and personalised approach for re-engaging ESL
Measures to enhance youth employability	• Apprenticeships and/or pre-apprenticeship (or pre-vocational) training • Structured traineeships that form part of a 'train-first' approach • Mentoring and support to young person throughout placement and beyond • Incentives and support to participating employers throughout placement • VET
Measures to facilitate school-to-work (STW) transitions	• Outreach and rehabilitation programmes • Intensive and personalised help and support, including individualised action planning through dedicated case workers and mentors • IAG and counselling, including individualised vocational &/or socio-pedagogical guidance • Early activation, e.g., intensive and personalised jobsearch assistance programmes combined with follow-up services • Special programmes addressing specific barriers faced by youth at risk, e.g., language courses, transport, living and/or childcare subsidies
Employment measures	• Subsidised employment programmes, e.g., well-targeted employer subsidies

References

Hadjivassiliou, Kari P., Catherine Rickard, Chiara Manzoni and Sam Swift. 2016. *Database of effective youth employment measures in selected Member States.* STYLE Working Paper WP4.4b

Hadjivassiliou, Kari P., Arianna Tassinari, Werner Eichhorst and Florian Wozny. Forthcoming. 'How does the Performance of School-To-Work Transition Regimes in the European Union Vary?' In *Youth Labor in Transition*, edited by Jacqueline O'Reilly, Janine Leschke, Renate Ortlieb, Martin Seeleib-Kaiser and Paola Villa. New York: Oxford University Press.

Petmesidou, Maria, and María González Menéndez. Forthcoming. 'Policy Transfer and Innovation for Building Resilient Bridges to the Youth Labor Market'. In *Youth Labor in Transition*, edited by Jacqueline O'Reilly, Janine Leschke, Renate Ortlieb, Martin Seeleib-Kaiser and Paola Villa. New York: Oxford University Press.

Smith, Mark, Janine Leschke, Helen Russell and Paola Villa. Forthcoming. 'Stressed Economies, Distressed Policies, and Distraught Young People: European Policies and Outcomes from a Youth Perspective'. In *Youth Labor in Transition*, edited by Jacqueline O'Reilly, Janine Leschke, Renate Ortlieb, Martin Seeleib-Kaiser and Paola Villa. New York: Oxford University Press.

Learning from the Dutch case: innovating youth (un)employment policies in Amsterdam, Eindhoven and Tilburg

Marc van der Meer, **Ruud Muffels** and **Sonja Bekker**

Introduction

Youth unemployment is a complex problem that has no simple, one-size-fits-all solution. Over the last couple of years after the economic crisis, youth unemployment has dropped substantially in the Netherlands, although it remains high among youngsters without a starting qualification and among ethnic minorities. A substantial minority of youngsters, about 5%, belong to the NEET category, this however is the lowest percentage in Europe. In addition many youngsters are out of the picture of the usual statistics because they are not registered as unemployed while still seeking proper employment.

The current drop in youth unemployment suggests that for a better understanding of the low level of Dutch youth unemployment, we have to understand how and with which effect Dutch policies responded to the crisis. During the crisis important policy changes were launched in the Netherlands, notably the decentralization of social policies to the local level, the austerity policies, and the concluding of the social accord in 2013 that changed the employment protection rules affecting youngsters in particular. The combination of decentralization and restrained budgets for social policy created the need as well as the opportunity to develop innovative regional- and municipal-level cooperation between public authorities, business and schools. The national government is governing this process with subsidies to support innovative projects combatting youth unemployment or to set up public–private partnership projects, e.g. to improve job-to-job mobility or to develop labor market expertise. The policies to implement the European "Youth Guarantee" appeared to be very modest and left to the regions.

Regional 'multiple helix' governance

In this context, the question is to what extent the modest national ambitions to tackle youth unemployment have triggered learning at the regional level. In this contribution we have a brief look at policy developments in the capital city Amsterdam, in the economically advanced Eindhoven 'Brainport' region and the Tilburg labour market region where a novel 'youth unemployment free zone' has been set up. At first sight, the approach in the three regions appears to be quite similar. All three regions have adopted a triple-helix network approach in which government, employers, and knowledge institutions have set up a stakeholder network of public-private partnerships to design new practices and to achieve: fairly ambitious targets with respect to youth unemployment (Tilburg); top-talent management in the high-tech industry and creating career-long employment security (Eindhoven); and development of intermediate-level vocational education for low-skilled youngsters as part of a broader economic agenda (Amsterdam). All three have established a development organization, although they are not all equally robust. In Amsterdam, the network approach is very much initiated by the Economic Board, in which various stakeholders (government, education, business) are involved, though a political change was needed to bring in the VET schools as a vital part of the network. Also in the Brainport region, a development organization facilitates the network-based collaboration. In Amsterdam, as in Eindhoven, top-talent development for the labor market is high on the agenda, although Eindhoven mainly focuses on technical and IT professionals, whereas Amsterdam covers wider range of professions, skills and talent management. Tilburg stands out for its in European terms unique ambition with collaborative actions and practices.

Critical conditions

The operation or impact of such network communities is always limited by the time and resources devoted to their functioning but especially by the authority assigned to and the power these networks can unfold which are required to change existing practices. In the case of cross-cutting themes encompassing two or more policy domains such as education and social policy, the demands or requirements for collaboration or cooperation become more explicit. In the field of education and work, they are twofold, first, the definition of a new mission and style of cooperation between school and companies is required to connect the processes of learning and working. Secondly, a deepening is needed of the content of learning and working so as to improve and upgrade the skill levels of youngsters. This points to the role of prevention through reduction of early school leaving and making use of a backbone of labour market information, including a set of signaling indicators on the development of the youth labour market.

Thus, at regional level, as part of the triple-helix approach, a further prioritization of ambitions and goals in policy making is necessary. For this reason, the implementation of a "Youth Guarantee" in Amsterdam, Eindhoven, and Tilburg requires a tailor-made approach with room for mediation and individual coaching to match youngsters to work. This also means the support and involvement of the parents or the household in which the youngster lives. Youngsters dropping out of the school system early on should set policy alarm bells ringing immediately. Moreover, sound statistics on school progress, school-to-work transitions, and inactivity are necessary conditions for success. A preventive approach also requires that one reach out to vulnerable youth as early as possible. Another issue is the unfavourable position of low-educated migrant workers facing higher barriers to finding work than native youngsters, even when they have similar qualifications. This has not changed during the recent economic recovery. For this challenge, a concerted approach on the three domains of employment, education, and social policy is required.

Conclusion

In spite of their short-time horizon, the emergence of a "Dutch triple- or multi-helix" approach in the three regions under scrutiny is promising to tackle youth unemployment at first sight. Stakeholders start learning from each other about the bottlenecks of the regional labour market and about how to improve policies to combat youth unemployment, which is a difficult issue to resolve. We argue that these novel modes of "governance" can receive support and feedback from stakeholders at local level. This innovative approach represents a shift from the classical modality of governance—which is project-oriented, subsidy-based, and coupled to financial incentives—to a network-based collaborative and more proactive and preventive approach that is conducive to innovative practices. Ideas have been proposed and partly tested in practice; now they need to be translated into sustainable practices and researched in depth to understand the factors behind their failure or success.

References

Bekker, Sonja, Marc van der Meer and Ruud Muffels. 2015. *Barriers to and Triggers for Innovation and Knowledge Transfer in the Netherlands.* STYLE-D4.1 Country Report Netherlands

Muffels, Ruud, Marc van der Meer, Sonja Bekker. 2017. *Regional Governance of Youth Unemployment: A Comparison of three Innovative Practices of Multilevel Cooperation in the Netherlands.* Unpublished Manuscript, Tilburg Law School.

What have we learnt about policy innovation and learning?

Maria Petmesidou, **María C. González Menéndez** and **Kari Hadjivassiliou**

Facilitators of learning and innovation

In most of the countries studied, local/regional administrations and agencies exchange knowledge on policy processes and tools among themselves and are involved in EU-wide mutual policy learning.

The role of policy entrepreneurs in promoting policy transfer and learning – initially in the context of sectoral and/or local pilot initiatives, subsequently to be spread nationally – has been highlighted in a few countries (e.g., Slovakia, France and partly Greece and Spain).

EU level strategies, such as the Youth Guarantee and the European Alliance for Apprenticeships, recently opened up windows of opportunity for policy entrepreneurs.

Equally important for policy innovation is local knowledge accumulated by key actors in policy design and delivery institutions, which enables them to build trust and working relationships with major stakeholders.

Innovative practices and added value

Innovative practices at the local/regional level draw on the added value that is created for existing policies by local partnerships and networks among major actors (regional/municipal authorities, PES, employers, youth agencies, educational and training institutions, social enterprises and other relevant stakeholders).

A comprehensive and integrated perspective for promoting youth employment is considered to be the added value. This combines early intervention, personalised guidance and individualised action planning for young people in taking the initial step into employment (with a specific emphasis on subgroups of NEETs).

Successful cases of innovative practices

Our analysis highlighted a number of promising (but still at an initial stage) or already successful cases of innovative practices at the regional/local level involving policy learning and transfer.

The Mid-Brabant Pact in South Netherlands, signed by major stakeholders in order to develop interventions that are expected to lead to a 'Youth-Unemployment-Free Zone' within a three-year period (from 2015 to 2018) emulates successful network-based strategies for employment growth and youth labour market integration in another region of the country (the Southeastern Brainport region).

The UK implementation of the Youth Contract in the region of Wales demonstrates ample scope for spreading innovation further.

The Community Centres in Slovakia targeted at young Roma introduced significant innovation in helping disadvantaged youth to develop soft skills for jobsearch. Epistemic communities and international NGOs transferred expertise for the establishment of these Centres.

The 'Local Missions' and the 'Pôles emploi' in France, which function as main hubs of wider partnerships at the local level, promote innovation through coordination of measures aimed at NEETs.

Inter-regional spread of the JEEP (Jeunes, école, emploi) initiative, initially introduced by the Forest municipality of the Brussels region in order to inform and counsel young people about their future employment before they leave compulsory education, is another successful case.

Also in Spain, some local pilot projects involve cross-regional learning (e.g., Aragón imitated the employers' space of Lugones, and Gijón learnt from Cartagena the value of partnerships),

Governance barriers to learning and innovation
However, for the above initiatives to yield results with regard to sustained labour market integration of youth at the national level, a policy environment conducive to co-ordinated sharing and diffusion of knowledge between different levels of administration and joint stakeholders' bodies is required.

In some countries (e.g., Denmark), corporatist governance highly supports systematic bottom-up and top-down learning and policy innovation, while in other countries fragmented governance hinders co-ordinated learning exchange.

Major barriers are presented by fragmentation of competencies among different levels of administration, which leads to inconsistent cooperation across regions and across other actors, slowing innovation diffusion (e.g., in Belgium and Spain).

Over-centralised administrative structures, dominance of fragmented project-based solutions and the inability to convert such projects into long-term sustainable policies (in Greece and Turkey) are another barrier.

Political culture and values (e.g., a strong liberal tradition in the UK) and party-political expediency (e.g., in Slovakia), do not always favour a systematic and co-ordinated flow of information into high levels of (strategic) policy decision-making.

Hence, the improvement of coordination capacities vertically and horizontally among key policy actors is crucial for facilitating the spread of good practices nationwide.

Foci of policy innovation: 'Triple' helix, the Youth Guarantee and apprenticeships
The main foci of innovation regarding effective STW transition strategies consist in:

(a) a novel mode of governance in policy design and delivery often referred to as a 'triple' or 'multiple' helix, which involves collaboration between the public administration, professional bodies and education/training providers, employers, youth associations and other stakeholders regarding employment growth and youth labour market integration;

(b) a commitment to the Youth Guarantee through an integrated preventive and proactive approach that combines services and provides comprehensive support tailored to individual needs; and

(c) the strengthening of traineeships and apprenticeships (such as the dual VET) as a significant tool for enhancing youth employability in parallel with the mobilisation of employers to play a more active role in this respect.

Future challenges
In the countries considered, front-runners in active ALMPs have developed upper-secondary vocational programmes comprising schooling and work-based training (e.g., Denmark, Netherlands). The main policy challenges for them are to:

- improve the image of VET (set in the context of an integrated service provision to youth),

- strengthen the commitment of employers to offer apprenticeship places, and

- promote dissemination of knowledge about the matching of skills to the needs of industry.

In the UK and France, the key challenges are how to:

- mobilize employers, in collaboration with professional bodies and training providers in order to reconsider the knowledge base, learning methodology and delivery of VET, and

- develop new apprenticeship standards.

In Greece, Spain and Slovakia, the challenges with the expansion of dual learning models in VET are:

- the needs to be supported, with the aim of improving the content and quality of dual VET,

- strengthening feedback mechanisms between VET and the labour market, and

- raising VET's public visibility and attractiveness for young people.

In these latter countries, the reform of VET and apprenticeships is closely linked with another major policy challenge concerning the delivery of integrated, individualised services under the Youth Guarantee. Improving the quality and capacity of PES operation is of paramount importance in this respect.

Finally, in all countries, a more consistent policy approach to tackling the intersection of disadvantage linked to youth, gender, ethnic and migrant status needs to be developed from an early stage of the education path through to labour market entry.

Policy pointers drawing on database analysis
An analysis of the database's programmes has highlighted a number of policy pointers that can serve as recommendations for successful policy learning and innovation in relation to effective school-to-work transitions in the EU. These are presented below.

- Prevention and early intervention at key transition stages over the full cycle of school-to-work transition

- Policies designed with enough flexibility to cater for the different needs of specific sub-groups of NEETs, or targeted at particular sub-groups

- Proactive outreach work, including through active involvement of NGOs and/or youth organisations and e-outreach

- Systems for diagnosing vulnerable young people's specific needs

- Early, integrated and person-centred interventions to address complex needs

- Effective case management combined with individualised action planning together with personalised mentoring, help and support, as well as follow-up well after the end of the intervention

- Sufficient PES capacity and resources to properly service youth at risk who require much more intensive and personalised attention

- Programmes integrating and combining services to offer a comprehensive approach tailored to young people's individual needs in relation to school-to-work transition

- Involvement of all relevant stakeholders, including youth organisations and youth workers

- Partnership/multi-agency working and co-ordination for an integrated service to youth at risk, especially at local level

- Individualisation of learning pathways based on a good understanding of how the young person actually learns; flexible/modularised curricula and alternative learning environments together with a focus on attitudes/self-esteem, and 'soft' and basic skills

- Programmes combining work and study such as quality apprenticeships, traineeships and work experience placements together with, where required, pre-vocational/pre-apprenticeship training

- Financial support acting as a safety net for vulnerable NEETs taking part in an intervention

References

Petmesidou, Maria, María C. González Menéndez and Kari Hadjivassiliou. 2016. *Policy Synthesis and Integrative Report.* STYLE Working Paper WP4.4a Policy Synthesis and Integrative Report

Hadjivassiliou, Kari P., Arianna Tassinari, Werner Eichhorst and Florian Wozny. Forthcoming. 'How does the Performance of School-To-Work Transition Regimes in the European Union Vary?' In *Youth Labor in Transition*, edited by Jacqueline O'Reilly, Janine Leschke, Renate Ortlieb, Martin Seeleib-Kaiser and Paola Villa. New York: Oxford University Press.

Petmesidou, Maria, and María González Menéndez. Forthcoming. 'Policy Transfer and Innovation for Building Resilient Bridges to the Youth Labor Market'. In *Youth Labor in Transition*, edited by Jacqueline O'Reilly, Janine Leschke, Renate Ortlieb, Martin Seeleib-Kaiser and Paola Villa. New York: Oxford University Press.

Further reading on policy innovation, learning and transfer

Country Reports

Martellucci, Elisa, and Gabriele Marconi. 2015. *Barriers to and Triggers for Innovation and Knowledge Transfer in Belgium.* STYLE-D4.1 Country Report Belgium

Carstensen, Martin B., and Christian Lyhne Ibsen. 2015. *Barriers to and Triggers for Innovation and Knowledge Transfer in Denmark.* STYLE-D4.1 Country Report Denmark

González-Menéndez, Maria, Ana Guillén, Begoña Cueto, Rodolfo Gutiérrez, Javier Mato and Aroa Tejero. 2015. *Barriers to and Triggers for Innovation and Knowledge Transfer in Spain.* STYLE-D4.1 Country Report Spain

Smith, Mark, Maria Laura Toraldo and Vincent Pasquier. 2015. *Barriers to and Triggers for Innovation and Knowledge Transfer in France.* STYLE-D4.1 Country Report France

Petmesidou, Maria, and Periklis Polyzoidis. 2015. *Barriers to and Triggers for Innovation and Knowledge Transfer in Greece.* STYLE-D4.1 Country Report Greece

Bekker, Sonja, Marc van der Meer and Ruud Muffels. 2015. *Barriers to and Triggers for Innovation and Knowledge Transfer in the Netherlands.* STYLE-D4.1 Country Report Netherlands

Veselkova, Marcela. 2015 *Barriers to and Triggers for Innovation and Knowledge Transfer in Slovakia.* STYLE-D4.1 Country Report Slovakia

Gökşen, Fatoş, Deniz Yükseker, Sinem Kuz and Ibrahim Öker. 2015. *Barriers to and Triggers for Innovation and Knowledge Transfer in Turkey.* STYLE-D4.1 Country Report Turkey

Hadjivassiliou, Kari, Arianna Tassinari and Sam Swift. 2015. *Barriers to and Triggers for Innovation and Knowledge Transfer in the UK. STYLE-D4.1 Country Report UK*

Petmesidou, Maria, and María González Menéndez. 2016. *Policy Learning and Innovation Processes.* STYLE Working Paper WP4.2 Policy learning and innovation processes drawing on EU and national policy frameworks on youth – Synthesis Report

Gökşen, Fatoş, Alpay Filiztekin, Mark Smith, Çetin Çelik, İbrahim Öker and Sinem Kuz. 2016. *Vulnerable Youth and Gender Mainstreaming.* STYLE Working Paper WP4.3 Vulnerable Youth & Gender in Europe

Petmesidou, Maria, María C. González Menéndez and Kari Hadjivassiliou. 2016. *Policy Synthesis and Integrative Report.* STYLE Working Paper WP4.4a Policy Synthesis and Integrative Report

Hadjivassiliou, Kari P., Catherine Rickard, Chiara Manzoni and Sam Swift. 2016. *Database of Effective Youth Employment Measures in Selected Member States.* STYLE Working Paper WP4.4b

Hadjivassiliou, Kari P., Arianna Tassinari, Werner Eichhorst and Florian Wozny. Forthcoming. 'How does the Performance of School-To-Work Transition Regimes in the European Union Vary?' In *Youth Labor in Transition*, edited by Jacqueline O'Reilly, Janine Leschke, Renate Ortlieb, Martin Seeleib-Kaiser and Paola Villa. New York: Oxford University Press.

Leschke, Janine, and Mairéad Finn. Forthcoming. 'Labor Market Flexibility and Income Security: Changes for European Youth during the Great Recession'. In *Youth Labor in Transition*, edited by Jacqueline O'Reilly, Janine Leschke, Renate Ortlieb, Martin Seeleib-Kaiser and Paola Villa. New York: Oxford University Press.

Petmesidou, Maria, and María González Menéndez. Forthcoming. 'Policy Transfer and Innovation for Building Resilient Bridges to the Youth Labor Market'. In *Youth Labor in Transition*, edited by Jacqueline O'Reilly, Janine Leschke, Renate Ortlieb, Martin Seeleib-Kaiser and Paola Villa. New York: Oxford University Press.

Smith, Mark, Janine Leschke, Helen Russell and Paola Villa. Forthcoming. 'Stressed Economies, Distressed Policies, and Distraught Young People: European Policies and Outcomes from a Youth Perspective'. In *Youth Labor in Transition*, edited by Jacqueline O'Reilly, Janine Leschke, Renate Ortlieb, Martin Seeleib-Kaiser and Paola Villa. New York: Oxford University Press.

Skills and education mismatch

Introduction: Skills and education mismatch

Seamus McGuinness

The various transitions that young people make between school and work and the decisions they take regarding their human capital development have substantial implications for their future life prospects. The research undertaken here seeks to inform policy with respect to the following key aspects of young people's lives:

(a) the nature of human capital development in third-level institutions,

(b) transitions from education to work, and

(c) the relative exposure to employment mismatch and separation in employment.

The nature of human capital development in third-level institutions
Two aspects of human capital development are considered

- the implications of the composition of higher education delivery for subsequent labour market outcomes (McGuinness, Bergin and Whelan 2015a; 2015b), and
- the impact of part-time working among students on the general labour market (Beblavý et al. 2016).

With respect to course composition, there is clear evidence that a higher concentration of work-related components such as research projects, work placements, the acquisition of facts/practical knowledge and project/problem-based learning can reduce the probability of graduate mismatch in first employment. The research shows that the probability of mismatch in the first job is highly reduced by a higher [aggregate] number of vocational course components in a degree programme. The pay-offs to increasing the practical aspects of programme delivery appear largest in degree courses that are generally classified as more academic in nature, suggesting that practical learning approaches and placements should be adopted in most, if not all, degree programmes.

In terms of the impact of part-time working, the evidence indicates that students are dispersed across the low- to medium-skilled segment of the labour market and are not exclusively concentrated in the least skill-intensive jobs/occupations. The findings support the 'complementarily view' of the co-existence of student employment and low-skilled employment rather than the crowding-out theory, whereby students would compete for job opportunities with low-skilled workers.

Transitions from education to work

In terms of routes into the labour market, we find that higher education work placements with the potential to develop into permanent posts and the provision of higher-education job-placement assistance have very substantial impacts in reducing the incidence of graduate overeducation.

Our findings support the view that by strengthening links with employers and investing more heavily in career-support functions, universities and third-level institutions can play an important role in matching graduates with jobs.

The research also shows that the use of private employment agencies significantly heightens the risk of subsequent mismatch. Therefore, higher education institutions can play an important role in terms of educating students in the jobsearch methods to utilise and to avoid.

Relative exposure to employment mismatch and separation in employment

Dealing firstly with young people's relative exposure to transition between the states of inactivity, unemployment and employment, we found that young people 'churn' through the labour markets relatively more frequently than prime-age workers. Specifically, young people are more likely to become unemployed (from employment) but are also more likely to move from unemployment to employment (relative to prime-age workers).

These patterns are consistent across countries, although there are some variations in the rates. With respect to the individual characteristics that influenced labour market transitions, higher levels of schooling were a key factor affecting the likelihood of exiting unemployment to enter employment. The result suggests that young people's relative exposure to job loss is particularly high during recession.

In terms of within-employment mismatch, the evidence indicates that while overeducation rates in Europe are converging upwards over time, the general pattern of overeducation is linked across many countries, suggesting that the phenomenon responds in a similar way to external shocks and, consequently, is likely to also react in similar ways to appropriate policy interventions. However, the evidence suggests that overeducation within peripheral states (Portugal, Ireland, Italy, Greece and Spain) evolves somewhat differently compared to the rest of Europe, so that a different policy response is likely to be appropriate in these countries.

While the overall results are complex for the determinants of youth overeducation, a number of impacts are consistently present for all or most country groupings. Specifically, youth overeducation is highly driven by the composition of education provision, and it will tend to be lower in countries with more developed vocational pathways.

Furthermore, youth overeducation tends to be heavily related to the level of aggregate labour demand, proxied in the model by variations in the participation rate and GDP per capita. Finally, youth overeducation tends to be lower the higher the employment share of part-time workers, suggesting that the phenomenon may be partly driven by labour market flexibility.

Is there a role for higher education institutions in improving the quality of first employment?

Seamus McGuinness, **Adele Whelan** and **Adele Bergin**

The problem of graduate employment

As labour market transitions for young people have become increasingly difficult in the past decade, alongside the growing population of university graduates, can HEI do more to help young people find their first job?

We focused on the labour market transitions of European university graduates and examined the factors influencing the likelihood of newly qualified university graduates becoming mismatched on entering the labour market.

The forms of mismatch considered are overeducation and over-skilling, whereby individuals are deemed to have education or skills in excess of those required in their current jobs. Both over-skilling and overeducation have consistently been found, in a large number of international studies, to be associated with lower wages and lower job satisfaction.

We explored the potential role of universities in reducing the extent of graduate mismatch through both the manner in which education is delivered within degree programmes and the part played by third-level institutions in smoothing the transition of graduates to the labour market. We addressed two key research questions:

- Is graduate mismatch related to the nature of the route into employment? Are certain modes of entry more heavily correlated with overeducation or over-skilling and do universities have a role in alleviating this?
- To what extent is labour market mismatch related to the variations in the structure of university degree programmes?

Higher education institutions have an important role to play

Graduate higher education work placements with the potential to develop into permanent posts provide an important route into the labour market. Assistance with job placements also has very substantial impacts in reducing the incidence of graduate overeducation and over-skilling.

Our research supports the view that by strengthening links with employers and investing more heavily in career-support functions, universities and other third-level institutions can play an important role in matching graduates with jobs.

Higher education institutions can also play an important role in terms of educating students in the jobsearch methods they should use and avoid. For example, the study shows that the use of private employment agencies significantly heightens the risk of subsequent mismatch.

With respect to course composition, we find clear evidence that a higher concentration of work-related components such as research projects, work placements, the acquisition of facts/practical knowledge and project/problem-based learning can reduce the probability of graduate mismatch in the first graduate job.

As the number of vocational course components in a degree programme increases, the probability of mismatch in a first job decreases.

The pay-off to increasing the practical aspects of programme delivery appears largest in degree courses that are generally classified as more academic in nature, suggesting that practical learning approaches and placements should be a key component of all European degree programmes, irrespective of field of study.

References

McGuinness, Seamus. Adele Whelan and Adele Bergin. 2015b. *Recruitment Methods & Educational Provision Effects on Graduate Over-Education and Over-Skilling*. STYLE Working Paper WP5.4 Report Recruitment Methods

McGuinness, Seamus. Adele Whelan and Adele Bergin. 2016. 'Is there a role for higher education institutions in improving the quality of first employment?' *The B.E. Journal of Economic Analysis & Policy* 16 (4). doi: ***https://doi.org/10.1515/bejeap-2016-0174***.

Are student workers crowding out low-skilled youth?

Miroslav Beblavý, **Brian Fabo**, **Lucia Mýtna Kureková** and **Zuzana Žilinčíková**

The consequences of a growing student population

One of the most noticeable long-term social changes across the EU in recent decades has been the massive increase in the numbers of young people going on to higher education. This is sometimes called the 'massification' of tertiary education.

Whereas higher education at university used to be something for the elites, it has now become something for the 'masses'. In some countries, this reflects a policy of encouraging a 'widening of participation' to include young people who have not traditionally participated in higher education beyond compulsory schooling.

Sometimes the catalyst for this development has been the promotion of democratic inclusion; sometimes it has also been propelled by the perceived requirements of the fourth industrial revolution, which is reshaping work in advanced industrial economies with a skill shortage for highly qualified labour from the indigenous population.

As a result of these different drivers, the proportions of students in higher education have grown significantly. For example, between 2001 and 2011, the population of students in the EU grew from 16.5 million to over 20 million, according to Eurostat, although it still varies enormously between EU countries and there are still a lot of young people who do not go on to higher education (see Table 1 in Beblavý et al. 2015).

Students no longer wait until they graduate to look for work; as student numbers have increased, so has the practice of combining work and study as a way of funding their education. However, this trend entails a potential risk, particularly for unskilled workers. They may find it more difficult to find jobs if they are being 'crowded out' by the cheaper, more highly qualified and more flexible student labour force. What are the consequences of these increases in the student population for youth employment and for young people outside HE looking for work?

Examining the problem

To address this question, we examined the structure of student employment: Who are student workers? What jobs do they do? How do typical student jobs differ from the jobs non-students do?

Our analysis of this issue employs a unique methodology. It combines data on the supply of student and non-student labour from the EU Labour Force Survey and the EUROSTUDENT project for EU countries. In addition, it provides an innovative analysis of labour demand using job vacancies posted at the leading Slovak and Czech job portal Profesia.

In the analysis of vacancies, we have built on a young but quickly growing stream of literature, which focuses on extracting data relevant to social scientists from job vacancies (see Mýtna Kureková, Beblavý and Thum-Thysen 2015; Beblavý et al. 2017 for a detailed overview of the state of the art in literature and applications).

This combined approach allowed us to gain more confidence in the results, given the high level of consistency of the findings obtained using the two distinct methodological approaches (see Beblavý et al. 2015 for the full analysis).

Diversity of employment for students

We found student employment to be highly diverse and not particularly limited to low-skilled, auxiliary occupations (Beblavý et al. 2015; 2017; Grotti, Russell and O'Reilly forthcoming). On the contrary, student work is heavily concentrated in (skilled) service and industrial work. Additionally, a non-negligible part of students in higher education already work in professional or associate professional occupations in line with their field of study, for example in the ICT sector or business services.

Precarious student jobs supplement rather than compete with core workers

At the same time, student work tends to be precarious, being associated with non-standard working time and very short contracts (Grotti, Russell and O'Reilly forthcoming).

Jobs advertised specifically for students come with fewer explicit skill and experience requirements compared to jobs not explicitly advertised for students.

The difference in skill expectations and the reduced length of work commitment suggests that there is little direct competition between student and non-student workers. It appears that student work is used to supplement the core, non-student workers, in particular at times of economic adjustment.

Rather than replacing non-students, employers appear to utilise the flexible student workers to smoothen the effects of the business cycle.

Student workers go hand in hand with a strong youth labour market

Where the labour market produces many standard jobs, such as in the Nordic countries or in Austria, student workers are also plentiful. On the contrary, in the Mediterranean countries, where work for young people is scarcer, the student worker population also appears meagre.

That does not necessarily mean, however, that Southern European students do not work as much as their Northern peers. Rather, we observe that student jobs are more likely to be advertised abroad (see Hyggen et al. 2016), adding the international mobility dimension to the flexibility characteristic of student work. This could potentially fuel internal mobility within the European Union, as explored by Hyggen et al. (2016).

Policy implications

Our research suggests that policy-makers should welcome the growth in student employment and do not need to fear a crowding-out effect whereby students are displacing other, less well qualified young workers.

Instead, attention should be given to matching the work that students undertake with their fields of study (see McGuiness, Bergin and Whelan 2015b), and to ensuring high-quality working conditions (including decent wages) for all young workers in general, irrespective of their student status.

References

Beblavý, Miroslav, Mehtap Akgüc, Brian Fabo, Karolien Lenaerts and Félix Paquier. 2017. *A Methodological Inquiry into the Data Generating Process Concerning New Jobs and Skills. Methodology.* Working paper, Leuven, FP7 InGRID project, M21.6.

Beblavý, Miroslav, and Brian Fabo. 2016. 'Impact of Student Workers on the European Labor Markets'. *Human Resource Management* 6: 27-41.

Beblavý, Miroslav, Brian Fabo, Lucia Mýtna Kureková and Zuzana Žilinčíková. 2015. *Are Student Workers Crowding out Low-Skilled Youth?* STYLE Working Paper WP5.3 Are student workers crowding out the low skilled youth

Grotti, Raffaele, Helen Russell and Jacqueline O'Reilly. Forthcoming. 'Where Do Young People Work?' In *Youth Labor in Transition*, edited by Jacqueline O'Reilly, Janine Leschke, Renate Ortlieb, Martin Seeleib-Kaiser and Paola Villa. New York: Oxford University Press.

McGuinness, Seamus, Adele Bergin and Adele Whelan. 2015b. *Recruitment Methods & Educational Provision effects on Graduate Over-Education and Over-Skilling.* STYLE Working Paper WP5.4 Report Recruitment Methods

McGuinness, Seamus, Adele Bergin and Adele Whelan. 2016. 'Is there a Role for Higher Education Institutions in Improving the Quality of First Employment?' *The B.E. Journal of Economic Analysis & Policy* 16 (4). doi: ***https://doi.org/10.1515/bejeap-2016-0174***.

Mýtna Kureková, Lucia, Miroslav Beblavý and Anna Thum-Thysen. 2015. 'Using Online Vacancies and Web Surveys to Analyse the Labour Market: A Methodological Inquiry'. IZA *Journal of Labor Economics* 4 (1): 1–20. doi:10.1186/s40172-015-0034-4.

Mýtna Kureková, Lucia, and Zuzana Žilinčíková. 2016. 'Are Student Jobs Flexible Jobs? Using Online Data to Study Employers' Preferences in Slovakia'. *IZA Journal of Labor Studies* 5: 20. doi:10.1186/s40174-016-0070-5 ***https://izajoels.springeropen.com/articles/10.1186/s40174-016-0070-5***

How different are youth and adult labour market transitions?

Vladislav Flek, **Martin Hála** and **Martina Mysíková**

Why are youth labour market transitions different?

Youth transitions are different for several reasons. First, only a fraction of school-leavers and university graduates immediately manage to find a stable and satisfactory job. The rest initially face unemployment or frequent job changes combined with repeated unemployment spells. This situation is attributed to educational mismatch, to a lack of work experience and to the absence of firm-specific skills. Second, youth employment tends to be unstable even when education, skills and other characteristics match the employer's requirements. Young employees are still more likely to be exposed to layoffs, for instance because of the practice of fixed-term labour contracts, seniority-weighted redundancy payments or last-in first-out rules.

These long-term patterns of youth transitions illustrate the marginalised status of young people on the labour markets. The Great Recession has further amplified the existing difficulties of young people – a situation that has resulted in youth (16-34) unemployment rates increasing faster than prime-age unemployment rates (35-54). Despite the reasonably good and varied amount of partial findings collected so far, we believed that a synthetic, cross-national view on youth labour market dynamics during the Great Recession was still largely lacking. To understand these effects, we analysed the youth labour market dynamics in selected EU countries over various stages of the Great Recession (Flek and Mysíková 2016; 2017). We were interested in a group of young individuals aged 16-34, and we compared these results with a reference group involving the prime-age population (35-54).

We wanted to find out:

1. How do the movements (gross flows) of young people between employment, unemployment and inactivity differ from the dynamics of the prime-age labour market?

2. What are the differences in the probabilities of young and prime-age individuals changing their labour market states?

3. Do the most marked differences between the evolution of youth and the prime-age unemployment rates lie in a relatively different exposure to job loss, in the prospects for exiting unemployment, or in transitions between inactivity and the labour market?

4. What individual characteristics affect youth/prime-age transitions from employment to unemployment?

5. How do unemployment durations and the characteristics of young/prime-age unemployed influence their chances of finding a job?

We used longitudinal data from the European Union Survey on Income and Living Conditions (EU-SILC) from January 2008 to December 2012. We provide analysis for a selection of countries that represent the south-west of Europe: France, Italy and Spain; the former communist economies of the East: Czech Republic and Poland; and Austria as a country with low levels of youth unemployment and high productivity. Applying estimation techniques such as variance decompositions, duration models and probit models, the analysis yields a number of key findings.

Findings:

Young people make more transitions than older workers

Youth is relatively more involved in gross flows than prime-age groups. This holds true uniformly across the countries analysed over the period 2008–2012 and supports the less recent evidence on a higher aggregate fluidity of youth labour markets compared to prime-age markets.

Young people face a higher probability of job loss

The policy priority should be to reduce the gap between the unemployment risks faced by a young and a prime-age worker. This gap is characteristic for all the labour markets analysed and concerns countries with substantially different labour market performance, institutions, EU-membership history and other national specificities.

Drivers of youth unemployment versus prime-age unemployment

Inflows of young workers into unemployment account for far higher increases in youth unemployment rates compared to prime-age unemployment rates where the inflows have not been as high. This finding additionally confirms the presence of a strong disparity in (formal and/or informal) employment protection between the two age groups analysed.

Experience and education reduce risk of job loss among youth

Young people need to gain work experience promptly so as to minimize the probability of job loss. Also, the effect of education on lowering the risk of job loss is significant for young people. Higher education actually decreases the probability of becoming unemployed more substantially for young workers than for prime-age workers.

Unemployment durations negatively affect the probability of finding a job

From 2010 onward, the job-finding prospects of young unemployed could be viewed as a diminishing function of unemployment duration in all countries analysed. This can be attributed to stigmatisation and discouragement effects of prolonged unemployment duration. However, prime-age unemployed are still likely to suffer relatively more heavily from this duration dependence effect.

The individual characteristics of young unemployed matter

Higher education significantly increases the job-finding probability of young unemployed. Furthermore, employers avoid hiring the relatively immature young unemployed aged less than 24. In the absence of other members in respondents' households, the pressure to find a job imposed on young unemployed appears to be significantly higher.

References

Flek, Vladislav, Martin Hála and Martina Mysíková. Forthcoming. 'How do youth labor flows differ from those of older workers?' In *Youth Labor in Transition*, edited by Jacqueline O'Reilly, Janine Leschke, Renate Ortlieb, Martin Seeleib-Kaiser and Paola Villa. New York: Oxford University Press.

Flek, Vladislav, and Martina Mysíková. 2016. *Youth transitions and labour market flows – who moves and how?* STYLE Working Paper WP5.2 Youth Transitions and Labour Market Flows

What are the drivers of overeducation?

Seamus McGuinness, **Adele Bergin** and **Adele Whelan**

What is overeducation and does it matter?

Overeducation describes the situation whereby individuals are employed in jobs for which the level of schooling required to obtain, or to carry out the job is below the level of schooling held by the worker. We argued that almost all of the relevant research to date has relied on country-specific cross-sectional data (with observations on variables at a given point of time) or panel data sets (containing observations of multiple variables obtained over multiple time periods for the same individuals; McGuinness, Bergin and Whelan 2015a).

Furthermore, studies have tended to focus on identifying individual or firm-level reasons to explain overeducation. Or, researchers have been interested in its impacts on individual outcomes such as income and job satisfaction: are people less satisfied doing jobs for which they are overqualified?

However, we do not know how overeducation evolves across countries over time or know which macroeconomic, demographic and institutional forces drive it. This is because of a lack of aggregate time-series data (i.e., where observations on a variable or set of variables covers several time periods).

How do trends in overeducation vary by country and over time?

To address this gap in our knowledge and using time-series data, we found that overeducation tends to rise over time in a number of European countries but that this is by no means a universal pattern. Overeducation was found to be static and had even declined in some European countries. Indeed, a positive finding was that overeducation had not risen in the majority of countries in our study. These findings can be seen in Figure 1 below, which plots the overeducation rates over time for both the entire sample of European countries and also, separately, for three groups of countries from Eastern, Peripheral and Central Europe.

Given that we are dealing with a large number of countries, for the purposes of our analysis we group these into three categories on the basis of common linkages in terms of geographical proximity, levels of economic development and access to the single market.

The first category is comprised of the countries that acceded to the EU from 2004, which are Bulgaria, Czech Republic, Estonia, Hungary, Lithuania, Latvia, Poland, Romania, Slovenia, and Slovak Republic, and are referred to as the 'Eastern' states.

The second category refers to Portugal, Ireland, Italy, Greece and Spain, the traditional 'Periphery' of the EU.

The third group ('Central') comprises the remaining countries located in central and northern Europe and includes Austria, Belgium, Denmark, Finland, France, Iceland, Luxemburg, Netherlands, Norway, Sweden and the UK.

The first thing that becomes apparent is that overeducation has remained remarkably stable: since 2003, just under 18% of people employed, across the EU28, reported being overeducated for the jobs they were doing.

There is evidence of slight cyclicality: overeducation rates rose somewhat following the onset of the Great Recession in 2008 before falling off again in 2010.

However, more variation is apparent when the data is analysed separately for the Central, Eastern and Peripheral country groupings. The peripheral countries have the highest rate of overeducation, at between 25% and 30%. These rates are also more volatile, with overeducation appearing to rise between 2003 and 2008 before falling thereafter.

Overeducation in Central European countries ranged between 17% and 20% and, in contrast to the Peripheral group, overeducation appeared to rise somewhat in the aftermath of the Great Recession before falling again after 2010. Finally, the incidence of overeducation appears most stable in the Eastern European countries, with the series appearing to fluctuate around a 15% average throughout the period.

Figure 1: *Mean overeducation rate (restricted to full-time employees), 2003-2013.*

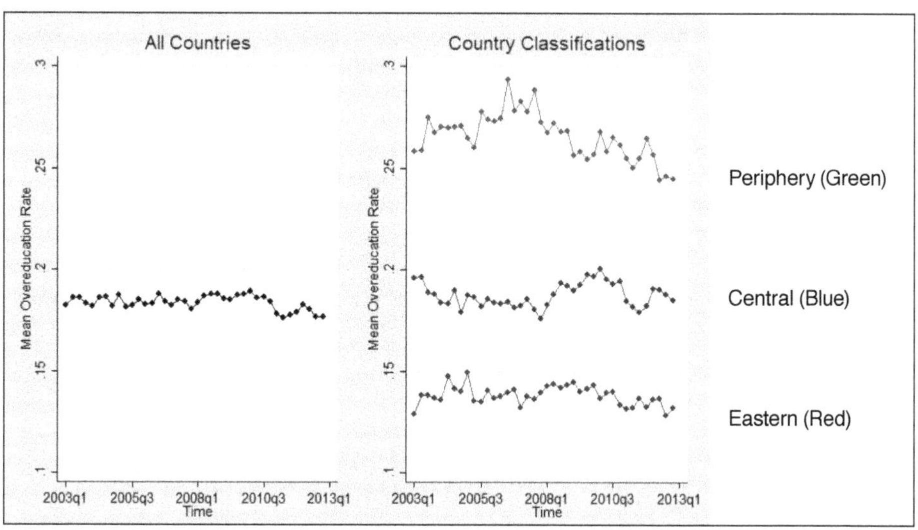

What are the long-run trends?

Despite such regional disparities, long-run trends and relationships were found to exist within and between countries. The evidence suggests that while overeducation rates in Europe are converging upwards over time, the general pattern of overeducation growth is related across many countries.

From a policy perspective, the extent to which overeducation could be suitable for a common policy approach, either at a European or a national level, will largely depend on the similarities in the evolution of overeducation over time both between and within countries. Therefore, while overeducation rates are generally converging to a higher level, they also tend to follow a similar pattern, suggesting that the phenomenon responds in a similar way to external shocks and, consequently, is likely to react in similar ways to appropriate policy interventions. However, the research indicates that overeducation within Peripheral states evolves somewhat differently relative to the rest of Europe, suggesting that a separate policy response is likely to be appropriate in these countries.

What are the long-term consequences?

For younger workers, less favourable outcomes early in their careers, such as overeducation, may negatively impact future labour market success, so it is important to understand the incidence of youth overeducation, its evolution over time and the drivers of youth mismatch.

Youth (15-24) and adult (25-64) overeducation rates were found not to move together in an equilibrium relationship within the majority of countries, and youth overeducation rates were found to be generally more volatile in nature.

Finally, in terms of the determinants of youth overeducation, some common themes emerge. Our studies find that youth overeducation is highly driven by the composition of education provision, aggregate labour demand and labour market flexibility.

References

McGuinness, Seamus, Adele Bergin and Adele Whelan. 2015a. *A Comparative Time Series Analysis of Overeducation in Europe: Is there a Common Policy Approach?* STYLE Working Paper WP5.1 Overeducation in Europe

McGuinness, Seamus, Adele Bergin and Adele Whelan. Forthcoming. 'Overeducation in Europe: Is there Scope for a Common Policy Approach?' In *Youth Labor in Transition*, edited by Jacqueline O'Reilly, Janine Leschke, Renate Ortlieb, Martin Seeleib-Kaiser and Paola Villa. New York: Oxford University Press.

Skills and education mismatch: Policy themes

Seamus McGuinness, **Lucia Mýtna Kureková** and **Vladislav Flek**

Based on these research report findings, important policy implications can be drawn regarding (i) human capital development in third-level institutions, (ii) transitions from education to work and (iii) relative exposure to employment mismatch and separation in employment.

Human capital development in third-level institutions
The findings from Beblavý et al. (2015), Mýtna Kureková and Žilinčíková (2016), Beblavý and Fabo (2016) and McGuinness, Bergin and Whelan (2015b) emphasise the importance of practical learning within degree programmes and suggest that students can further develop their human capital through part-time work while studying without imposing additional costs on low-skilled workers. In terms of university provision, the study by McGuinness, Bergin and Whelan (2015a) demonstrates that there are large positive impacts associated with learning elements such as research projects, work placements, the acquisition of facts/practical knowledge and project/problem-based learning.

The research also demonstrates that a graduate's likelihood of experiencing either overeducation or over-skilling on entering the labour market is lower the higher the number of practical learning elements within their degree programme. McGuinness, Bergin and Whelan (2015b) also show that the pay-off of practical learning tends to be highest within degree programmes that are traditionally considered to be academic in nature. Given that the negative impacts of worker mismatch are known to be substantial and long-lasting with respect to earnings, job satisfaction and career progression, the research suggests that the formulation of workplace and practical skills, specifically through elements such as work placements, should be a key component of all European degree programmes, irrespective of field of study.

The finding of the importance of work-relevant human capital formation deriving from McGuinness, Bergin and Whelan (2015b) also suggests that the experience of practical work-based learning through part-time employment, in combination with study, also has the capacity to enhance the quality of job match in first employment. The fact that Beblavý et al. (2015) show that students can acquire such skills without imposing additional costs on low- and medium-skilled workers is also a positive finding.

However, there is not sufficient evidence from either Beblavý et al. (2015) or McGuinness, Bergin and Whelan (2015b) to conclude that the impacts of part-time work on students' total human capital formation is strictly positive, as it is likely that an increase in part-time work may also have some negative impacts on classroom-based human capital formation. More research is needed to inform policy on the net effects of part-time work on subsequent total skill acquisition and labour market outcomes.

Transitions from education to work

McGuinness, Bergin and Whelan (2015b) generate important lessons for higher education institutions not only in terms of degree structure, but also with respect to routes into the labour market. The authors also show that acquiring a job with the aid of a university substantially reduces the incidence of labour market mismatch in first employment. By strengthening links with employers and investing more heavily in career-support functions, universities and third-level institutions can play an important role in matching graduates with jobs by eliminating many of the informational asymmetries that can lead to graduate mismatch. Higher education institutions can play an important role in terms of educating students in the jobsearch methods to employ and those to avoid. For instance, it is clear from the results of McGuinness, Bergin and Whelan (2015b) that the use of private employment agencies significantly heightens the risk of subsequent mismatch, perhaps because of the fact that such organisations are primarily motivated by achieving a job placement and have little incentive, or capacity, to ensure the quality of any match. A limitation of the study is that it focuses on a relatively narrow period following graduation, so that more research is certainly required into the more long-run impacts of the role of jobsearch on labour market outcomes.

Exposure to employment mismatch and separation in employment

Both Flek and Mysíková (2016) and McGuinness, Bergin and Whelan (2015a) indicate that, in many countries, young people face (a) a higher risk of job loss during recession and (b) a higher risk of exposure to overeducation throughout the economic cycle. Both reports suggest that young people are less likely to have their qualifications fully recognised within the labour market and are most likely to be fired during a downturn in economic condition.

McGuinness, Bergin and Whelan (2015a) and Flek and Mysíková (2016) suggest that policy has a role to play in reducing transitions into overeducation and unemployment, both of which have potentially devastating impacts on future labour market outcomes and progression amongst young workers. With respect to youth overeducation, the initial findings of McGuinness, Bergin and Whelan (2015a) show that the unrestricted expansion of higher education supply and increased labour market deregulation tend to stimulate rates of overeducation.

The principal policy implication from the study is that, in order to prevent an increase in overeducation, governments should take fuller account of the prevailing structure of labour demand within an economy before formulating policies around higher education expansion or greater labour flexibility.

With respect to the higher incidence of job loss amongst young workers, Flek and Mysíková (2016) suggest that policy be more focused on protecting the position of young workers in the labour market during recessions. While job losses are inevitable when growth declines, it is both inequitable and inefficient to have higher concentrations of unemployment amongst the youngest sections of society. The research by Flek and Mysíková (2016) points strongly at the need to strengthen employment protection for young people in order to align it more fully with the rights enjoyed by older workers.

Furthermore, this research by Flek and Mysíková (2016) also implies that at the outset of any recession, activation policy should be heavily focussed on developing strategies to incentivise employers to retain younger workers in order to stop any future rapid rise in rates of youth unemployment. Finally, again with respect to activation policy, Flek and Mysíková (2016) suggest that policy instruments that are triggered at a particular point in a claimant's unemployment spell, such as the Youth Guarantee, should be designed to take account of variations in the pattern of unemployment durations across countries.

Acknowledgements
The authors would like to thank Glenda Quintini (OECD) and the European Commission's DG for Employment, Social Affairs and Inclusion for comments on an earlier version of papers that contributed to this section.

References

Beblavý, Miroslav, Mehtap Akgüc, Brian Fabo, Karolien Lenaerts and Félix Paquier. 2017. *A Methological Inquiry into the Data Generating Process Concerning New Jobs and Skills.* Methodology. Working paper, Leuven, FP7 InGRID project, M21.6c.

Beblavý, Miroslav, and Brian Fabo. 2016. 'Impact of Student Workers on the European Labor Markets'. *Human Resource Management* 6: : 27-41.

Beblavý, Miroslav, Brian Fabo, Lucia Mýtna Kureková and Zuzana Žilinčíková. 2015. *Are Student Workers Crowding out Low-Skilled Youth?* STYLE Working Paper WP5.3 Are student workers crowding out the low skilled youth

Flek, Vladislav, and Martina Mysíková. 2016. *Youth Transitions and Labour Market Flows – Who Moves and How?* STYLE Working Paper WP5.2 Youth Transitions and Labour Market Flows

Grotti, Raffaele, Helen Russell and Jacqueline O'Reilly. Forthcoming. 'Where Do Young People Work?' In *Youth Labor in Transition*, edited by Jacqueline O'Reilly, Janine Leschke, Renate Ortlieb, Martin Seeleib-Kaiser and Paola Villa. New York: Oxford University Press.

McGuinness, Seamus, Adele Bergin and Adele Whelan. 2015a. *A Comparative Time Series Analysis of Overeducation in Europe: Is There a Common Policy Approach?* STYLE Working Paper WP5.1 Overeducation in Europe

McGuinness, Seamus. Adele Whelan and Adele Bergin. 2015b. *Recruitment Methods & Educational Provision effects on Graduate Over-Education and Over-Skilling.* STYLE Working Paper WP5.4 Report Recruitment Methods

McGuinness, Seamus. Adele Whelan and Adele Bergin. 2016. 'Is There a Role for Higher Education Institutions in Improving the Quality of First Employment?' *The B.E. Journal of Economic Analysis & Policy* 16 (4). doi: ***https://doi.org/10.1515/bejeap-2016-0174***.

McGuinness, Seamus, Adele Bergin and Adele Whelan. Forthcoming. 'Overeducation in Europe: Is There Scope for a Common Policy Approach?' In *Youth Labor in Transition*, edited by Jacqueline O'Reilly, Janine Leschke, Renate Ortlieb, Martin Seeleib-Kaiser and Paola Villa. New York: Oxford University Press.

Mýtna Kureková, Lucia, Miroslav Beblavý and Anna Thum-Thysen. 2015. 'Using Online Vacancies and Web Surveys to Analyse the Labour Market: A Methodological Inquiry'. *IZA Journal of Labor Economics* 4 (1): 1–20. ***https://izajole.springeropen.com/articles/10.1186/s40172-015-0034-4***.

Mýtna Kureková, Lucia, and Zuzana Žilinčíková. 2016. 'Are Student Jobs Flexible Jobs? Using Online Data to Study Employers' Preferences in Slovakia'. *IZA Journal of Labor Studies* 5 (20). doi:10.1186/s40174-016-0070-5 ***https://izajoels.springeropen.com/articles/10.1186/s40174-016-0070-5***

Flek, Vladislav, Martin Hála and Martina Mysíková. Forthcoming. 'How do youth labor flows differ from those of older workers?' In *Youth Labor in Transition*, edited by Jacqueline O'Reilly, Janine Leschke, Renate Ortlieb, Martin Seeleib-Kaiser and Paola Villa. New York: Oxford University Press.

McGuinness, Seamus, Adele Bergin and Adele Whelan. Forthcoming. 'Overeducation in Europe: Is there Scope for a Common Policy Approach?' In *Youth Labor in Transition*, edited by Jacqueline O'Reilly, Janine Leschke, Renate Ortlieb, Martin Seeleib-Kaiser and Paola Villa. New York: Oxford University Press.

Further reading on skills and education mismatch

These results are published in more depth in the STYLE Working Papers

http://www.style-research.eu/publications/working-papers

Beblavý, Miroslav, Brian Fabo, Lucia Mýtna Kureková and Zuzana Žilinčíková. 2015. *Are Student Workers Crowding out Low-Skilled Youth?* STYLE Working Paper WP5.3 Are student workers crowding out the low skilled youth

Flek, Vladislav, and Martina Mysíková. 2016. *Youth Transitions and Labour Market Flows – Who Moves and How?* STYLE Working Paper WP5.2 Youth Transitions and Labour Market Flows

McGuinness, Seamus, Adele Bergin and Adele Whelan. 2015. *A Comparative Time Series Analysis of Overeducation in Europe: Is there a Common Policy Approach?* STYLE Working Paper WP5.1 Overeducation in Europe

McGuinness, Seamus. Adele Whelan and Adele Bergin. 2015b. *Recruitment Methods & Educational Provision effects on Graduate Over-Education and Over-Skilling.* STYLE Working Paper WP5.4 Report Recruitment Methods

McGuinness, Seamus, and Vladislav Flek. 2016. *Policy Synthesis and Integrative Report.* STYLE Working Paper WP5.5 Policy Synthesis and Integrative Report on Mismatch Skills and Education

Migration and mobility

Changing patterns of migration in Europe

Mehtap Akgüç and **Miroslav Beblavý**

Since the end of World War II, Europe has experienced large-scale migration both internally and from the outside the EU. In this contribution, we focus on intra-European migration flows from Southern and Eastern Europe to the rest of Europe. We compare Southern and Eastern European migration patterns with figures on internal European migration from the rest of the EU and on migration from non-EU countries. This provides a broader picture of a changing and dynamic migrant reservoir in Europe over time. We use a combination of secondary sources, analysis of descriptive macro data on migration flows, and econometric analysis of micro data on labour market outcome of migrants with an emphasis on youth, in accordance with the STYLE project focus. Our research was concentrated on five key questions.

How do intra-European and non-EU migration flows compare over time?
The descriptive analysis using aggregate country data suggests that even though migration from non-European countries is very substantial, the intra-European flows from Southern and Eastern Europe are non-negligible, with comparable emigration rates and differing trends and composition in the post-war period.

How did the composition of intra-European flows change over time?
Has there been a shift with an increase of more young migrants from Southern Europe than from Eastern Europe? Geographical proximity matters: Spanish inflows to France or Polish inflows to Germany are very common. But since the early 2000s, Spanish migrants are heading instead to the UK and Polish migrants are going to Ireland.

How are migratory trends related to political developments?
The fall of the Iron Curtain and the expansion of EU membership saw new waves of migration in the past twenty years, which were further accelerated by the EU accession. Since the mid-1970s, post-war European guest-worker programmes have targeted low-skilled, male and relatively young workers from Southern Europe, Turkey, Yugoslavia and the Maghreb. More recent waves of migration have included more asylum-seekers and refugees since the 1990s. Only since the 2000s has high-skilled large-scale labour migration gained more prominence in Europe.

How do young EU migrants' outcomes differ from those of non-EU migrants? The econometric analysis, using pooled micro data from a Europe-wide survey, suggests that observable characteristics explain part, but not all, of the differential labour market performance of the migrants. Young migrants from both Eastern and Southern Europe are more likely to be overqualified than young native-born workers.

We also find important gender gaps: male migrants have higher rates of employment and work longer hours, across all migrant groups, especially amongst non-EU migrants, where more traditional gender norms may apply (Zuccotti and O'Reilly forthcoming). To address this gap, policy-makers could take a targeted approach, whereby they inform migrant women about existing facilities, such as family-friendly work schedules and access to childcare.

To tackle issues of persisting native–migrant gaps in labour market performance, policies could be geared toward further integration and non-discriminatory treatment of foreign-born residents in the destination labour markets. Employers could use anonymous job applications to avoid discriminatory hiring based on ethnicity.

On the education–occupation mismatch issue, better screening and more transparent evaluation schemes could be developed to compare and recognise the degrees, qualifications and skills possessed by migrants so that their skills and competences could be put to better use in destination countries. An innovative new tool – geared at non-EU nationals who are more disadvantaged in terms of labour market outcomes than EU migrants (Akgüç and Beblavý forthcoming; Spreckelsen, Leschke and Seeleib-Kaiser forthcoming) – is the development of a new EU Skills Profile Tool for Third Country Nationals. Similarly, mechanisms that facilitate international skill transferability and on-the-job training possibilities could be offered to young migrants so as to avoid skill mismatches in occupations.

References

Akgüç, Mehtap, and Miroslav Beblavý. 2015. *Re-emerging Migration Patterns: Structures and Policy Lessons.* STYLE Working Paper WP6.3 Re-emerging Migration Patterns: Structures and Policy Lessons

Akgüç, Mehtap, and Miroslav Beblavý. Forthcoming. 'What Happens to Young People Who Move Country to Find Work?' In *Youth Labor in Transition*, edited by Jacqueline O'Reilly, Janine Leschke, Renate Ortlieb, Martin Seeleib-Kaiser and Paola Villa. New York: Oxford University Press.

Spreckelsen, Thees, Janine Leschke and Martin Seeleib-Kaiser. Forthcoming. 'Europe's Promise for Jobs? Labor Market Integration of Young EU Migrant Citizens in Germany and the United Kingdom'. In *Youth Labor in Transition*, edited by Jacqueline O'Reilly, Janine Leschke, Renate Ortlieb, Martin Seeleib-Kaiser and Paola Villa. New York: Oxford University Press.

Zuccotti, Carolina V., and Jacqueline O'Reilly. Forthcoming. 'Do scarring Effects Vary by Ethnicity and Gender?' In *Youth Labor in Transition*, edited by Jacqueline O'Reilly, Janine Leschke, Renate Ortlieb, Martin Seeleib-Kaiser and Paola Villa. New York: Oxford University Press.

East2West and North2North: Youth migration and labour market intermediaries in Austria and Norway

Christer Hyggen, **Renate Ortlieb**, **Hans Christian Sandlie** and **Silvana Weiss**

An important aspect of migratory flows is the role of labour market intermediaries for youth mobility in Europe. Positioned between employers and jobseekers, labour market intermediaries are often involved in transnational recruiting processes. We analysed recruiting strategies of employers and jobsearch strategies of young migrants, thereby also considering the working conditions of the latter.

Research design

The research uses a comparative design, focusing on the situation of young EU8 migrants in Austria and of young Swedes in Norway. Austria and Norway provide particularly attractive job prospects to migrants. Here, in comparison with other countries, youth unemployment rates are low, wage levels are high and working conditions are good. Furthermore, in both countries, several industries are suffering labour shortages.

The research concentrates on three industries with a high demand for labour: tourism, care/health and high-tech. It draws on 116 interviews conducted with young migrants, employers, labour market intermediaries and other experts.

Employers need flexible workers

The results indicate that employers in Austria and Norway are interested in recruiting young migrants from neighbouring EU countries because they need large numbers of flexible workers.

Youth motivations

Young migrants are attracted by good job opportunities – in particular, by comparatively high salaries, attractive career prospects and good working conditions. Further important drivers for young people to apply for jobs in Austria or Norway are geographical proximity, good language skills and a certain spirit of adventure. On the other hand, major obstacles to job matching are information deficits, a lack of social networks and insufficient foreign language skills.

Labour market intermediaries

Labour market intermediaries can help to overcome these barriers within the transnational recruiting/jobsearch process. Intermediaries provide information and/or serve as matchmakers who manage the entire recruiting process. Some labour market intermediaries do the complete administrative work for both employers and young migrants.

According to our research findings, mainly private companies are involved in transnational recruiting/jobsearch processes. In contrast, public labour market intermediaries (i.e., employment service agencies) only play a minor role. The importance of intermediaries varies across industries and between the two countries. For instance, in the 24-hour care sector in Austria, they are key players who recruit women from EU8 countries to work in private households. Many of them receive support from other intermediary agencies located in EU8 countries in order to reach young people who are willing to work in Austria. In Norway, the role of labour market intermediaries is connected to the skill level. They are more important for high-skilled migrants than for the lower skilled.

In both countries, labour market intermediaries have powerful positions in the triangular relationship between themselves, employers and young migrants. Their impact on working conditions is strong, but ambivalent. On the one hand, they have the power to secure good working conditions for young migrants by counselling and controlling the employer. On the other hand, because usually they consider the employers to be their main clients, they feel more committed to employers than to migrants. As a consequence, the position of young migrants is weaker, bearing the risk of exploitation.

This research underlines the importance of labour market intermediaries for youth migration in Europe. However, we advocate for drawing more attention to the needs of young migrants. As one strategy to achieve this objective, we suggest that public labour market intermediaries should take a more active role in the transnational recruiting/jobsearch and matching processes of young migrants in Europe.

References

Hyggen, Christer, Renate Ortlieb, Hans Christian Sandlie and Silvana Weiss. 2016. *East-West and North-North Migrating Youth and the Role of Labour Market Intermediaries. The Case of Austria and Norway.* Style Working Paper WP6.2 Working conditions and labour market intermediaries Norway and Austria

Leschke, Janine, Martin Seeleib-Kaiser, Thees Spreckelsen, Christer Hyggen and Hans Christian Sandlie. 2016. *Labour Market Outcomes and Integration of Recent Youth Migrants from Central-Eastern and Southern Europe in Germany, Norway and Great Britain.* STYLE Working Paper WP6.4 Labour market outcomes and integration of recent youth migrants from Central-Eastern and Southern Europe in Germany, Norway and Great Britain

Ortlieb, Renate, Maura Sheehan and Jaan Masso. Forthcoming. 'Do Business Start-Ups Create High-Quality Jobs for Young People?' In *Youth Labor in Transition*, edited by Jacqueline O'Reilly, Janine Leschke, Renate Ortlieb, Martin Seeleib-Kaiser and Paola Villa. New York: Oxford University Press.

Four stories of migration

Christer Hyggen, **Renate Ortlieb**, **Hans Christian Sandlie** and **Silvana Weiss**

In the course of our fieldwork, we met many young people on the move, and their individual stories varied greatly. Here we present four typical stories of young migrants who moved to find a job in Austria and in Norway. Their stories are constructed on the basis of 116 interviews with migrants, employers and intermediaries.

József moved from Hungary to Austria to work in an engineering firm
József is a young Hungarian male, aged 24. He achieved his university degree in electrical engineering in Hungary and has been working in Austria for six months. Back home his team won first prize in a student industrial competition and the award was an internship for three months with an Austrian company. He was delighted with this opportunity, but it was difficult for him to move to Austria: he had problems finding an affordable place to live because as a student money was tight. Moving to Austria involved costs: for travelling, for the hotel that he needed until he found a place to live, for deposits and for basic living equipment. Furthermore, he had only basic German skills and so it was difficult to obtain information about room listings. A number of people on an online portal offered him a room, but because his spoken German was weak, and he needed a room for only a few months, he was not considered a very attractive applicant. After more than 30 attempts, he got the chance to rent a room in a shared apartment. On hearing of József's troubles, his two student colleagues in Hungary who also won the internships in Austria decided to stay at home.

So József came to Austria alone. He worked hard to convince his employer to offer him a more permanent position. Since he had been one of the best students at his university, he did well and was offered a job for another two years when the internship finished. Today he is thankful for the opportunity and still works hard hoping one day to get a permanent position. He often works nights and at the weekends and has few friends in Austria, so he uses his time mainly for work. He enjoys his job because he is in the R&D department and is working with new and exciting technology. However, sometimes he wishes he had more spare time and more friends in Austria.

But József is grateful to have this job because at home he would not earn as much. Even if he only gets the minimum wage as defined by the collective agreement for his profession, he earns much more than his friends who stayed in Hungary. He is not sure if he will ever return home. Perhaps he will stay in Austria or move to Germany where job opportunities are even better.

Zuzana moved from Slovakia to Austria to become a care worker
Zuzana is a 32-year-old woman from Slovakia. After highschool, she worked in different offices as a secretary. She married at 26 and had her first child at 27. One year later she divorced, and since then she has experienced financial problems. She has to pay back a loan in order to keep the apartment where she lives with her daughter. This made Zuzana decide to work as a 24-hour carer in Austria. She knew women who worked in Austria and she heard the pay was good. And so she took a 200-hour course for care workers provided by the Red Cross. In a course folder, she found information about an agency in Bratislava that helps women to find a job as carers in Austria. She called and they gave her an exam date to prove her German skills. Unfortunately, she failed, so she then set about improving her German skills over the next two months using her sister's old school textbook. She passed the exam on the second attempt and got a job offer within two weeks. Two cooperating agencies, one in Austria and the other in Slovakia, managed all the paper work and they sent a taxi to her apartment that took her directly to an Austrian household.

Zuzana has been working in Austria as a carer since 2011. She is usually available in a household for 24 hours over two weeks. When this two-week shift is over, another Slovak woman arrives in a taxi to replace her and the same taxi takes Zuzana back to Slovakia for two weeks. Her parents look after her daughter while she is working in Austria.

Zuzana is a self-employed worker, but the intermediary companies take care of all the legal formalities. She pays around 350 euros per year for their services. Even if she hardly ever needs the help of the agencies, she is willing to pay the fee because should she lose her current client, the agency would then find her a new one within a few days or weeks. At the moment, she is pleased with her job: she lives with a friendly family who treat her well. However, she has worked in households with very difficult and unfriendly clients. Once the situation was so bad that she decided to leave. The employment agency supported her, but she now believes it would be better not to make any complaints about a future client.

Zuzana is happy with her situation because she earns good money and is able to pay back her loan. In the two weeks when she is at home, she can spend a lot of time with her daughter. However, it's hard to be separated from her for the other two weeks. Furthermore, she feels isolated working in a household in the Austrian countryside. Apart from the relatives of the client she cares for, she meets no Austrians. Since she must always be available for the client when she is in Austria, she has no possibility to get in contact with other Austrians or build up any social network of her own. Zuzana hopes to pay off her debts as soon as possible so she can return to Slovakia and live with her daughter.

Fredrik moved from Sweden to Norway to work in bars and then in IT
Fredrik came to Norway from a small town in the north of Sweden to find work. Having finished highschool with only an IT specialisation, his career prospects at home were

poor. Many of his friends (those who had not already left for other countries or larger Swedish cities to work or study) were unemployed. Fredrik had a job in Sweden – a fixed-term, relatively poorly paid position with an IT company. His employer expected him to work hard and never be absent from work; he was let know that others could fill his position with a day's notice. Fredrik wanted to get away – to discover the world.

Through his network of friends, he knew that there were job opportunities in Norway and that the wages were considerably higher than in Sweden. He had some savings and borrowed money from his grandmother before heading to Norway with the telephone number of a friend of a friend where he could stay for a couple of nights. Through his contact he was encouraged to contact a Swedish Association in Norway. This association offers cheap lodgings and he had a room within a week. In the lobby, he met a group of other Swedes on their way to the tax office to get a necessary "D-number" and they told him to set up an account with a Norwegian bank.

At the same time, he applied for a range of jobs through the Internet and visited bars and restaurants to look for job openings. On the third day, he contacted a temporary job agency and was offered a two-week engagement in a restaurant starting the following week. At first it was a bit of an adventure, he gained many new friends and had fun. But he soon discovered that the cost of living was high in Norway and he was running short on funds. It took him only a week to land his first job, but he wasn't going to get his first pay cheque for a month. Fredrick's living quarters were not suited for a long stay and he started looking for a place to live. He was offered a room in a shared dwelling with other Swedes in an apartment downtown, but in addition to paying the first month's rent, he had to come up with a two-month security deposit. If his family had not come up with the funds, his adventure would have ended there.

Two years later, Fredrik is still in Norway. After working on different short-term IT project contracts, he was offered a permanent position in a firm that he had been working for through a temporary jobs agency. The company then paid to buy him out of his contract with the agency and he now works in a large private IT organisation with good training and career opportunities. He still dreams of travelling the world, but he may have to wait for the holidays.

Lisa moved from Sweden to Norway to work as a nurse

Lisa worked as trained nurse in a Swedish hospital in a large city not far from the Norwegian border. She graduated from her university two years ago and has been working in the same hospital for the past year. At a training seminar, a representative approached her from an employment agency offering her the same amount of pay in two weeks that she now made in a month if she was willing to move to Norway. She accepted and was offered a flat on the hospital grounds in Norway, and assistance in going through the formal procedures for the accreditation required to work in a Norwegian hospital and the formalities related to taxes. Two months later, she started working in Norway with colleagues and patients that could understand her native language and she even found a few work friends from her hometown.

However, problems arose with the limitations on working hours. Ideally, she would work as much as possible over two weeks in Oslo, but her hours are limited by labour regulations. She now plans to move back home to Sweden to be closer to friends and family.

What happens to young people moving to Germany, Norway and the UK to find work?

Janine Leschke, **Martin Seeleib-Kaiser** and **Thees Spreckelsen**

Research questions

One of the most distinctive characteristics of youth employment in recent years has been the large proportion of young people who move abroad to find work (O'Reilly et al. 2015). But how well integrated are these young EU migrants? Are they offered new opportunities by these jobs or are they part of an increasingly marginalised and precarious labour force?

Research design

To examine these questions, we set about comparing the different circumstances of young people who had moved to work in Germany, Norway and the UK. These three countries have very different ways of including young people in the labour market (Hadjivassiliou et al. forthcoming). We were interested in finding out if the country they moved to made much difference to their outcomes. We focused on young people who had come from Central and Eastern Europe (CEE; EU8), Bulgaria and Romania (EU2) and Southern Europe, compared to young people from Western and Northern EU countries (EU15 without EU-South), as well as third-country nationals, i.e., people who had come from outside the EU.

We use national Labour Force Survey data for the pre-crisis and crisis period and for the most part show simple proportions and means across the different migration groups, not controlling for additional characteristics such as skills level so as to reflect the public debates (for the full analysis including tables and figures, see Leschke et al. 2016, and for a more integrated analysis on the British and German case, only see Spreckelsen, Leschke and Seeleib-Kaiser 2016).

We examine the labour market integration of young EU migrant workers in both its quantitative (employment, unemployment and inactivity rates) and qualitative aspects. We measured qualitative labour market integration by capturing several dimensions of working conditions: the prevalence of atypical employment (e.g., non-permanent employment and solo self-employment); working hours and earnings; and occupation-skills mismatch. To capture wider social integration, we also consider social benefit receipt.

Our analysis is novel in three ways:

1. its comparative perspective among the destination countries,
2. its focus on recent EU youth migrants (those who moved country in the previous five years), as well as
3. its distinction of migrants by regions of origin.

Does it make a difference which country they moved to?
Regarding the destination countries, we compared the UK (with its open general skills labour market) with Norway and Germany (which have more closed labour markets focused on specific skills). The three destination countries differed considerably in their economic trajectories in the post-2008 economic crisis, with the UK experiencing (relatively) higher levels of unemployment than Norway and Germany.

After the 2004 and 2007 EU enlargements, the countries differed in the way they allowed workers from the accession countries to move and work within their borders; these restrictions were called 'transitional arrangements'. The UK's initial openness to Central and Eastern European citizens compared to Germany's restrictiveness and Norway's gradual opening of its labour market provide a good test case for investigating the importance of region-of-origin and economic crisis effects.

Previous research was largely focused on assessing the labour market integration of all migrants, thereby ignoring the potential double disadvantage of young migrants as being migrants and in transition from education into the labour market. Our focus is very policy relevant given the youth unemployment crisis of, particularly, the Southern European countries.

Third, and crucially, this study is original in investigating how well EU youth migrants do in the labour market given their region of origin. Usually, EU migrant citizens' labour market situation is assessed by comparing migrants from EU15 with those from EU8 and EU2 countries of Central and Eastern Europe. However, the labour market situation and institutions of the Southern EU countries are very different, even more so after the recent economic and debt crisis, particularly for young people. This potentially influences the labour market outcomes of young migrants by region of origin, which is a new form of stratification.

How well did they do?
Two positive findings of the study are that *young EU migrant citizens are rather well integrated quantitatively in the respective labour markets when it comes to employment.* This is not the case for third-country youth nationals.

The second positive observation is that the *economic crisis does not seem negatively related to young EU migrant citizens' labour market integration in the respective destination countries*. In the German case, the post-2008 period even saw an improvement of the situation for youth from Central and Eastern Europe with respect to some of the indicators.

Our most important finding is that there is a surprising similarity in the qualitative labour market integration (working conditions) of young EU migrant citizens across Germany, Norway and the UK.

Does it matter where you come from?
For migrants who arrived in the last five years, their region of origin mattered more in determining labour market success than institutional differences between their new host countries.

Young people from Central Eastern Europe (EU8) and from Bulgaria and Romania (EU2) were the least successful. Youth from the EU-South were moderately successful, and those from Northern and Western EU (+EFTA) countries in some cases even did better than their native peers. This ranking or stratification of labour market outcomes was consistent across Germany, (Norway) and the UK; it was not possible to include Norwegian data on Southern European youth migrants in the analysis.

This raises the question as to how stratification of labour market integration by region of origin can be explained. A possible explanation is the *wage differentials* between the country of origin and the destination country, whereby migrants from countries with low wages are willing to accept less well-paid and poorer quality jobs. Likewise, social benefits can be exported from the country of origin for a transition period, and this transportability of benefits provides EU migrants from high-benefit countries with an opportunity to look for better jobs in the destination countries. Both explanations relate to the idea of a reservation wage, that is, the minimum wage at which a worker is willing to take a job.

Our results hint at the fact that recent youth migrants from a *higher-paying, mature welfare state (Western and Northern EU countries and EFTA)* have qualitatively better jobs than those from emerging welfare states.

In addition, our results suggest that intra-EU migration of youth should not only be seen as a Western EU (EU15) versus Central and Eastern EU issue. Rather than this dichotomy, young EU migrant citizens form distinct groups according to their regions of origin. Future official statistics and academic research should take this more detailed view into account.

In conclusion, the question arises from our research whether migrating within the EU actually improves young EU citizens' labour market position and thereby contributes to an economically closer European Union – an often-propagated aim of the European Commission. Future analyses of trends over time will give a more definitive answer to this question.

References

Hadjivassiliou, Kari P., Arianna Tassinari, Werner Eichhorst and Florian Wozny. Forthcoming. 'How Does the Performance of School-To-Work Transition Regimes in the European Union Vary?' In *Youth Labor in Transition*, edited by Jacqueline O'Reilly, Janine Leschke, Renate Ortlieb, Martin Seeleib-Kaiser and Paola Villa. New York: Oxford University Press.

Leschke, Janine, Martin Seeleib-Kaiser, Thees Spreckelsen, Christer Hyggen and Hans Christian Sandlie. 2016. *Labour Market Outcomes and Integration of Recent Youth Migrants from Central-Eastern and Southern Europe in Germany, Norway and Great Britain.* STYLE Working Paper WP6.4 Labour market outcomes and integration of recent youth migrants from Central-Eastern and Southern Europe in Germany, Norway and Great Britain

Spreckelsen, Thees, Janine Leschke and Martin Seeleib-Kaiser. 2016. *Labour Market Integration of Young EU Migrant Citizens in Germany and the UK.* STYLE Working Paper 6.4a Labour market integration of young EU migrant citizens in Germany and the UK

Spreckelsen, Thees, Janine Leschke and Martin Seeleib-Kaiser. Forthcoming. 'Europe's Promise for Jobs? Labor Market Integration of Young EU Migrant Citizens in Germany and the United Kingdom'. In *Youth Labor in Transition*, edited by Jacqueline O'Reilly, Janine Leschke, Renate Ortlieb, Martin Seeleib-Kaiser and Paola Villa. New York: Oxford University Press.

How well integrated are young EU migrants in the UK workforce?

Thees Spreckelsen and **Martin Seeleib-Kaiser**

Migration and the principle of free movement within the EU are one of the main issues in the debate over whether Britain should remain in the European Union. Polls suggest that the public is very sympathetic to the idea that the UK should restrict immigration and that it is the source of numerous problems. But why is this? And are these fears justified?

There is a great deal of heat generated in the media on this subject, but very little of it is based on fact. Our research intends to contribute some evidence to this debate. We studied the levels of young people migrating to the UK from across the EU and elsewhere, their qualifications and what kind of jobs they did when they arrived.

We found that young EU migrant citizens are well integrated in the UK labour market. They have higher employment rates, work longer and are less likely to receive jobseeker's allowance than their UK peers.

Nevertheless, we can also clearly identify differences in the pay and conditions they will accept. The wages of young EU migrant citizens from Central and Eastern European (CEE) countries are often lower, and the contracts are more likely to be precarious. Moreover, these workers are very often overqualified for the jobs they are doing.

We focused on six different groups of young people in the UK. Everyone in the study was aged between 20 and 34 (60% of all migrants who had arrived in the UK in the last five years are in this age group). Specifically, we focused on those who had been born outside the UK with no UK citizenship and were resident in the UK for one year or more, having arrived in the UK within the past five years. Our analysis is based on pooled data from the UK Labour Force Survey (2010-2014), a large quarterly survey of the UK resident population.

We divided the sample into the following groups: CEE (Czech Republic, Estonia, Hungary, Latvia, Poland, Slovakia and Slovenia); Bulgaria and Romania; Southern European countries (Cyprus, Greece, Italy, Malta, Portugal, Spain); remaining EU countries (Austria, Belgium, Netherlands, Luxembourg, Denmark, Finland, France, Germany, Ireland and Sweden); and migrants from the rest of the world.

High employment

Overall, EU migrant citizens have relatively high employment rates. Young migrant workers from CEE have an employment rate of 82%, compared with an employment rate of 73% among young people born in the UK. While workers born in the UK on average worked a 40-hour week, most EU migrant citizens worked at least one hour more per week.

Our analysis shows that while 8.5% of those born in the UK were unemployed between 2010 and 2014, just 5% of migrants from CEE said they had been without a job during that period. Moreover, the probability of receiving jobseeker's allowance is about 20% among unemployed EU migrant citizens and 38% among young UK citizens.

Minimising skills shortages

Free movement of workers also contributes to reducing skill shortages. EU migrant citizens from CEE are much more likely than UK nationals to work in manufacturing, thereby positively contributing to the much-heralded 'rebalancing of the UK economy'.

Young people from Bulgaria and Romania are more likely than any other group to work in construction, thereby reducing the shortage of construction workers and positively contributing to the building of much-needed housing and infrastructure.

Somewhat more surprisingly, especially if compared to the oft-used image of poverty migration, young EU migrant citizens from Bulgaria and Romania are as likely to work in financial services as UK youths.

Highly qualified

Many of the EU migrant citizens are highly qualified. Recent young European migrant workers from CEE are often overqualified for the jobs in which they are working. But young migrants from the rest of the EU and outside Europe did better than expected in the jobs they secured when matched with the median for qualifications held by others in the same occupation.

Paid less

On average, young migrant citizens from CEE as well as Bulgaria and Romania are paid around one-fifth less than their UK peers in gross hourly wages. Meanwhile, other EU migrant citizens do much better: those from southern Europe receive comparable rates to UK peers, while those from the rest of Europe (mostly from France and Germany) earn on average more than 20% higher hourly wages than their UK peers. Workers from the EU were overall more likely to be employed on a fixed-term contract or by a temping agency.

Conclusion

Overall, young EU migrant citizens are well integrated into the UK labour market. But there are significant differences when it comes to how much their pay and skills match. Migrants from CEE countries and Bulgaria and Romania are at a disadvantage on this front.

The reasons why – whether it is discrimination against hiring Eastern Europeans or a failing on their part – are questions for future research to address. What is clear in the context of the EU referendum debate, however, is that EU migrant citizens contribute to an overall high employment rate and the diverse workforce in the UK – by providing sorely needed skills in various sectors of the economy.

Figure 1: *Young people with qualifications higher than median qualifications in occupation*

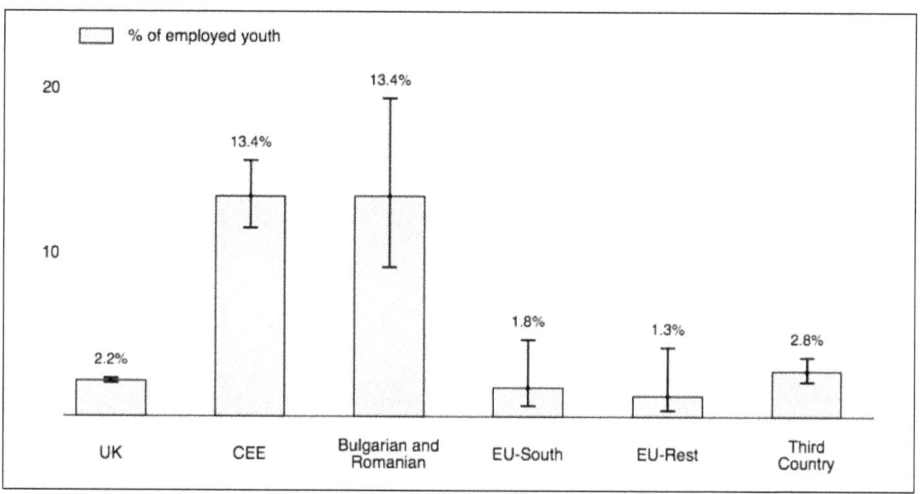

Data: *Pooled UK quaterly labour force survey, 2010-2014: weighted estimates adjusted for sampling design.*
*Recent migrants: *arrived within last 5 years, country of birth not UK and no UK citizenship.*

Figure 2: *Youth migrant citizens' gross hourly wages* relative to UK youth*

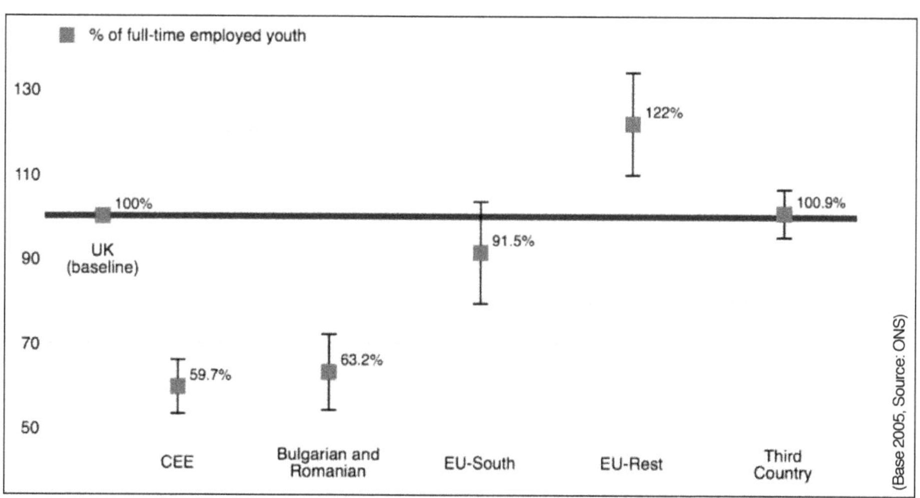

Data: *Pooled UK quaterly labour force survey, 2010-2014: weighted estimates adjusted for sampling design.*
*Hourly wage: *Estimates of the logarithm of gross hourly pay (HOURPAY variable) adjusted for CPI.*

References

Spreckelsen, Thees, Janine Leschke and Martin Seeleib-Kaiser. Forthcoming. 'Europe's Promise for Jobs? Labor Market Integration of Young EU Migrant Citizens in Germany and the United Kingdom'. In *Youth Labor in Transition*, edited by Jacqueline O'Reilly, Janine Leschke, Renate Ortlieb, Martin Seeleib-Kaiser and Paola Villa. New York: Oxford University Press.

An earlier version of this was originally published in The Conversation:
https://theconversation.com/hard-evidence-how-integrated-are-young-eu-migrants-into-the-uk-workforce-56714

Gender and migrant workers' fragile transitions from education to employment

Fatoş Gökşen and **İbrahim Öker**

Gender, migrant status and school-to-work transition

Despite advances in recent decades, women have faced considerable wage differentials, segregated job opportunities and an underrepresentation in senior positions. These gender differences within and outside the labour market have created risks of vulnerability that interact with other dimensions to change or exacerbate the same risks over the life cycle.

One significant dimension of vulnerability is migrant status (Meeuwisse et al. 2010). Young migrants generally face non-recognition of training credentials, which results in 'de-skilling', whereby they can only obtain jobs beneath their qualifications (Cortina et al. 2014). This may mean unregulated, precarious and poorly paid work for migrants, producing divisions among young workers. A particular focus on the interaction of migrant status and gender is necessary to understand the school-to-work (STW) transition pathways of vulnerable groups in Europe.

To account for this, we map vulnerability in STW transitions across gender and migrant status. We consider the extent to which policies directed at young people recognise the multiplicity of factors that affect women's and migrants', and particularly migrant women's transition from education to the labour market. We show the role of intersectionality of gender and migrant status in maintaining and, in some cases, increasing vulnerability regarding various labour market outcomes.

In our EU-wide comparative analyses, we use the EU-SILC (cross-sectional) waves from 2005 to 2013. When engaging in cross-national comparative analyses, it is important to consider the institutional environment that might aid or hinder a smooth transition into the labour market. The extent of vulnerabilities and gender differences are influenced by young people's context (Whelan and Maître 2010). Thus, we use a sample of countries in order to represent four types of regimes for STW transitions – universalistic (Denmark and the Netherlands), liberal (UK), employment-centred (France and Belgium) and subprotective countries (Spain, Greece and Turkey); where the data permit, we also include an analysis of Slovakia as an example of a post-communist regime.

The context matters in vulnerable transitions

Our comparative analysis of vulnerabilities across different regimes of STW transitions points to a critical effect of intersectionality, which results in different routes and fragmented transitions between school and the labour market, with women and migrants often suffering the most. Nevertheless, school-to-work regimes reproduce different regularities of inequalities in varying degrees.

Our findings show that regimes characterised by an institutionalised Vocational Education Training (VET) system and strong counselling support for training and employment such as found in Denmark, tend to perform relatively well in facilitating STW transitions of different vulnerable groups. By contrast, France's employment-centred regime, characterised by fewer second-chance options, creates early disconnection of immigrant youth from education and the labour market. The UK is an interesting case in which vulnerability is not directly correlated with immigration or minority status. In subprotective Spain and Greece, transitions are the most heterogeneous, non-linear and unpredictable. Limited standard workplaces, unprotected living conditions, and a large informal economy combine with an underdeveloped VET system to make gender and migrant status strong determinants of youth unemployment.

Gender and migrant status matter in vulnerable transitions

Our analysis of the EU-SILC data points at strong evidence of the intersectionality of youth, gender and other forms of vulnerability linked to migrant status.

Young migrant males typically participate more in education than young native males across Europe. In contrast, fewer young migrant females are in education compared to their native counterparts in all countries, with the exception of the Netherlands and the UK.

Our findings also show that in all European countries, except the UK, females had a higher unemployment rate before the crisis, but that the rise in the unemployment rate for young males meant that gender gaps closed and, in some cases, were reversed. As for migrants, they tend to have higher unemployment rates than EU nationals. Particularly in employment-centred France and Belgium, the young migrant unemployment rate is over 25%.

We also found that being a NEET is a more critical issue for females. A larger share of young females stays out of both the labour force and education in Greece, Spain, France and the UK; Denmark reported no significant difference between young women and men. In Greece and Spain, furthermore, NEET rates have been persistently higher among women. The persistence of the gender gap (albeit significantly reduced) indicates continued barriers to employment, education and training for young women.

Our results also suggest that NEET status is more common among migrants than EU nationals; the number of migrant NEETs has grown much faster than that of native

NEETs. Between 40% and 50% of migrants are NEETs in Spain and Greece, while in employment-centred France and Belgium, the rate of joblessness among migrants is as high as in southern European countries.

Intersectionality matters in vulnerable transitions

Our results suggest that migrant females are the most disadvantaged group in terms of unemployment in all countries. The risk of unemployment is higher for more educated migrant females in employment-centred and subprotective countries. Similarly, the risk of inactivity is highest among migrant females.

In our analysis of STW transitions, we do not consider part-timers as having successfully transited to employment, since temporary work may be associated with insufficient income and a lack of job permanency. Hence, we treated part-time employment as another indicator of vulnerability. The results show that migrant females are the least likely to be in full-time employment, regardless of their educational attainment.

Finally, we analysed occupations and wages as indicators of the quality of the school-to-work transitions of vulnerable groups. Our findings suggest that both females and migrants, but especially migrant females, are more likely to be disadvantaged. In addition, we observed that young females earn 25% less than the native males in all countries. Even if these groups have the 'privilege of being employed', their jobs tend to enjoy lower wages. It is likely that the low occupational scores of migrant women result from human capital issues (lack of language proficiency, unfamiliarity with the labour market of the receiving country), and systemic barriers that may not be intentionally discriminatory but whose end result is disadvantage (Rubin et al. 2008).

Policy implications

Our analysis of the policy environment shows that policy towards youth labour markets is often gender blind and that there is limited evidence of consistent gender mainstreaming. Given the gender gap and its interaction with migrant status identified in our mapping exercise, policies could be more efficient if they recognised gender differences – for example, school drop-out rates for boys, segregation of training opportunities for girls, and the interaction of gender and migrant status in educational choices. Although we find some evidence of good practice that recognises gender differences at the margins and indeed the intersectionality of youth, more could be done for gender and other forms of vulnerability.

There is a growing acceptance of gender mainstreaming, which aims at reversing the tendency to treat gender as a 'specialist' field of policy and advocates decentralising institutional responsibility for gender (Daly 2005). While this appears to be a positive development, critical scholars show the concept's vagueness, divergent interpretations and implementations, and limited impact on gender equality. We suggest that greater consideration of the intersectionalities of gender with other demographic factors can help explain the segmentation of the youth labour market and understand the life-long repercussions for the risk of vulnerabilities.

References

Cortina, Jeronimo, Patrick Taran, Jerome Elie and Alison Raphael. 2014. *Migration and Youth: Challenges and Opportunities*. Global Migration Group by UNICEF http://unesdoc.unesco.org/images/0022/002277/227720e.pdf.

Daly, Mary. 2005. 'Gender Mainstreaming Theory and Practice'. *Social Politics* 12 (3): 433-450.

Gökşen, Fatoş, Alpay Filiztekin, Mark Smith, Çetin Çelik, İbrahim Öker and Sinem Kuz. 2016. *Vulnerable Youth and Gender Mainstreaming*. STYLE Working Paper WP4.3 Vulnerable Youth & Gender in Europe

Meeuwisse, Marieke, Sabine E. Severiens and Marise Ph. Born. 2010. 'Reasons for Withdrawal from Higher Vocational Education. A Comparison of Ethnic Minority and Majority Non-Completers'. *Studies in Higher Education* 35 (1): 93–111. doi:10.1080/03075070902906780.

Rubin, Jennifer, Michael S. Rendall, Lila Rabinovich, Flavia Tsang, Constantijn van Oranje-Nassau and Barbara Janta. 2008. *Migrant Women in the European Labor Force*. Santa Monica: Rand Corporation. http://www.rand.org/content/dam/rand/pubs/technical_reports/2008/RAND_TR591.pdf.

Whelan, Chris T., and Bernard Maître. 2010. 'Welfare Regime and Social Class Variation in Poverty and Economic Vulnerability in Europe: An Analysis of EU-SILC'. *Journal of European Social Policy* 20 (4): 316-332.

Return Migration to CEE after the crisis: Estonia and Slovakia

Jaan Masso, **Lucia Mýtna Kureková**, **Maryna Tverdostup** and **Zuzana Žilinčíková**

The enlargement of the European Union in 2004 opened up the European labour market for the new, mainly Central and Eastern European (CEE), countries. Many people, especially the young, chose to seize the opportunity and seek employment in Western Europe. Patterns of East-West migration have been diverse: some of the migrants settled in the host countries, others stayed abroad for longer periods, while an important part of migration has been temporary or seasonal.

Research questions

The heterogeneity of migration strategies opens up a number of questions. In our research, we addressed two of them. First, we were interested in how the characteristics of return migrants differ from those who did not return; and second, how well returnees have integrated into the home labour market shortly after their return. These issues are critical from the perspective of home countries for evaluating the benefits and costs of intra-EU mobility. The focus on the years during and following the economic crisis in 2008 reflects the impact of the crisis on the return migration processes.

Research design

The analysis focused on two CEE countries – Estonia and Slovakia. We used EU-LFS data from the years 2008 to 2013 that, despite certain dissimilarities, are suitable for a cross-country comparative analysis of young adults aged 15-34 years. While the two small economies are comparable in their migration rates, they differ in other important aspects, including labour market conditions, the severity of the economic crises in 2008-2009, and social protection spending.

The comparison of these two countries enabled us to identify common patterns of return migration and integration into the home labour market, on the one hand, and particularities of these processes, on the other. We were especially attentive to the role of qualification mismatch while working in a host country, and to the role of macroeconomic factors – GDP per capita and unemployment rate – on the specific characteristics of returnees and their short-term labour market outcomes.

Comparing Estonia and Slovakia

In Estonia, the share of returnees was high and rising between 2008 and 2013 and, by the end of the period, the rate of return exceeded the rate of out-migration. In Slovakia, the proportion of returnees to migrants was rather modest, not exceeding 20% in any of the observed years, hence out-migration was never balanced by a sizeable return.

Regarding education, we did not observe a great differences between young returnees and non-migrants or migrants in either of the countries. However, the mismatch between the level of formal education gained in the home country and employment while abroad was an important predictor of return in Estonia. This suggests that the decision to return may have been driven by more optimistic prospects of employment in the home country. On the contrary, the qualification mismatch abroad did not have any influence on Slovak returnees.

In Slovakia, those who were self-employed while working abroad were less likely to become returnees, and those who were out of the labour market a year prior to the interview, especially students and unemployed, were more likely to return.

The effect of macro-economic variables is also different across the two countries. Whereas in Estonia the return of young migrants is associated with decreasing unemployment rates, in Slovakia the opposite seems true.

Do returnees have higher rates of unemployment?

We also observed that returnees had a higher probability of being unemployed following return than the general population; in other words, those without recent migration experience. This is, however, likely to be short-term unemployment because we captured the returnees in a transition period.

Importantly, using complementary analyses based on administrative data and interviews, we found that returnees can afford a longer jobsearch period thanks to accumulated savings from abroad and possibly also the opportunity to transfer unemployment benefits from the host country (Hazans 2008; Zaiceva and Zimmermann 2016).

Overall, this indicates a better match to skills and experience upon return.

From a cross-country comparative perspective, the unemployment rates of returnees were much higher in Slovakia than in Estonia, which we attribute to a worse performing labour market in Slovakia.

Conclusion

In conclusion, we observed different stories of return migration in Slovakia and Estonia. We not only observed different shares of returnees, but also different underlying reasons for return amongst young migrants, in particular.

Policy-wise this implies that there is no single recommendation concerning return migration to CEE countries. Country-specific contexts are important for gaining a thorough understanding of the processes and their individual and macro-economic implications.

References

Hazans, Mihails. 2008. *Post-Enlargement Return Migrants' Earnings Premium: Evidence from Latvia.* University of Latvia and BICEPS, http://ssrn.com/abstract=1269728.

Masso, Jaan, Lucia Mýtna Kureková, Maryna Tverdostup and Zuzana Žilinčíková. 2016. *Return Migration Patterns of Young Return Migrants after the Crises in the CEE Countries: Estonia and Slovakia.* STYLE Working Paper WP6.1 Return migration patterns of young return migrants after the crisis in the CEE countries: Estonia and Slovakia

Masso, Jaan, Lucia Mýtna Kureková, Maryna Tverdostup and Zuzana Žilinčíková. Forthcoming. 'What are the Employment Prospects for Young Estonian and Slovak Return Migrants?' In ***Youth*** *Labor in Transition*, edited by Jacqueline O'Reilly, Janine Leschke, Renate Ortlieb, Martin Seeleib-Kaiser and Paola Villa. New York: Oxford University Press.

Mýtna Kureková, Lucia, and Zuzana Žilinčíková. 2016. What is the Value of Foreign Work Experience? IZA *Journal of European Labor Studies* 5, no. 1 (2016): 20.

Zaiceva, Anzelika, and Klaus F. Zimmermann. 2016. 'Returning Home at Times of Trouble? Return Migration of EU Enlargement Migrants During the Crisis'. In *Labor Migration, EU Enlargement, and the Great Recession,* edited by Martin Kahanec and Klaus F. Zimmermann, 397-418. Berlin: Springer. https://link.springer.com/book/10.1007/978-3-662-45320-9

Emerging policy lessons for youth migration

Lucia Mýtna Kureková and **Renate Ortlieb**

The set of contributions in this section of the volume, together with the entire research of the STYLE project around migration and mobility, converge on a set of policy themes that we identify below in greater detail.

Anti-discriminatory practices and integration tools for intra-EU and third-country mobility
Intra-EU and third-country migrants have poorer labour market outcomes compared to nationals. However, these differences varied for youth migrants in terms of the quality of employment and wages, which were found to be stratified depending on the migrants' region of origin. Youth migrants from CEE (EU8), Bulgaria and Romania (EU2) proved to be doing worst; youth migrants from EU-South had a middle position; and youth from the remaining EU countries were doing better than their native peers. This might reflect the fact that policies continue to be designed in such a way that migrant workers have suboptimal social conditions and limited civil rights (transitional arrangements, temporary working schemes for third-country nationals).

We find that labour market intermediaries are not necessarily neutral and often serve the interests of employers first, rather than those of migrants. While they help facilitate access to foreign labour markets, they can in some cases also contribute to leaving young migrants in jobs with poor working conditions: low pay for long working hours and short-term contracts, rather than counterbalancing these phenomena.

Among policy tools to address the existing labour market segmentation of CEE migrants, in particular, we suggest:

- strengthening the role of public labour market intermediaries
- increasing monitoring and regulation of private intermediaries to secure good working conditions for young migrants
- improving career and training opportunities to help young migrants to develop their skills at work and to participate in training programmes that support them in gaining access to jobs that fit their skills and interests

- considering providing financial support to young migrants (see Jobbresan as an example of best practice).

Example of best practices: Jobbresan (job travel)
In response to soaring youth unemployment in some Swedish municipalities, an innovative project was launched in collaboration between the municipality, the public employment service and the social security administration. The project was coordinated by the Nordic Council of Ministers. Focusing on the needs of the young unemployed, a model called Söderhamnsmodellen was developed, consisting of three steps aimed at removing the main obstacles faced by young labour migrants from Sweden to Norway:

- a lack of capital and work experience,

- a lack of networks in the country of destination

- advice on how to find work and a place to live in Norway.

The project recruited long-term unemployed living off unemployment benefits or social assistance in Sweden. The young unemployed were offered some initial courses in writing CVs, applying for jobs, how to perform in a job interview and general training in Norwegian language and culture.

After a short period of training, they were sent by bus to the Norwegian capital Oslo. In Oslo, they were offered shared housing with expenses paid for a month. During the first few days, they were instructed on practicalities related to bank accounts, work permits and jobsearch, and invited to an introductory meeting with local representatives from the labour union providing information on rights and obligations in the Norwegian labour market.

The participants reported positive experiences: they enjoyed being together as a group sharing information and experiences, and they had readily available assistance to assess job offers and contracts. As a result, a large share of these young people found jobs within a short period of time.

Gender is a salient factor in migration and return
Youth labour mobility and return migration are gendered phenomena. For example, Hyggen et al. (2016) found that young men are somewhat more mobile than young women. Furthermore, we found the typical gender segregation between different industries, with a larger number of women working in caring professions – as 24-hour caregivers in Austria or as nurses in Norway – and a large share of men working in technical fields. In the 24-hour care sector in Austria, there is also an obvious vertical gender segregation: most of the caregivers from EU8 countries are women while many of the intermediating persons are men.

The analysis of return migration finds that foreign work experience and returns might contribute to reducing the gender pay gap in the home labour market, as evidenced by the Estonian case. The benefit of return migration for the Estonian labour market materialises through a decrease in the gender wage disparity, particularly among youth. Also, gender intersects with other dimensions, such as the migratory experience, in predicting labour market outcomes in the destination country.

Policy-makers should have these gender issues in mind and adjust policies so as to acknowledge that gender might be a further intervening factor in migration processes and in returning to the home country. It significantly affects choices and alternatives in destination countries as well as in the country of origin when returning.

Public institutions can better facilitate the labour market integration of migrants and returnees

We find that the role of public institutions in improving the labour market integration of migrants and returnees could be enhanced. First, labour market intermediaries, like the local public employment services or educational institutions, could play a more salient role as information providers for youth who are interested in moving abroad to get a job. We suggest fostering further international collaboration of the public employment services, for instance in the form of the EURES network established for this purpose. Furthermore, social media should be considered as an important communication tool to reach young people. Second, there is scope for public institutions to provide better assistance upon return and to facilitate integration. For example, return migrants can become a target category in labour offices. Importantly, inequalities exist among returnees and not all returnees are on an equal footing in terms of their abilities. While many returnees circumvent formal institutions, there are still many who approach them and can be reached by effective policy. In particular, returnees disadvantaged in terms of gender, age or ethnicity might be of more need of assistance from public intermediaries in their re-integration process.

Skill matching continues to be a challenge

Overqualification of intra-EU migrants and poor matching continue to be a challenge. We find that the implications of skill mismatch are important. For returnees, it matters what type of experience migrants gain abroad, whether it is relevant to their field and whether it results in a demonstrable set of hard and soft skills. From this perspective, tools facilitating the matching of migrants to jobs, such as EURES, employment agencies or well-designed job portals, can be very useful. Matching should be encouraged by decreasing information asymmetries in intra-EU mobility.

A further focus to enhance matching should be given to improving the language skills of migrants. Insufficient languages skills make it difficult to get in contact with people in the country of destination so as to have better access to housing. Programmes that help to improve language skills and to foster transnational networks are helpful in overcoming obstacles at this stage of the process. An increased focus on intra-EU exchange during education may be one way, while subsidised language courses or increased opportunities for financial support for participating in language training are further forms of facilitating language skill development.

The non-recognition of foreign qualifications and experience and the above-mentioned insufficient language skills may force young migrants to take up jobs below their skill levels. This may negatively affect matching quality as well as work contracts and working conditions for the young migrants. Here again, public (or private) labour market intermediaries or labour unions could be mediators that stand between employers and employees in negotiating working contracts and working conditions. These services could be set up as a web-based service or as an actual contact point for migrants. Continued efforts to standardise educational criteria and to develop a European dictionary of education and grades may be another strategy to help migrants to achieve adequate positions, and to help employers find employees and workers with the right qualifications and motivation.

At the same time, the research findings indicate that intra-EU wage differentials may present an obstacle for young people from Eastern Europe in developing professional careers. For instance, young women from Slovakia working as 24-hour caregivers in private households in Austria receive comparatively high wages, but these jobs do not offer long-term career development opportunities. Thus, it might be important for young people to have opportunities to put less emphasis on current income and to also invest in professional training that will open up long-term career prospects.

Methodological implications

Our research has several methodological implications. First, across research tasks we faced difficulties with the suitability and quality of representative data sets for migration research: the samples are often small and representative data sets and databases might not capture the large variety of existing migration patterns: e.g., commuting, seasonal working, student working, short-term employment, posting, etc. For example, 24-hour care workers usually work in two-week cycles with the primary residence in their home country. Thus, they might not appear in the official statistics of the receiving country, even if their number is considerably high. Furthermore, the analysis of integration patterns of young migrants most likely included a 'better integrated' group of recent migrants and those with sufficiently good language skills to participate in the survey. There is therefore a great need for better data about migration.

Second, given the limitations of representative data sets (LFS, ESS), we showed that new sources of data, such as online data (online CVs, web surveys) can be used to analyse labour mobility from perspectives that representative data sets do not allow. Third, our research has shown that comparative frameworks – both from the sending and the receiving country perspectives – can help us understand the role of institutional or macroeconomic factors, or find important differences across countries and over time that help us to better understand underlying causes and consequences of intra-EU mobility. Fourth, because of the diversity of migration patterns, the combination of qualitative and quantitative methods is very useful and it enables us to capture a more holistic picture of youth migration in Europe.

References

Mýtna Kureková, Lucia. 2016. STYLE Policy Brief No 6: Mismatch Migration and Mobility

Mýtna Kureková, Lucia, and Renate Ortlieb. 2016. Policy synthesis and integrative report. STYLE Working Paper WP6.5

Further reading on youth labour mobility and migration

Akgüç, Mehtap, and Miroslav Beblavý. 2015. *Re-emerging Migration Patterns: Structures and Policy Lessons.* STYLE Working Paper WP6.3 Re-emerging Migration Patterns: Structures and Policy Lessons

Akgüç, Mehtap, and Miroslav Beblavý. Forthcoming. 'What Happens to Young People Who Move Country to Find Work?' In *Youth Labor in Transition*, edited by Jacqueline O'Reilly, Janine Leschke, Renate Ortlieb, Martin Seeleib-Kaiser and Paola Villa. New York: Oxford University Press.

Hyggen, Christer, Renate Ortlieb, Hans Christian Sandlie and Silvana Weiss. 2016. *East-West and North-North Migrating Youth and the Role of Labour Market Intermediaries.* The Case of Austria and Norway. Style Working Paper WP6.2 Working conditions and labour market intermediaries Norway and Austria

Leschke, Janine, Martin Seeleib-Kaiser, Thees Spreckelsen, Christer Hyggen and Hans Christian Sandlie. 2016. *Labour Market Outcomes and Integration of Recent Youth Migrants from Central-Eastern and Southern Europe in Germany, Norway and Great Britain.* STYLE Working Paper WP6.4 Labour market outcomes and integration of recent youth migrants from Central-Eastern and Southern Europe in Germany, Norway and Great Britain

Masso, Jaan, Lucia Mýtna Kureková, Maryna Tverdostup and Zuzana Žilinčíková. 2016. *Return Migration Patterns of Young Return Migrants after the Crises in the CEE Countries: Estonia and Slovakia.* STYLE Working Paper WP6.1 Return migration patterns of young return migrants after the crisis in the CEE countries: Estonia and Slovakia

Masso, Jaan, Lucia Mýtna Kureková, Maryna Tverdostup and Zuzana Žilinčíková. Forthcoming. 'What are the Employment Prospects for Young Estonian and Slovak Return Migrants?' In *Youth Labor in Transition*, edited by Jacqueline O'Reilly, Janine Leschke, Renate Ortlieb, Martin Seeleib-Kaiser and Paola Villa. New York: Oxford University Press.

Mýtna Kureková, Lucia, and Renate Ortlieb. 2016. *Policy Synthesis and Integrative Report.* STYLE Working Paper WP6.5

Mýtna Kureková, Lucia. 2016. STYLE Policy Brief No 6: Mismatch Migration and Mobility

Ortlieb, Renate, and Silvana Weiss. Forthcoming. 'How do Labor Market Intermediaries Help Young Eastern Europeans find work?' In *Youth Labor in Transition,* edited by Jacqueline O'Reilly, Janine Leschke, Renate Ortlieb, Martin Seeleib-Kaiser and Paola Villa. New York: Oxford University Press.

Spreckelsen, Thees, Janine Leschke and Martin Seeleib-Kaiser. 2016. Labour Market Integration of Young EU Migrant Citizens in Germany and the UK. STYLE Working Paper 6.4a Labour market integration of young EU migrant citizens in Germany and the UK

Spreckelsen, Thees, Janine Leschke and Martin Seeleib-Kaiser. Forthcoming. 'Europe's Promise for Jobs? Labor Market Integration of Young EU Migrant Citizens in Germany and the United Kingdom'. In Youth *Labor in Transition,* edited by Jacqueline O'Reilly, Janine Leschke, Renate Ortlieb, Martin Seeleib-Kaiser and Paola Villa. New York: Oxford University Press.

Family matters

Introduction: How do families matter in helping young people find work?

Tiziana Nazio and **András Gábos**

Family legacies affect young people's strategies and decisions around finding work and moving into independent living. Where one comes from has always affected young people's job opportunities and paths out of school. These effects are becoming increasingly polarised both within and across European societies along a variety of dimensions that cannot simply be read off in terms of ethnicity, class, gender, the original nationality of one's parents, or even the society young people from different backgrounds find themselves in.

Understanding the long-term implications of these social divisions is central to knowing which kinds of policy interventions might be most effective in addressing current levels of youth unemployment.

Here, we examine how families help young people to find work, what effects brothers and sisters have, or what effect having parents who do not work has on young people finding work themselves. We also look at what happens to young people who leave home and/or set up their own families, and whether the recent recession has increased the risk of them returning to their parental home.

What difference does the family make?
The resources brought into young people's lives by their families can play a crucial role in shaping their employment and career prospects. Equipped themselves with different capacities to support their young adult children, whether living at home or independently, families contribute to stratifying their children's educational and occupational achievements, their opportunities, strategies and prospects in the labour market. They do so through both direct and indirect mechanisms.

Higher-class families are more successful in informing and supporting young people's employment decisions. They do this through: advice and guidance; social networks and building expectations and aspirations; and economic support. These resources mean that children from wealthier families are better equipped to manage risky transitions that may entail longer periods of non-employment, more precarious jobs or a need for financial support. Securing more equal opportunities for young people requires addressing the effects of these inter-family differences.

Research gaps

Much research has focused on the intergenerational transmission of inequalities through education. Less attention has been paid to how families back up children in their transition to the labour market. We focused on several ways in which families, with their differing resources, aid or hinder their children's employment prospects. We analysed the effect of social background on occupational outcomes, on degree of success in early careers, and on sharing of economic resources within and between households.

We used several comparative data sources for different analyses: the European Union Statistics on Income and Living Conditions (EU-SILC), the Gender and Generation Survey (GGS), and the Survey of Health, Ageing and Retirement in Europe (SHARE). We estimated the association between various individual, family and country characteristics, and several young people's outcomes: their occupational circumstances; their occupational success up to five years from finishing education; the distribution of money within the household (when co-resident with their parents); and receipt of regular transfers (when they had left the parental household).

Findings:

Coming from a work-poor household

Coming from work-poor households both strongly and negatively affects young people's employment opportunities. Berloffa et al. (2016) point to the legacy of parents' working status during adolescence for young people aged 25-34: growing up in a work-poor household, where no one is working, makes for a higher risk of unemployment and inactivity than growing up in a work-rich household where both parents are working. The study provides evidence of an intergenerational persistence of worklessness, with some important differences for young men and women.

Going into higher education

Young people living in households where neither parent was working are considerably less likely to be in education (Berloffa et al. 2015). While higher education is a major stepping-stone to a professional job and a successful integration into the labour market, the chance of going on to tertiary education still largely depends on family social-class background and parents' own involvement in the labour market.

The brothers and sisters effect

Wider family (dis)advantages are also reproduced through members of the family who no longer live in the parental home. It is not the number of brothers or sisters that matter, but whether they are employed or not. Siblings' employment seems to be associated with young people's chances of being employed. Employed brothers or sisters might possibly guide the young people still at home by helping them look for a job, or by referring them to someone in their social network, thus enhancing the young person's employment chances. It may also reflect shared family values or aspirations and expectations.

Staying at home longer

Young people's step into independent living may actually be improved by staying longer in the parental home. Most young adults in Europe seem to benefit from living with their parents when we take into account how resources are shared within the household (Filandri et al. 2016).

This happens because of two mechanisms: parents typically have higher incomes compared to their young adult children and they also share a larger fraction of their incomes with other household members. From a poverty risk point of view, young people living in their parental home face lower risks than their counterparts who are already living independently. In some cases, as shown by Medgyesi and Nagy (*forthcoming*), young working members of the family also stay at home to support their families, and are more likely to share their financial resources with more vulnerable members of their family.

Sharing financial resources

There are strong differences across countries regarding the likelihood of being a recipient of regular cash transfers from the parental household. Young people in the south of Europe are much less likely to receive cash transfers from their parents compared to young people from Northern Europe.

However, in the Southern countries, higher rates of material support are provided through longer periods of co-residence. Our research reveals two drivers of regular financial transfers: the probability of receiving regular economic support increases where families are wealthier, but also with their children's need (i.e., when they are not employed). Parental resources are more important than young people's needs when parents provide financial support. In other families, it is the young people themselves who are helping to support the family by sharing their financial resources.

Conclusions

The family that young people grew up in not only shapes their choices around education and career tracks, it also influences their performance in the labour market. The number of employed family members can affect their capacity to secure employment. Social class background is associated with different levels of occupational success: higher social classes seem better able to give their children successful outcomes.

Intra-household sharing of resources and regular cash transfers seem to be an additional way in which social inequalities and unequal transmission of opportunities are being maintained and reproduced across generations.

Family resources (from co-resident and non-co-resident members) can strongly affect opportunities for young people in terms of guiding them through employment paths and also helping them avoid employment traps, gain access to social networks, develop soft skills, acknowledge their potential and interests, and select and afford investments in education.

Policy implications

In order to secure similar opportunities, policy interventions should aim at changing the intergenerational transmission of disadvantages. In particular, policies focused on the most disadvantaged families could address the trend of increasing polarisation of opportunities. Given the salience of early stages of the employment career for later outcomes, policies should consider a comprehensive investment strategy in young people's transition to employment from an early stage, already when education decisions are being made and right upon school leaving.

A strategy to foster more equal access to job opportunities would entail:

1. increasing opportunities for disadvantaged children, as well as for low work-intensity households, so as to have their children pursue higher education;

2. on completion of studies, offering guidance around young people's strategic planning through the initial steps of their employment careers; and

3. devising cash benefits aimed at supporting the income level of the less advantaged social groups, especially during non-employment, through a universal system of unemployment benefits for young people that are unrelated to the previous contribution history.

References

Berloffa, Gabriella, Marianna Filandri, Eleonora Matteazzi, Tiziana Nazio, Nicola Negri, Jacqueline O'Reilly, Paola Villa and Carolina Zuccotti. 2015. *Work-Poor and Work-Rich Families: Influence on Youth Labour Market Outcomes.* STYLE Working Paper WP8.1 Work-poor and work-rich families

Berloffa, Gabriella, Marianna Filandri, Eleonora Matteazzi, Tiziana Nazio, Nicola Negri, Jacqueline O'Reilly, and Alina Şandor. 2016. *Family Strategies to Cope with Poor Labour Market Outcomes.* STYLE Working Paper WP8.2 Family strategies to cope with poor labour market outcomes

Berloffa, Gabriella, Eleonora Matteazzi and Paola Villa. Forthcoming. 'The Worklessness Legacy: Do Working Mothers Make a Difference?' In *Youth Labor in Transition*, edited by Jacqueline O'Reilly, Janine Leschke, Renate Ortlieb, Martin Seeleib-Kaiser, and Paola Villa. New York: Oxford University Press.

Filandri, Marianna, András Gábos, Márton Medgyesi, Ildikó Nagy and Tiziana Nazio. 2016. *The Role of Parental Material Resources in Adulthood Transitions.* STYLE Working Paper WP8.4

Medgyesi, Márton, and Ildikó Nagy. Forthcoming. 'Income Sharing and Spending Decisions of Young People Living with their Parents'. In *Youth Labor in Transition*, edited by Jacqueline O'Reilly, Janine Leschke, Renate Ortlieb, Martin Seeleib-Kaiser and Paola Villa. New York: Oxford University Press.

Does families' working behaviour affect their children's school-to-work trajectories?

Gabriella Berloffa, **Eleonora Matteazzi** and **Alina Şandor**

Labour market success or failure in the early years of adulthood is the outcome of a number of potentially complex interactions involving an individual's ability and personality, family background, educational attainment and country-specific characteristics (education systems, labour market institutions, macroeconomic conditions) (Hadjivassiliou et al. *forthcoming*; Grotti, Russell and O'Reilly *forthcoming*). We know that parents matter in determining how well their children are likely to do when it comes to finding a job, and a good quality job at that.

To examine how the family affects what kind of job young people find, we focused on the importance of the family's socio-economic characteristics for young people's employment outcomes. Studies suggest that young individuals with a 'poor' family context (in terms of education, economic resources and networking) are more disadvantaged in terms of labour market performance.

However, the vast majority of these studies focus on intergenerational effects (Raitano and Vona 2015; Berloffa, Matteazzi and Villa 2015a), with very few studies considering the contemporaneous effect of parental employment on children's employment (Kind 2015; Berloffa, Matteazzi and Villa 2015b). Additionally, these studies generally examine the evolution of individual's employment statuses over time, by looking at year-to-year transitions.

Instead, we study the impact of the family employment structure on young people's school-to-work trajectories so as to analyse more accurately the transitory and more persistent labour market conditions.

Dynamic school-to-work trajectories and family employment condition

The contribution of this work is threefold. First, we examine the impact of family employment conditions on the entire labour market entry process of young individuals. Second, we distinguish the working status of parents from that of other working-age family members (siblings), to check whether they have different effects on youth school-to-work trajectories. Third, we also consider separately the employment status of the mother and the father to examine whether there exists a father-son and a mother-daughter type of effect.

We focus on young Europeans aged 16-34 who have just exited full-time education, and we look at their labour market pathway from this point forward over a period of three years.

We use monthly information on employment statuses to identify school-to-work (STW) trajectories. In each month, individuals can be employed, unemployed, in education or inactive.

STW trajectories are defined over a 36-month period and are classified according to the time needed to reach employment and the pathway that led to the first relevant employment spell, that is, an employment spell lasting for at least six consecutive months. These trajectories are classified as follows:

Speedy: a relevant employment spell is achieved within six months after leaving full-time education;

Long-search: a relevant employment spell is achieved after more than six months in unemployment or inactivity;

In&out successful: various non-relevant employment spells, interspersed by short periods in unemployment or inactivity, end up in a relevant employment spell;

In&out unsuccessful: various non-relevant employment spells, interspersed by short periods in unemployment or inactivity, do not end up in a relevant employment spell

Continuous unemployment and/or inactivity: only spells of unemployment or inactivity;

Return to education: a spell in education lasting at least six consecutive months experienced at least six months after having left full-time education.

Our main interest is in the role of the family employment structure in influencing young people's STW trajectories. We consider household members' employment status over the six-month period around the month in which young people left full-time education, that is, the three months before and the three months after. We measure the intensity of their work participation over that six-month period and we keep distinct the work intensity of the mother, of the father and of the other working-age family members. We perform separate analyses for young males and females.

Does parental employment affect children's labour market entry?

Yes! Parental working conditions are of crucial importance in explaining youth STW trajectories. Having a mother or father who worked continuously during the six-month period increases the probability of being speedy and long-search, while it reduces the probability of being continuously unemployed/inactive.

Does the presence and the working status of other family members affect youth labour market entry?
Yes! The presence of some working-age family members reduces the likelihood of having a rapid labour market entry, while it increases the probability of being continuously unemployed/inactive. However, this negative effect is overcome if they are working (at least some of them for at least some months). Specifically, when other working-age family members are employed, the probability of a speedy trajectory is much higher; and the likelihood of being continuously unemployed/inactive is much lower compared to households where all other family members do not work.

What counts more, a working parent or a working sibling?
The employment status of parents and siblings has an equivalent effect on youth STW trajectories. It is enough that someone in the family works to significantly increase youth probabilities of being on a speedy trajectory into work themselves, and it decreases their likelihood of being continuously at the margin of the labour market.

Is there a mother-daughter or father-son effect?
Mothers' and fathers' working status have similar effects on adult children's probability of being on a speedy trajectory. However, the working status of the mother is more effective in reducing the children's probability of being continuously unemployed/inactive. When other working-age individuals (apart from the parents) are present in the household, the mother's employment condition has a larger positive effect than the father's employment status on their sons' probability of staying continuously at the margin of the labour market; however, the opposite is found for sons' likelihood of rapidly entering into paid work.

What can policies do for young people from work-poor families?
A stable working condition on the part of parents is associated with more favourable entry trajectories for both males and females. The working status of other working-age family members also has important consequences.

If no one in the household is working, this seems to have a negative effect on young people finding work on leaving education. However, this effect is reduced if there are no other unemployed siblings in the same household. If other brothers and sisters are working, this reduces the effect of young people not finding work.

From a policy perspective, our empirical findings suggest that it is important to consider the employment structure of young people's families around the time they leave education. In particular, policy interventions should be targeted at young people living in households where parents or other family members do not work. These interventions should focus not only on young people's motivations and perceptions, but also on supporting them with access to effective jobsearch services and training opportunities.

References

Berloffa, Gabriella, Eleonora Matteazzi and Paola Villa. 2015a. 'Family Background and Youth Labour Market Outcomes across Europe'. *In Work-Poor and Work-Rich Families: Influence on Youth Labour Market Outcomes*, edited by Gabriella Berloffa, Marianna Filandri, Eleonora Matteazzi, Tiziana Nazio, Nicola Negri, Jacqueline O'Reilly, Paola Villa and Carolina Zuccotti. STYLE Working Paper WP8.1 Work-poor and work-rich families

Berloffa, Gabriella, Eleonora Matteazzi and Paola Villa. 2015b. 'Households and Youth Employment'. In *Work-Poor and Work-Rich Families: Influence on Youth Labour Market Outcomes*, edited by Gabriella Berloffa, Marianna Filandri, Eleonora Matteazzi, Tiziana Nazio, Nicola Negri, Jacqueline O'Reilly, Paola Villa and Carolina Zuccotti. STYLE Working Paper WP8.1 Work-poor and work-rich families

Berloffa, Gabriella, Gabriele Mazzolini and Paola Villa. 2015. 'From Education to the First Relevant Employment Spell'. In *Youth School-To-Work Transitions: From Entry Jobs to Career Employment*, edited by Gabriella Berloffa, Eleonora Matteazzi, Gabriele Mazzolini, Alina Şandor and Paola Villa. STYLE Working Paper WP10.2 Youth School-To-Work Transitions: from Entry Jobs to Career Employment

Berloffa, Gabriella, Eleonora Matteazzi and Paola Villa. Forthcoming. 'The Worklessness Legacy: Do Working Mothers Make a Difference?' In *Youth Labor in Transition*, edited by Jacqueline O'Reilly, Janine Leschke, Renate Ortlieb, Martin Seeleib-Kaiser, and Paola Villa. New York: Oxford University Press.

Grotti, Raffaele, Helen Russell and Jacqueline O'Reilly. Forthcoming. 'Where Do Young People Work?' In *Youth Labor in Transition*, edited by Jacqueline O'Reilly, Janine Leschke, Renate Ortlieb, Martin Seeleib-Kaiser, and Paola Villa. New York: Oxford University Press.

Hadjivassiliou, Kari P., Arianna Tassinari, Werner Eichhorst and Florian Wozny. Forthcoming. 'How Does the Performance of School-To-Work Transition Regimes in the European Union Vary?" In *Youth Labor in Transition*, edited by Jacqueline O'Reilly, Janine Leschke, Renate Ortlieb, Martin Seeleib-Kaiser, and Paola Villa. New York: Oxford University Press.

Kind, Michael. 2015. *Start Me Up: How Fathers' Unemployment Affects Their Sons' School-To-Work Transitions* Ruhr Economic Papers 583. ***http://www.rwi-essen.de/media/content/pages/publikationen/ruhr-economic-papers/rep_15_583.pdf***

Raitano, Michele, and Francesco Vona. 2015. *'Measuring the Link between Intergenerational Occupational Mobility and Earnings: Evidence from Eight Countries'. Journal of Economic Inequality* 13: 83-102.

Acknowledgements

The authors would like to thank participants at the STYLE General Assembly Project Consortium Meeting (Copenhagen, January 11-12, 2016), IWPLMS 37th Annual Conference (Barcelona, July 6-8, 2016) and TIY 24th Annual Workshop (Trento, September 7-10, 2016) for helpful comments and suggestions on earlier drafts of these papers.

Workless parents, workless children?

Gabriella Berloffa, **Eleonora Matteazzi** and **Paola Villa**

In 2015, more than 6.6 million young people (aged 15-24 years) were neither in employment nor in education or training (NEETs) in the EU, and the overall employment rates for young people (33%) were still four percentage points lower than they were in 2008 (37%) (Mascherini *forthcoming*).

At the European level, efforts to facilitate young people's inclusion in the labour market have been notable (O'Reilly et al. 2015). The total budget of the Youth Employment Initiative is €6.4 billion for the period 2014-20, and it will be increased by a further €2 billion for 2017-2020 if the Council and the European Parliament adopt the Commission's proposal. Understanding when, how and for whom we need to intervene to enhance young people's employment prospects is crucial so that public resources can be used effectively, and to ensure that young individuals have as equal opportunities as possible.

A key factor influencing young people's skill formation and attitudinal development is the family environment. The role of the family in shaping children's tastes for education and in developing their skills has been largely documented. But these effects can go beyond education and also directly affect young individuals' labour market outcomes. Therefore, we need to know whether individuals who grew up in families with certain characteristics face more difficulties than others in participating in the labour market or in finding/keeping a job when adults.

The effects of parents' employment on their children's labour market outcomes
Various authors have shown that children's unemployment or inactivity is closely related to their fathers' and mothers' employment status. Experiencing parental worklessness during adolescence may impact on young adults' aspirations and attitudes towards the labour market (different evaluations of work and sense of stigma, different attitudes towards relying on welfare benefits), as well as the type of social networks on which they can rely when searching for a job.

But we know little about the extent to which these effects vary across European countries, and even less about the relative role of fathers and mothers. We analysed the extent to which parents' worklessness during children's adolescence (around 14 years of age) affects their children's employment outcomes as young adults (around 30 years of age) across various European country groups, and considering the gender of both parents and children (Berloffa, Matteazzi and Villa 2017; Berloffa, Matteazzi and Villa *forthcoming*).

We used a European-harmonised household survey (EU-SILC), which contains information about the employment condition of young adults (aged 25-34) in 2005 and 2011 and about the working condition of their parents when these young adults were aged about 14. We estimated the impact of various individual, family and country characteristics on young adults' likelihood of being employed, NEET or in education for five groups of countries: Nordic, Continental, English-speaking, Mediterranean and Eastern European countries.

The apple *doesn't* fall far from the tree

We found that, after controlling for education and other individual and country characteristics, mothers' worklessness increases their daughters' likelihood of being workless by about 20%-40% in all European country groups, both before and during the crisis (see Table 1 below). In contrast, maternal employment affects sons' worklessness only during the crisis.

The effects of fathers' employment during children's adolescence are less widespread compared to those associated with maternal employment status. Fathers' worklessness increased their sons' and daughters' likelihood of being workless both before and during the crisis only in Mediterranean countries. Here, in 2011, young men who had a workless father during their adolescence had a double probability of being workless themselves compared to the sons of working fathers. In other country groups, the effects of fathers' worklessness is generally limited to sons and to specific years (before the crisis in Continental countries and after the crisis in Eastern European countries).

Interestingly, we find a similar likelihood of being workless for children who grew up in workless households, independently of whether one or two parents were present.

For those who grew up with a single parent (usually a mother), and where that parent was working, their likelihood of being without work was comparable with those who grew up in male-breadwinner families.

Our findings suggest that mothers' influence on their daughters is related to some structural phenomena as well as the likely transmission of attitudes to gender roles. However, mothers' role for their sons seems more related to the intergenerational transmission of skills or attitudes.

Fathers' employment appears particularly important in Mediterranean countries, especially when labour market conditions deteriorate. This could suggest that working fathers are able to utilise their networks more to find work for their children. Results for the other country groups are more difficult to explain and deserve further investigation.

Policies for workless parents

Our results highlight the importance of mothers' employment for their children's future prospects. Indeed, the adolescents who grew up in the years of the Great Recession with workless mothers might suffer in the future when they start their working life. This calls for new policy initiatives aimed at helping mothers with adolescent children to enter, remain or re-enter paid work. It is also necessary to support children of non-working mothers.

Policy-makers should also pay attention to children of non-working fathers, especially in Mediterranean countries, designing new strategies to foster equality of opportunities in access to jobs.

Table 1: *Percentage difference in the likelihood of being NEET for young adults (aged 25-34) with the same individual characteristics – by their parents' employment status (when young adults were 14)*

	The role of **mothers' employment**: male-breadwinner families vs. dual-earner families				The role of **fathers' employment**: workless families vs. male-breadwinner families			
	Daughters		Sons		Sons		Daughters	
	2005	2011	2005	2011	2005	2011	2005	2011
Nordic countries	+38%*	0	0	0	0	+81%*	0	0
English-speaking countries	**+46%**	**+24%**	0	**+55%**	+33%*	0	0	+31%*
Continental countries	**+29%**	**+34%**	0	**+33%**	**+90%**	0	0	0
Mediterranean countries	**+17%**	**+20%**	**+10%***	**+17%**	**+33%**	**+97%**	**+16%**	**+19%**
Eastern countries	**+21%**	**+38%**	**+37%**	**+42%**	0	**+45%**	0	**+16%***

Notes: (*) The difference is significant only at the 10% level

Source: Authors' estimation based on EU-SILC data.

References

Berloffa, Gabriella, Marianna Filandri, Eleonora Matteazzi, Tiziana Nazio, Nicola Negri, Jacqueline O'Reilly, Paola Villa and Carolina Zuccotti. 2015. *Work-Poor and Work-Rich Families: Influence on Youth Labour Market Outcomes.* STYLE Working Paper WP8.1 Work-poor and work-rich families

Berloffa, Gabriella, Eleonora Matteazzi and Paola Villa. 2017. *The Intergenerational Transmission of Worklessness in Europe. The Role of Fathers and Mothers.* Working Paper 4. Trento: Department of Economics and Management, University of Trento.

Berloffa, Gabriella, Eleonora Matteazzi and Paola Villa. Forthcoming. 'The Worklessness Legacy: Do Working Mothers Make a Difference?' In *Youth Labor in Transition*, edited by Jacqueline O'Reilly, Janine Leschke, Renate Ortlieb, Martin Seeleib-Kaiser, and Paola Villa. New York: Oxford University Press.

Mascherini, Massimiliano. Forthcoming. 'Origins and Future of the Concept of NEETs in the European Policy Agenda'. In *Youth Labor in Transition*, edited by Jacqueline O'Reilly, Janine Leschke, Renate Ortlieb, Martin Seeleib-Kaiser, and Paola Villa. New York: Oxford University Press.

O'Reilly, Jacqueline, Werner Eichhorst, András Gábos, Kari Hadjivassiliou, David Lain, Janine Leschke, Seamus McGuinness, Lucia Mýtna Kureková, Tiziana Nazio, Renate Ortlieb, Helen Russell and Paola Villa. 2015. 'Five Characteristics of Youth Unemployment in Europe: Flexibility, Education, Migration, Family Legacies, and EU Policy'. SAGE Open 5 (1): 1–19. ***http://journals.sagepub.com/doi/abs/10.1177/2158244015574962***

Acknowledgements

The authors would like to thank Thomas Biegert, Fatoş Gökşen, Chiara Saraceno, participants at the STYLE General Assembly Project Consortium Meetings (Grenoble, March 23-24, 2015; Turin, June 13-15, 2016; Krakow, January 29-31, 2017), at SASE 27th Annual Conference (London, July 2-4, 2015), at ECINEQ 6th Meeting (Luxembourg, July 13-15, 2015) and at SIE 57th Annual Conference (Milan, October 20-22, 2016) for helpful comments and suggestions.

What a difference a mum makes

Mark Smith and **Genevieve Shanahan**

Most people know all the reasons why they need to be grateful to their mothers, for all that was learned, loved and nurtured throughout the years. However, research shows we should in fact also be grateful to all our 'mothers' – including our mothers-in-law – for what they pass on to us. Not least some protection against the challenges of the modern-day labour market for young women and men.

Thanks Mum!

Our parents are one of the key influences on our values, our attitudes and our life chances. For good, and sometimes bad, they shape how we approach most aspects of our lives, from leisure to education to work, and also to our own couple relations. Research shows that children tend to adopt similar attitudes to trust and risk as those held by their parents (Dohmen et al. 2012). Mothers tend to have a greater influence, particularly as regards trust. Indeed, these attitudes pervade the way we subsequently approach all spheres of life, including health, finance and work.

Like mother like daughter, like father like son

It is no surprise that we follow in the footsteps of our parents. A study by a team at Stanford University entitled 'It's a Decent Bet That Our Children Will Be Professors Too' shows how social classes and socio-economic status are transmitted from one generation to the next to the extent that offspring are quite likely to emulate the specific occupations of their parents (Jonsson et al. 2011). While it's widely accepted that kids inherit their parents' general, all-purpose social capital, networks and resources, the Stanford team found that these advantages can be occupation-specific too. So, your lawyer Mum might instil you with a professional comportment and self-confidence, and offer you connections to her various professional-class friends. On top of that, the fact that you are more likely to talk about law at the dinner table might mean you thereby learn how to think and speak specifically like a lawyer.

Dads have a role too. A 2011 Canadian study (Corak and Piraino 2011), for instance, found that approximately two in five young men were at some point employed by an employer who also employed their father, and that almost 10% stuck with that employer long term. Two broad theories emerge to explain this tendency of young adults to work where their parents work. The first is nepotism – where parents or their friends have some power, they may use it to give preference to their kids. A second theory suggests, however, that early socialisation by parents might also indicate the young person's superior suitability for the job, given all they have learned about the role from their parents. Exploitation of the early training that seemingly arises naturally within families might be a particularly efficient and productive use of resources, and therefore beneficial for the economy as a whole. However, such processes may reinforce inequalities for those who do not have parents in well-paid occupations or prestigious networks.

Mothers' transmission of attitudes to their daughters

Much of the focus on intergenerational transmission of occupations focuses on fathers and sons, primarily because there are more data for men's jobs than for women's, and also because of the perceived greater complexity of women's occupational choices. Expectations that men will work full time are consistent over time and across countries in spite of the advancement of women in the workplace and calls for men to take on a greater role in the home. By contrast, women's opportunities for work outside the home vary and continue to be shaped by caring responsibilities. Nevertheless, the transmission of attitudes from mothers to daughters demonstrates the important impact of such attitudes on labour market participation.

These impacts span generations and can be seen as an 'inheritance' of daughters from their mothers for their labour market participation. Even more interesting, perhaps, is that there is not only an increased likelihood that a mother's daughter will work, but also that her daughter-in-law will work. Men might choose women who are similar to their mothers, and witnessing the benefits of a working mother in their childhoods might motivate them to replicate that arrangement in their own families. There is some evidence that mothers may also inculcate their sons with the skills and values necessary to create more egalitarian households (Campos-Vazquez and Velez-Grajales 2014).

Working mothers as insurance against the economic crisis

Recent research on the impacts of the economic crisis shows that the effects of a working mother and father reduce the risk of their children being without work, and that these effects hold across countries and time. The insuring effect of working fathers against worklessness among their children declined over the crisis, but this was not the case for mothers. Comparing the situation across European countries, one of the studies found that having had a working mother increased the probability of being employed and reduced that of being inactive (Berloffa et al. 2015; Berloffa et al. forthcoming). This is especially important because being inactive – not working and not looking for work – is a particularly risky status for young people. Having two working parents is associated with higher employment rates, or reduced worklessness, for both sons and daughters.

Benefits of equality across the generations

The influence of parental occupational and labour market behaviour underlines the benefits and risks of the intergenerational transfer of values and norms. For those who grew up in households with working mothers and fathers, labour market outcomes were generally better in terms of avoidance of worklessness during the crisis and gaining access to good networks. This can be viewed as another positive outcome of gender equality, for fostering mothers' employment during children's adolescence can have a positive effect on children's likelihood of youth employment success. However, the flip side is that those coming from workless households face greater risks of being without work and poor labour market outcomes (Berloffa et al. 2015). The lesson for families and policy-makers alike is that facilitating work for both parents, and particularly mothers, has both short- and long-term benefits for households and wider society.

References

Berloffa, Gabriella, Marianna Filandri, Eleonora Matteazzi, Tiziana Nazio, Nicola Negri, Jacqueline O'Reilly, Paola Villa and Carolina Zuccotti. 2015. *Work-Poor and Work-Rich Families: Influence on Youth Labour Market Outcomes.* STYLE Working Paper WP8.1 Work-poor and work-rich families

Campos-Vazquez, Raymundo Miguel, and Roberto Velez-Grajales. 2014. 'Female Labour Supply and Intergenerational Preference Formation: Evidence for Mexico'. *Oxford Development Studies* 42 (4): 553-569

Corak, Miles, and Patrizio Piraino. 2011. 'The Intergenerational Transmission of Employers'. *Journal of Labor Economics* 29 (1): 37-68.

Dohmen, Thomas, Armin Falk, David Huffman and Uwe Sunde. 2012. 'The Intergenerational Transmission of Risk and Trust Attitudes'. *Review of Economic Studies* 79: 645–677.

Jonsson, Jan O., David B. Grusky, Matthew Di Carlo and Reinhard Pollak. 2011. 'It's a Decent Bet That Our Children Will Be Professors Too'. In *The Inequality Reader. Contemporary and Foundational Readings in Race, Class, and Gender*, edited by David B. Grusky and Szonja Szelényi, 499-516. Boulder, Co: Westview Press.

Is any job better than no job?

Marianna Filandri, **Tiziana Nazio** and **Jacqueline O'Reilly**

How do we evaluate the quality of transitions young people make when they succeed in finding employment? To answer this question, we developed a typology of 'successful', 'investment', 'need' and 'failed' transitions, using the characteristics of the occupation, the skills required and the wages obtained (Filandri, Nazio and O'Reilly *forthcoming*). We looked specifically at transitions made in the three to five years after leaving education. One of the distinctive contributions of the study is to show the kinds of trade-offs young people might have to make and how family characteristics might influence how long young people can wait so as to make successful transitions.

Successful, investment and failed transitions

- A 'successful' transition is when a young person found a skilled and well-paid job.
- 'Well paid' is defined as above the median wage of all employed individuals by all ages in each country, each year.
- An 'investment' transition is where a skilled position has been achieved but with a trade-off of accepting a lower salary (skilled but low-paid job). Jobs requiring higher skills or qualifications may initially be poorly paid if entry positions are used by employers as screening devices. Over time, however, such jobs can result in increasing wage returns.
- A 'need' transition is where the job is low or unskilled and the wages can be either high or low.
- A 'failed' transition is where the wages are low and the job is unskilled; a failed transition also includes those who end up in unemployment or inactivity.

Findings

Empirical evidence is based on longitudinal EU-SILC data (with a longitudinal sample of monthly employment records over 36 months for the period 2005-2012) restricted to five selected countries: Finland, France, Italy, Poland and the UK.

We find that although both an early start and continuous employment are associated with more favourable outcomes (especially a higher rate of 'success' and higher paid occupations for young people above 24 years), these effects were relatively small and did not support the idea that any job is necessarily always better than joblessness.

A well-matched start with the trade-off of a lower salary (or of a somewhat longer jobsearch), in terms of skills level, might often be a better strategy for securing better outcomes in the long run, especially for university graduates.

We also found evidence that an investment transition into an initially poorly paid but skilled occupation could constitute an opportunity for young people that can soon turn into a successful positioning in the labour market.

Need and failed transitions via unskilled occupations for qualified young people could become an employment trap that is difficult to reverse in the long run.

Higher education seems to be a major stepping-stone to a professional job and successful establishment in the labour market. Also, the likelihood of moving from 'investment' to 'success' positions is higher for tertiary educated young people.

We also found that the capacity of young people to pursue tertiary education is still strongly stratified by family social class background and household work intensity (Berloffa et al. 2016).

What difference does the family make in how long you can wait?
These findings suggest a strong familial influence on young people's employment outcomes. Families of origin first influence their children's capacity to pursue higher studies and, later, their chances to transform these educational investments into successful employment careers. They point to mechanisms related to a more successful role of higher-class families in informing (through advice and guidance), supporting (through social networks, aspiration building, more effective guidance through the education and employment systems) and backing up (economic support and/or longer co-residence) young people's employment decisions.

The most promising career strategies often entail initial losses and some higher risks. For example, some young people either have to wait longer or are more likely to experience unemployment, or they make a trade-off in an 'investment' strategy accepting lower rates of pay.

Children from wealthier families are better equipped to face these risks. These findings complement those of McGuinness et al. (forthcoming) on the risk of educational mismatch and on labour market flows and unemployment duration affecting successful jobsearch (Flek, Hála and Mysíková forthcoming).

Finally, we found that, as inequalities widen, parents' ability to invest in their children's success not only remains salient but also becomes more unequal, again increasing the pertinence of policy intervention.

References

Berloffa, Gabriella, Marianna Filandri, Eleonora Matteazzi, Tiziana Nazio, Nicola Negri, Jacqueline O'Reilly, and Alina Şandor. 2016. *Family Strategies to Cope with Poor Labour Market Outcomes*. STYLE Working Paper WP8.2 Family strategies to cope with poor labour market outcomes

Filandri, Marianna, Tiziana Nazio and Jacqueline O'Reilly. Forthcoming. 'Youth Transitions and Job Quality: How Long Should They Wait and What Difference Does the Family Make?' In *Youth Labor in Transition*, edited by Jacqueline O'Reilly, Janine Leschke, Renate Ortlieb, Martin Seeleib-Kaiser, and Paola Villa. New York: Oxford University Press.

Flek, Vladislav, Martin Hála and Martina Mysíková. Forthcoming. 'How do Youth Labor Flows Differ from Those of Older Workers?' In *Youth Labor in Transition*, edited by Jacqueline O'Reilly, Janine Leschke, Renate Ortlieb, Martin Seeleib-Kaiser, and Paola Villa. New York: Oxford University Press.

McGuinness, Seamus, Adele Bergin and Adele Whelan. Forthcoming. 'Overeducation in Europe: Is There Scope for a Common Policy Approach?' In *Youth Labor in Transition*, edited by Jacqueline O'Reilly, Janine Leschke, Renate Ortlieb, Martin Seeleib-Kaiser, and Paola Villa. New York: Oxford University Press.

The luck is in the family: Continued financial support after leaving the nest

Marianna Filandri and **Tiziana Nazio**

Family support beyond co-residence

Parental support, or the lack of it, is pivotal in providing young people with skills, values, orientation and support during their transition to adulthood. And parental support continues even after young people have left home. This life stage is becoming increasingly uncertain as the duration of the transition period to economic adulthood lengthens and because of the retrenchment of welfare states and the increasing liberalisation of labour markets across Europe.

Some see these recent trends as a sign of convergence in European countries: increasingly, families are meant to step in, as they have done in the Southern and Eastern models of welfare provision (Viazzo 2010). But because not all families have the same resources to support these transitions, some young people are more exposed to the risk of poverty.

Regular monetary support

Parents can provide 'occasional' and 'exceptional' gifts in the form of economic support for education, home purchases (Druta and Ronald 2016) or weddings, as well as significant transfers of property and wealth during their life time and after their death. However, smaller amounts of regular monetary support have received much less academic attention. We were interested in finding out:

- How do familial resources help young people? And is this only relevant for wealthier families?

- Do young people's employment circumstances make a difference? Do those in need receive more?

Using data from the EU-SILC for 2011, we took into consideration all young adults (aged 25-34 years) in and out of work, excluding students. We selected 25 European countries with valid information on the receipt of regular cash transfers on a monthly, quarterly or annual basis (if they were received over several consecutive years). We also included information on social class measured in terms of the highest education level of either parent.

Regular inter-household cash transfers are regular payments received during the previous year by young adults from other non-co-resident household members (usually their parents). We excluded compulsory and voluntary alimony received on a regular basis. We used probit regression models to predict how the probability of receiving regular economic support varied according to socio-economic characteristics of recipients and donors.

Parental generosity: Same principle (need), different affordability (resources)
Across Europe, in all 25 European countries analysed, families supported their children in economic need – albeit to varying extents depending on their own economic circumstances. This included both regular forms of financial support as well as support in exceptional circumstances. Parents were equivalently generous in countries where welfare provisions were both more extensive and where they were more meagre. Nevertheless, there were also some interesting differences between countries, with no transfers being reported in Spain and Portugal, whereas in Cyprus and Bulgaria approximately 13% of young adults reported receiving regular payments.

We examined if differences were accounted for by the economic status of the parents or by the extent of the young person's need. Young people from more advantaged backgrounds, as well as those not employed, were the most likely to benefit from these transfers. Non-employed young people from a lower social class were more likely to receive help compared to their peers with jobs. Employed young people from a higher social class received similar or more transfers than non-employed young people from lower classes.

Polarising opportunities
It is worth drawing attention to the fact that young people from a higher social class had a noticeable advantage in how their parents helped them through both difficult and more stable periods. This financial buffer affects their ability to take up unpaid work experiences and internships, and to take lower paying job opportunities that may result in better career trajectories in the long run. It also reinforces the fact that non-employed young people from lower socio-economic classes are less well protected. Within this framework of cumulative disadvantage for the weakest, income support measures in the form of housing allowances or unemployment benefits would greatly help those struggling the most and those who are more exposed to the risk of a sudden income loss when not employed.

References
Druta, Oana, and Richard Ronald. 2016. 'Young Adults' Pathways into Homeownership and the Negotiation of Intra-Family Support: A Home, the Ideal Gift'. *Sociology* 51 (4): 783-799. http://journals.sagepub.com/doi/abs/10.1177/0038038516629900

Filandri, Marianna, András Gábos, Márton Medgyesi, Ildikó Nagy and Tiziana Nazio. 2016. *The Role of Parental Material Resources in Adulthood Transitions.* STYLE Working Paper WP8.4

Viazzo, Pier Paolo. 2010. 'Family, Kinship and Welfare Provision in Europe, Past and Present: Commonalities and Divergences'. *Continuity and Change* 25 (1): 137-159.

Acknowledgements
The authors would like to thank Fatoş Gökşen, Chiara Saraceno and the participants at the STYLE General Assembly Project Consortium Meetings (Grenoble, March 23-24, 2015; Turin, June 13-15, 2016; Krakow, January 29-31, 2017), at SASE 27th Annual Conference (London, July 2-4, 2015), AIEL Annual conference (Trento, 22-23 September 2016) and at the ESRC Annual conference (Oxford, September 22-24, 2016) for helpful comments and suggestions.

Leaving and returning to the parental home during the economic crisis

Fatoş Gökşen, **Deniz Yükseker**, **Alpay Filiztekin**, **İbrahim Öker**, **Fernanda Mazzotta** and **Lavinia Parisi**

Leaving and returning the parental home in hard economic times

Families can often provide a 'haven in a heartless world' for young people looking for work by providing housing, resources and finance in adverse times. Being unemployed or inactive makes it harder for young people to move into independent living or think about forming their own family. Has the recent economic crisis made it more difficult for the young to leave home? And, what evidence is there of a 'boomerang generation', whereby young people are more likely to return to their parents when they become unemployed?

Gökşen et al. (2015) describe the possible economic, institutional and cultural factors affecting the process of transition to adulthood and independent living. Across Europe, the share of young adults (below the age of 35) living with their parents has increased over time. Whereas this share of those still living at home is below 50% in Northern and Continental countries, it is above 65% in Mediterranean and over 70% in Central-Eastern European and Baltic countries. The increase in those staying at home accelerated after the 2008 crisis, particularly in Northern and Continental European countries.

Leaving and returning decisions: Between (un)employment and partnership

We wanted to find out what affect the Great Recession had on young people leaving (or returning) home? What difference does having a job or a partner have on their ability to live independently? And, are there significant differences across country groups?

Mazzotta and Parisi (*forthcoming*) analysed the process of leaving and returning to the parental home for young people in 14 European countries: these included Continental countries like Austria, Belgium, France, and Luxembourg, four Southern countries (Cyprus, Italy, Portugal and Spain), three Eastern countries (Czech Republic, Poland, and Slovakia) and three Baltic countries (Estonia, Lithuania, and Latvia).

Using data from the European Union Statistics on Income and Living Conditions (EU-SILC), we predicted the probability of youth (aged 18–34) leaving the parental home and, in turn, their probability (when aged 20–36) of returning to live with their parents (i.e., boomeranging) in a four-year period. Given the strong interdependence between living independently, finding employment and being in a partnership, we simultaneously modelled these three states for each of the two transitions: leaving and returning home. Net of other individual characteristics, we imagined the effects of the Great Recession as being to reduce the probability of leaving home and increase that of returning to the parental home.

Leaving home is getting harder

The lowest percentage of youth leaving the parental home each year is found in the Eastern, Baltic, and Southern European countries (3.0%, 4.5%, and 5.9%, respectively, on average over the entire period 2005-2013). It is here that young people postpone exit the longest. The highest rate of exit is in the Continental countries (13.6% on average, over the entire period). There has been a decrease in the share of young people leaving home between 2005 and 2013, except for the Eastern countries, where the exit rate is very low over the entire period.

Having a job is often a prerequisite for leaving home and also for forming a partnership. The Baltic and Eastern European countries have particularly high shares of people in a partnership still living with their parents. In general, for all groups of countries, forming a partnership seems to be more predictive than having a job in explaining why young people leave home. However, if the partnership breaks up (not having a partner), this is more likely to result in a return home – compared to losing one's job.

Apart from individual and family characteristics, the availability of housing and housing market circumstances strongly influence the opportunities for young adults to leave their parents' homes. A combination of high levels of home-ownership, difficult access to mortgages and high housing prices seems to constitute a significant obstacle to young people's residential independence and family formation.

Returning home is rare but is becoming more likely

Having left, returning to the parental home is a rather unlikely event; return rates amounted to less than 1% per year on average, across all country groups. Nevertheless, differences emerged during and after the economic crisis: there was an increased return to the parental home in all country groups, with the exception of the Eastern countries.

The Continental and Eastern countries have the lowest percentage of young people returning home, with an increase right after the onset of the crisis (2009–2010), while in the Baltic countries recorded an increase that lasts longer—from 2008–2009 until 2010–2011.

In the Southern countries, the probability of returning home increased constantly across all periods, indicating that it is structurally more difficult for young people to live independently in the South. There was also evidence of a long-term trend in boomeranging (returning home) in the Southern countries.

Union dissolution is a key determinant of returning home in all countries, while not being employed increases the probability of returning home in the Continental, Southern and Baltic countries. We also found that earnings help maintain independence: the higher the relative personal income of young people, the lower the likelihood of them returning home in all country groups in the analysis.

The importance of a job: Harder to leave and more likely to return
The levels of completed education are an important predictor of people's choice of living arrangements: those with higher education are more likely to live independently, even though there are variations across countries.

We found that the Great Recession reduced the probability of leaving home; it also increased the probability of young people returning home, although there were significant differences between countries.

- Young people from Continental countries were more likely to leave home, but these numbers also declined during the Great Recession.

- Young people from Southern and Eastern European are less likely to leave home when they are very young, and during the Great Recession those leaving also declined; there was an increase in those who returned to the family home in Southern Europe.

Decisions to leave or return home were less affected by whether or not the young person had a job; being in a partnership had more influence in this respect (leaving upon family formation and returning upon partnership dissolution).

When families matter more, state support can make a greater difference
More than in previous recessions, families seem to play a protective role by allowing their adult children to stay longer at home, thus enabling young adults to overcome the economic difficulties faced during the Great Recession. When it is families who increasingly bear the responsibility for buffering their adult children against market failure, being born in a more affluent family becomes more important in defining individuals' opportunities – and, in turn, their capacity to form a family – along the life course.

Public housing policies such as housing allowances and rent-controlled or free (social) housing seem to have a considerable impact on the decision to leave and return to the parental home. With the exception of Central-Eastern European countries, benefiting from housing allowances seems associated with a higher probability of leaving the parental home across all welfare regimes. Housing allowance also plays a role in the reverse decision: its lack seems to be associated with more frequent decisions to return to the parental home. Returners are more likely to be found among home-owners and private tenants.

The findings support the idea of an association between the household resources of young people's families and their decisions to leave or return to the parental home. Stronger parental resources seem to facilitate transitions into adulthood, whereas the consequences of unemployment and precarious work negatively reflect on young people's opportunity to establish their own families. Economic independence, promoted through employment, income support or housing allowance, is thus critical to dismantling the barriers encountered in the transition to independent adulthood.

References

Gökşen, Fatoş, Deniz Yükseker, Alpay Filiztekin, İbrahim Öker, Sinem Kuz, Fernanda Mazzotta and Lavinia Parisi. 2016. *Leaving and Returning to the Parental Home during the Economic Crisis.* STYLE Working Paper WP8.3 Leaving and returning to the parental home during the economic crisis

Mazzotta, Fernanda, and Lavinia Parisi. Forthcoming. 'Stuck in the Parental Nest? The Effect of the Economic Crisis on Young Europeans' Living Arrangements'. In *Youth Labor in Transition*, edited by Jacqueline O'Reilly, Janine Leschke, Renate Ortlieb, Martin Seeleib-Kaiser and Paola Villa. New York: Oxford University Press.

When do you start your own family?

Elena Mariani and **András Gábos**

Family background and transition to adulthood

Young people are finding it increasingly difficult to achieve independence from their parents and make a speedy transition to adulthood. They may want to establish their independence by moving out of the parental home and starting their own families, but financial constraints are often a major barrier. As a result, some young people postpone these significant steps, or may even decide to have children early on, even if they are not fully financially independent. Their options are significantly influenced by their own family background, which can reinforce social inequalities and intergenerational mobility amongst different groups of young people (Sirniö et al. 2016).

How does family formation differ by social background?

Considering the relevance of both its short- and long-term consequences, we focus on social gradient in the timing of family formation according to parental background. We explore whether parental background can shield some young people's family formation plans from the adverse effects of labour market disadvantage. Specifically, we asked the following questions.

1. Do young people from families with varying socio-economic background follow different family formation strategies?

Our expectation is that young people from lower socio-economic families have both their first marriage and their first child earlier than young people from higher socio-economic families.

2. What role does parental background play in mitigating the effect of unemployment in family formation strategies?

Expectedly, young people from higher socio-economic backgrounds, but with lower labour market attachment, still form their own families later than young people from lower socio-economic families in similar circumstances.

A comparison of four countries

To answer these questions, we used multivariate statistical methods on the first two waves of the longitudinal database of the Generations and Gender Programme (GGP) for four countries: Austria, Bulgaria, the Czech Republic and France. The selection of countries was constrained by the availability of harmonised information on demographic history, by the coverage of European countries and by the availability of measures of parental background. These constraints led to a small sample of countries in our analysis, which limits its generalisability.

Family background shields when employment fails

We found that the role of parental background is very important in terms of family formation, especially for less advantaged young people. The importance of the parental background during adverse employment circumstances is especially crucial for childbearing: having more parental resources avoids unfavourable outcomes, such as having a child when financial independence is lacking.

Family background can influence the timing of marriage, too. Young men and women from low socio-economic status families tend to get married earlier. This finding suggests that union formation may be particularly attractive for these groups, who may value gains from marriage in terms of economies of scale and pooled incomes to a greater extent than well-off young people.

We also found no strong gender differentials in the way in which labour market status affects family formation strategies, suggesting that young women in Europe are using the labour market to gain financial independence just as much as young men.

Parental background is a resource young people may fall on in the event of difficulties establishing independence with other means. This is especially so for childbearing: when young people are scarred by unemployment, they are more likely to delay family formation if they come from a high socio-economic status family.

In general, having more parental resources is associated with a lower risk of having a child when still financially dependent. But also, marriage is affected by family background. Young men and women from low socio-economic status families tend to get married earlier, suggesting that this may be a possible strategy towards gaining independence.

Families can amplify social inequalities

We found some evidence that those with low parental resources follow family formation strategies that are unfavourable for young people in terms of career and education investment and also for their offspring.

The role of parental resources is heightened when young people experience difficulties in the labour market. Since those from low socio-economic status families are also more likely to experience disadvantage in the labour market, the social disparities coming from family formation strategies are amplified.

From a policy perspective, designing benefit systems and employment programmes that take into account the situation of the parental home of young workers would reduce the disparity in access to resources among young people.

Because unemployment at the beginning of the working career has a scarring effect not just regarding labour market engagement but family formation as well, policies could be targeted at offering career guidance to young people from families with low resources, with a view to increasing their engagement with the labour market.

References

Filandri, Marianna, András Gábos, Elena Mariani and Tiziana Nazio. 2016. *Family Formation Strategies, Unemployment and Precarious Employment.* STYLE Working Paper WP8.5 Family formation strategies among the youth

Sirniö, Outi, Pekka Martikainen and Timo Kauppinen. 2016. 'Entering the Highest and the Lowest Incomes: Intergenerational Determinants and Early-Adulthood Transitions'. *Research in Social Stratification and Mobility* 44: 77-90.

Policy themes on family matters

Tiziana Nazio and **András Gábos**

The research work being carried out on the influence of the family of origin is informative to policy-making around several key aspects of young people's jobsearch and insertion process. We studied how employment outcomes are connected to family social background and how they reflect on young people's plans for family formation or their decision to return to the parental home. In particular, important findings and policy implications can be drawn regarding

1. employment services and guidance for young people
2. more gender-equal opportunities in the labour markets and
3. income support measures for unemployed and first-time jobseekers.

Employment services and guidance for young people

Research findings suggest that family resources, both economic and non-economic (from co-resident and non-co-resident members), can strongly stratify opportunities for young people (Berloffa et al. 2015; 2106). Family resources seem strategic in guiding them through employment paths and helping them to avoid employment traps, gain access to social networks, develop soft skills, acknowledge their potential and interests, and select and afford educational investments. Our results revealed that the tightened labour market conditions for youth over the crisis period might even sharpen existing differences, which would suggest a need for better employment services for young people. These findings highlight the opportunities for policy interventions aimed at re-addressing the intergenerational transmission of (dis)advantages, especially in Anglo-Saxon and Mediterranean countries, where the effects are stronger.

Given the relevance of early stages of the employment career for later outcomes (Berloffa et al. 2016), a comprehensive investment strategy in young people's transition to employment should become a priority. Key steps would be: (1) increasing opportunities for low- and middle-class children, and for those from low work-intensity households, to pursue higher education; and (2) offering later guidance for young people's strategic planning through the initial steps of their career.

In particular, policy interventions should be targeted at young people living in households where parents or other family members do not work. These interventions should focus both on young people's aspirations and motivation, and on giving them access to an effective jobsearch service.

Interventions might comprise raising awareness among parents on the importance of their expectations, guidance role, and array of options with respect to their children's educational routes (length and affordability) and potential returns. Policies should also focus on offering career guidance, especially for young people from poorer backgrounds, so as to increase aspirations and recognise and plan viable strategies towards the achievement of short- and long-term career goals.

Further, policy interventions should aim at securing more even access to tertiary education by family background, especially in those countries where tuition fees are high and young people are excluded from entitlement to economic support while studying, or where residential costs are an obstacle to the pursuit of higher-level studies. Research results (Berloffa et al. 2016; Filandri et al. 2016a) also revealed family influences on the educational routes pursued by young people, with children from households with poor attachment to the labour market entering employment earlier and being exposed to higher risks of unemployment or future employment traps.

Further, all empirical evidence provided around family effects in the STYLE project revealed the strong capacity that the family background has to affect young people's life chances (both in the labour market and around family formation). Policies and interventions should invest in educational programs (already at younger ages) to increase self-awareness about one's abilities and interests; to increase equality in educational aspirations and expectations; and to provide more broadly some of the soft skills that better-off parents can afford to give their children (this might include self-confidence, leadership, resilience, diplomacy, cooperative teamwork and mediation).

Finally, providing wider and more homogeneous access to opportunities for internships or company-based training might contribute to counterbalancing wealthier families' higher capacity to access these resources through personal networks. This could be achieved through investments in educational institutions' career-support functions or through employment agencies. Policies should provide young people with opportunities for exchange, mentoring and guidance within mixed environments, for sharing opportunities and social networks, and for enjoying the experience of a larger array of strategies and possible outcomes. This is strategic insofar as perceptions become highly selective in closed social circles, while attitudes are actually formed and strategies are pursued on the basis of the perceived available options.

More gender-equal opportunities in the labour markets

Our research provided evidence that securing better employment prospects for women (i.e., the mothers of young labour market entrants) would both benefit employment outcomes for young people and favour family formation (Berloffa et al. 2015; Filandri et al. 2016b). In particular, we revealed a strong association between mothers' employment and children's later occupational outcomes (with speedier transitions and increased employment participation of daughters, among other results). This suggests the utility of implementing policies aimed at favouring mothers' employment in order to prevent more difficulties for future generations. Our results also revealed that, for younger cohorts in recent times, a more gender-equal participation in the labour market is associated with a greater advancement in the transition to adulthood – for both genders (Filandri et al. 2016b). Results indicated the relevance of labour market structure, specifically of women's participation in the labour market (i.e., higher female employment rate), being significantly associated with all outcome states around family formation (employment and residential independence, partnership and parenthood). These results offer insights into a growing gender equality and a shift, especially for younger generations, to a double-breadwinning model in families, where two jobs (and income sources) are needed, desired or might be normatively perceived as appropriate for family formation. With growing levels of education and of uncertainty in the labour markets, self-realisation and personal autonomy (also through gaining an independent income) might be increasingly perceived as a necessary precondition to family formation by both male and female young people.

Addressing gender gaps early in the life course could help avoiding later inequalities and their long-term consequences. Gökşen et al. (*in this volume*) showed that gender mainstreaming has not been systematically applied to youth labour market policies in several case-study countries. Results from the research on family effects support the view that anti-discrimination policies that promote gender-equal access to employment and equal career opportunities might support young people in establishing an independent living and forming their own families, while also contributing to pursuing the objective of more inclusive and sustainable growth at the societal level. These measures also include conciliation policies to retain women in the labour force, such as paid leaves, long-term contracts (as opposed to fixed-term), care services and flexible working hours.

Income support for unemployed and first-time jobseekers

As of now, in most European countries, flexible jobs (agency work, fixed-term contracts, part-time work, mini-jobs, some forms of self-employment) risk becoming a lower segment of the labour force, catering especially for young people. These jobs often provide poor protection against risks such as, unemployment, illness, or providing the guarantee of a secure income in old age. Research results (Berloffa et al. 2015; 2016; Filandri et al. 2016a) suggested that relaxing hiring and firing legislation without compensating with generous social protection and active labour market policies, while also increasing the retirement age, risks affecting young people's capacity to establish themselves in employment in a way that strongly stratifies their life opportunities according to their class of origin. In the absence of a universal income provision for the unemployed, children from wealthier families may, with economic support from their families, bridge unemployment or non-employment much more easily than others. Especially Filandri et al. (2016a) indicated that both social origin and occupational circumstances were predictors of the likelihood of receiving regular income support. Non-employed children were more likely to benefit from parental support throughout, as are those from higher social classes. However, parental resources seemed stronger predictors than young people's needs: in all countries, employed children from higher social backgrounds had a similar (if not higher) likelihood of receiving regular transfers than unemployed children from the lower class.

Further, increases in unequal access to employment and household income would further jeopardise lower-class young peoples' life chances and opportunities. They would also, at the country level, increase losses in productivity (with a tremendous loss of productive potential) and raise the pressure for more passive income support measures. Alternatively, they would unevenly strain families who have to compensate for retrenching welfare and increasingly fragile markets.

A growing use of temporary contracts (relaxing hiring and firing regulations), without strong and universal income support measures, may exacerbate the turbulence experienced by young people in the initial steps of their careers (by increasing overall unemployment duration and 'need' strategies and recourse to 'failure' strategies or informal work). It may also increase young people's dependence on their families of origin, further diversify their destinies on the basis of their social origin, and worsen their prospects of a successful employment outcome in the longer term.

These findings suggest that benefit systems should be harmonised to include young people, because labour market segmentation, prolonged turbulence and informal work can easily become traps for youngsters in need of gainful employment. These inequalities could be redressed by means of redistributive policies aimed at supporting the income level of the lower class, especially during non-employment, either through a universal system of unemployment benefits for young people (unrelated to the previous contribution history) and/or housing allowances. The analyses from Task 8.4 and Task 8.5 support measures whereby government social protection programmes guarantee regular cash transfers to poor young adults in periods of non-employment, conditioned either on active jobsearch or participation in ALMPs.

References

Berloffa, Gabriella, Marianna Filandri, Eleonora Matteazzi, Tiziana Nazio, Nicola Negri, Jacqueline O'Reilly, Paola Villa and Carolina Zuccotti. 2015. *Work-Poor and Work-Rich Families: Influence on Youth Labour Market Outcomes.* STYLE Working Paper WP8.1 Work-poor and work-rich families

Berloffa, Gabriella, Marianna Filandri, Eleonora Matteazzi, Tiziana Nazio, Nicola Negri, Jacqueline O'Reilly, and Alina Şandor. 2016. *Family Strategies to Cope with Poor Labour Market Outcomes.* STYLE Working Paper WP8.2 Family strategies to cope with poor labour market outcomes

Filandri, Marianna, András Gábos, Márton Medgyesi, Ildikó Nagy and Tiziana Nazio. 2016. *The Role of Parental Material Resources in Adulthood Transitions.* STYLE Working Paper WP8.4

Filandri, Marianna, András Gábos, Elena Mariani and Tiziana Nazio. 2016. *Family Formation Strategies among the Youth.* STYLE Working Paper WP8.5 Family formation strategies among the youth

Gábos, András, and Tiziana Nazio. 2017. *Family drivers of youth unemployment and adulthood transition.* STYLE Policy Brief No 8: Family Drivers

Gökşen, Fatoş, Deniz Yükseker, Alpay Filiztekin, İbrahim Öker, Sinem Kuz, Fernanda Mazzotta and Lavinia Parisi. 2016. Leaving and Returning to the Parental Home during the Economic Crisis. STYLE Working Paper WP8.3 Leaving and returning to the parental home during the economic crisis

Nazio, Tiziana, and András Gábos. 2016. *Policy Synthesis and Integrative Report on Family and Cultural Drivers of Youth Unemployment and Adulthood Transitions.* STYLE Working Paper 8.6. Brighton: CROME, University of Brighton.

Further reading on family matters

Berloffa, Gabriella, Marianna Filandri, Eleonora Matteazzi, Tiziana Nazio, Nicola Negri, Jacqueline O'Reilly, Paola Villa and Carolina Zuccotti. 2015. *Work-Poor and Work-Rich Families: Influence on Youth Labour Market Outcomes.* STYLE Working Paper WP8.1 Work-poor and work-rich families

Berloffa, Gabriella, Marianna Filandri, Eleonora Matteazzi, Tiziana Nazio, Nicola Negri, Jacqueline O'Reilly, and Alina Şandor. 2016. *Family Strategies to Cope with Poor Labour Market Outcomes.* STYLE Working Paper WP8.2 Family strategies to cope with poor labour market outcomes

Berloffa, Gabriella, Eleonora Matteazzi and Paola Villa. Forthcoming. 'The Worklessness Legacy: Do Working Mothers Make a Difference?' In *Youth Labor in Transition*, edited by Jacqueline O'Reilly, Janine Leschke, Renate Ortlieb, Martin Seeleib-Kaiser, and Paola Villa. New York: Oxford University Press.

Filandri, Marianna, András Gábos, Márton Medgyesi, Ildikó Nagy and Tiziana Nazio. 2016. *The Role of Parental Material Resources in Adulthood Transitions.* STYLE Working Paper WP8.4

Filandri, Marianna, Tiziana Nazio and Jacqueline O'Reilly. Forthcoming. 'Youth Transitions and Job Quality: How Long Should They Wait and What Difference Does the Family Make?' In *Youth Labor in Transition*, edited by Jacqueline O'Reilly, Janine Leschke, Renate Ortlieb, Martin Seeleib-Kaiser, and Paola Villa. New York: Oxford University Press.

Gábos, András, and Tiziana Nazio. 2017. *Family Drivers Of Youth Unemployment And Adulthood Transition.* STYLE Policy Brief No 8: Family Drivers

Mazzotta, Fernanda, and Lavinia Parisi. Forthcoming. 'Stuck in the Parental Nest? The Effect of the Economic Crisis on Young Europeans" Living Arrangements'. In *Youth Labor in Transition*, edited by Jacqueline O'Reilly, Janine Leschke, Renate Ortlieb, Martin Seeleib-Kaiser, and Paola Villa. New York: Oxford University Press.

Medgyesi, Márton, and Ildikó Nagy. Forthcoming. 'Income Sharing and Spending Decisions of Young People Living with their Parents. In *Youth Labor in Transition*, edited by Jacqueline O'Reilly, Janine Leschke, Renate Ortlieb, Martin Seeleib-Kaiser, and Paola Villa. New York: Oxford University Press.

Flexible working and precariousness

Introduction: Balancing flexibility and security for young people during the crisis

Raul Eamets, **Katrin Humal**, **Miroslav Beblavý**, **Ilaria Maselli**, **Kariappa Bheemaiah**, **Mark Smith**, **Mairéad Finn** and **Janine Leschke**

The balance of flexibility and security for labour market participants is a perennial challenge for policy-makers. In the late 1990s, the term 'flexicurity' seemed to offer a solution to this balancing act. Indeed, in the first decade of this century, 'flexicurity' became a dominant theme at the European and national level, and although its use has declined in recent years, the flexibility/security balance has remained a central factor in determining labour market outcomes – particularly for young people.

However, the concept of 'flexicurity' received a lot of criticism, often related to a lack of clarity in its definition. On the one hand, this definitional ambiguity helps explain why the concept was picked up so easily at the policy level across a wide variety of stakeholders and national contexts. On the other hand, the ambiguity also explains how policies resulting in an overemphasis on (external) flexibility and employability, with little emphasis on job and income security, were developed. Whatever the term used, the balance of flexibility and security remains a key dimension in understanding the plight of young people entering the labour market, and the economic crisis only served to further expose the uneven security afforded to different labour market groups.

Young people tend to accumulate negative flexibility outcomes in that they have more limited contractual security, and a greater risk of working on non-standard contracts and of losing their jobs more quickly than the comparable adult population. At the same time, young people also have less job and income security because of their lower seniority and more limited employment histories. Furthermore, in most European countries, workers on non-standard contracts have more limited access to unemployment benefits than workers on standard employment contracts. These are all factors that can exacerbate the position of vulnerable labour market groups, which are often disproportionally engaged on such contracts – young people, women and people with lower education levels. The crisis exacerbated the risks of these negative outcomes.

Mapping flexibility and security for young people

In order to identify clusters of policy-making and flexibility-security outcomes, including key trends during the crisis period, it is important to explore the balance between flexibility and security for young people and to map flexibility-security indicators for EU member states.

Using national-level data from the OECD and Eurostat, this mapping exercise shows that, in terms of institutional settings of flexibility and security, there are a number of clear clusters – Eastern European countries consistently group together, as do Nordic countries with the Netherlands and Germany. These results are generally in line with earlier attempts to cluster flexibility-security regimes (see, for example, EC 2006). Although there are data limitations, the comparison of selected national-level outcome indicators shows that country groups with similar institutional settings do not necessarily have similar labour market and/or social outcomes for young people.

These results also support earlier findings that institutional and outcome-type measures of flexibility and security might not be correlated and should be examined separately (Chung 2012). These results suggest that there are a range of forces that shape outcomes on the youth labour market. Within-cluster, and indeed within-country, variations need to be taken into account in explaining these outcomes – further underlining for policy-makers and researchers alike that youth are far from a homogenous group.

Nevertheless, the results confirm that, overall, young people tend to have worse flexibility-security outcomes, especially after the initial effects of the crisis. Vulnerable groups on the labour market, such as youth, the elderly, women, the long-term unemployed and temporary employees, do not experience the same benefits that regular employees might gain from flexibility-security policies (see, for example, Leschke 2012).

Income security is a key measure

Young people's levels of financial security are closely linked to their flexibility outcomes – both in the labour market (external flexibility) and within firms (internal flexibility). To complement the mapping exercise, a detailed policy analysis of security measures highlights some of the tensions and contradictions that exist in policy-making, while also charting the direction of travel for policy aimed at youth labour markets in recent years. Making use of Europe-wide data (Eurostat LFS and other sources), we observe that older youth are better off than their younger counterparts in terms of external – but not internal – numerical flexibility. Older youth are also better off than the youngest with regard to income security, yet both groups do worse than adults on all three dimensions. More detailed, age-specific information on some security measures would help shed more light on these age differences.

These policy analyses emphasise the complexity of income security measures – such as unemployment benefit schemes. Their coverage and generosity, and the availability of secondary schemes, combined with the impact of frequent and not necessarily coherent adjustments during the first part of the economic crisis, all add to the complexity. Thus, comparative analysis of various aspects of access to benefits, and the impact upon young people, is not straightforward.

Which measure of unemployment?
In order to analyse the performance of European labour markets, adequate metrics are also required. For both younger and older workers, some conventional measures show weaknesses when they are applied to the relative performance of youth labour markets. Unemployment rates measure the share of the active population looking for work, while unemployment ratios capture the share of the age group as a whole (O'Reilly et al. 2015). By comparing ratios across age groups, we can assess relative risks.

The analysis of relative unemployment ratios for youth and adult populations, based on labour force survey data, shows that the labour market for workers below the age of 25 is more volatile, especially for the 20-24 age group. Cross-country differences are, nevertheless, remarkable, despite the greater risks generally experienced by young people and the widespread impact of the crisis.

The ratios of both youth and teen unemployment to prime-age unemployment tend to be stable and, in some cases, have improved over time rather than worsening. In other words, over the last 15 years, the relative disadvantage of young people in the 20-24 age group compared to prime-age individuals has been declining in Europe – a trend that did not change with the crisis.

Youth labour markets need special attention from researchers and policy-makers
These results underline that young people are not a homogenous group, either within or across countries, and suggest that the analysis of the youth labour market needs to capture this diversity, adopting a range of metrics to analyse complex trends. Furthermore, additional work is required to improve the reliability of certain institutional-level data – for example, information on benefit coverage rates in a cross-national perspective and in relation to young people.

The research demonstrates variations in a range of outcomes over the crisis period between age groups within the wider youth category and between young women and men. Policy-makers thus need to adopt a holistic view of the challenges facing young people. Further, policy needs to address the security deficit for young people, given that they are not only more prone to falling out of employment or failing to regain employment, but are also less likely to have access to income security provided by unemployment benefits, thereby accumulating negative outcomes of flexibility.

References
Chung, Heejung. 2012. 'Measuring Flexicurity: Precautionary Notes, a New Framework, and an Empirical Example'. *Social Indicators Research* 106 (1): 153-171. ***http://doi.org/10.1007/s11205-011-9800-2***

Eamets, Raul, Miroslav Beblavý, Kariappa Bheemaiah, Mairéad Finn, Katrin Humal, Janine Leschke, Ilaria Maselli and Mark Smith. 2015. *Mapping Flexibility and Security Performance in the Face of the Crisis.* STYLE Working Paper WP10.1 Mapping flexibility and security performance in the face of the crisis

European Commission. 2006. *Employment in Europe 2006*. Luxembourg: Office for Official Publications of the European Communities

Leschke, Janine. 2012. *Has the Economic Crisis Contributed to More Segmentation in Labour Market and Welfare Outcomes?* ETUI Working Paper 02. Brussels: European Trade Union Institute.

Leschke, Janine, and Mairéad Finn, 2016. *Tracing the Interface between Numerical Flexibility and Income Security for European Youth During the Economic Crisis.* STYLE Working Paper WP10.1a Tracing the interface between numerical flexibility and income security for European youth during the economic crisis

O'Reilly, Jacqueline, Werner Eichhorst, András Gábos, Kari Hadjivassiliou, David Lain, Janine Leschke, Seamus McGuinness, Lucia Mýtna Kureková, Tiziana Nazio, Renate Ortlieb, Helen Russell, and Paola Villa. 2015. 'Five Characteristics of Youth Unemployment in Europe: Flexibility, Education, Migration, Family Legacies, and EU Policy'. *SAGE Open* 5 (1): 1-19. http://journals.sagepub.com/doi/abs/10.1177/2158244015574962 ***http://sgo.sagepub.com/content/5/1/2158244015574962***

The quality of young Europeans' employment: A dynamic perspective

Gabriella Berloffa, **Eleonora Matteazzi**, **Alina Şandor** and **Paola Villa**

The quality of employment is usually evaluated by considering various dimensions of people's jobs: for example, the quality of earnings (both in absolute and relative terms), job security (type of contract or unemployment risk), education and training, work-life balance and gender equality, and the working environment (Burchell et al. 2014; OECD 2014). However, labour markets are increasingly characterised by workers moving frequently between jobs, combined with spells without work.

Therefore, if we are interested in evaluating workers' well-being, we need to develop new concepts of employment quality that capture individuals' employment conditions over time, instead of at a single moment.

Researchers evaluating the consequences of increased labour market flexibility (less stringent regulation of permanent and temporary contracts) have tended to focus on the type of contract and, in particular, the use of fixed-term contracts. However, there is a wide degree of variation in the security and other working conditions experienced by 'permanent' and temporary employees across countries. Thus, even when examining job security, we should adopt a definition that is not solely based on the type of contract, but also on the evolution over time of individuals' employment status (Berloffa et al. 2016).

What is a 'good job' in today's dynamic labour markets?

In this study, we present a new definition of (objective) employment quality, based on various dimensions of individuals' labour market experience over a two-year period. In particular, we consider four dimensions – employment security, income security, income success and a successful match between education and occupation. These are defined as follows:

- **employment security**: if a young person experienced employment spells lasting (each) at least six months and non-employment spells lasting (each) at most three months over the 24 months of observation;

- **income security**: if the annual labour earnings in both years of observation are above the at-risk-of-poverty threshold and are not decreasing over time;

- **income success**: if monthly labour earnings in both years of observation are larger than the country-year-education specific median earnings, and are not decreasing over time;

- **educational-occupational success**: if a young person is not over-educated, and does not move from one occupation category to an inferior category during the two-year period of observation.

The novelty of this approach is twofold. First, we evaluate the quality of individuals' employment conditions, and not the quality of the specific job they hold. Second, we adopt a dynamic perspective to assess employment quality, by considering evolution over time using the four dimensions.

This new approach allows us to analyse and compare young Europeans' employment quality. In particular, using EU-SILC data, we focus on individuals aged 16-34 around five years after leaving full-time education, and examine how individual characteristics and labour market institutions (in particular, employment protection legislation and expenditure for active labour market policies, ALMP) affect the probability of finding secure and/or successful employment conditions.

Gender and education matter in achieving a good-quality employment condition
The results show that around five years after having left education, women are less likely than men to achieve employment security. However, if they are able to follow a stable employment trajectory, they have more chance of being income-secure. Nevertheless, females are always less likely to be successful, even when they manage to remain continuously employed.

In terms of security, the key obstacle for women is remaining continuously in employment, that is, reducing the number and length of periods without work. Yet for those who succeed in achieving a stable and continuous employment path, inequalities remain in terms of income success, though not income security. Overall, we find that education allows young people to have more stable and continuous employment trajectories, while also increasing their chances of being income-secure.

Employment quality and labour market policies
Analysis of the policy environment suggests that loosening the rules on the use of temporary contracts reduces the chances for all young people of achieving a sufficiently secure employment condition, generating more difficulties for women and low-educated individuals. However, stricter rules for individual dismissals and higher expenditure on ALMP appear to have positive effects on employment-secure trajectories. In some cases, however, negative effects in terms of income security arise from these more protective policies – for example, for women and low-educated individuals.

Policies for the most disadvantaged: Women and the lower educated

Our results show that, in the EU, women and the lower educated tend to face greater difficulties in obtaining good-quality employment conditions. In particular, the research demonstrates the need to enhance women's chances of remaining continuously in employment and of moving up in the labour income distribution. Recent labour market reforms that have tended to loosen the rules on the use of temporary contracts or on individual dismissals create more difficulties for women and for low-educated individuals. The results underline the need for more specific and targeted interventions to improve the quality of employment of the most disadvantaged groups.

Descriptive statistics of employment quality for young people (aged 16-34) around five years after leaving education in 17 European countries (shares)

	Secure employment condition			Successful employment condition		
	Employment security	Income security	**Employment & income security**	Income success	Education-Occupation success	**Income & education occupation success**
All sample	0.67	0.37	**0.35**	0.18	0.53	0.14
Gender						
Male	0.72	0.41	**0.39**	0.24	0.57	0.18
Female	0.62	0.33	**0.31**	0.13	0.49	0.10
Education						
Low	0.40	0.16	**0.14**	0.12	0.36	0.09
Medium	0.65	0.36	**0.34**	0.18	0.55	0.14
High	0.78	0.44	**0.42**	0.21	0.57	0.15
Country group						
Nordic	0.69	0.39	**0.35**	0.19	0.60	0.15
Continental	0.74	0.40	**0.38**	0.21	0.56	0.15
Southern	0.58	0.31	**0.29**	0.16	0.44	0.12
Eastern	0.69	0.39	**0.38**	0.19	0.57	0.15
Observation period						
2006-2007	0.69	0.44	**0.41**	0.21	0.56	0.16
2010-2011	0.66	0.31	**0.30**	0.16	0.49	0.12

Notes: *Education: Low: lower-secondary education; Medium: upper-secondary education; High: tertiary education.* Country groups: *Nordic: DK, FI, SE; Continental: AT, BE, FR, NL; Southern: EL, ES, IT, PT; Eastern: CZ, EE, HU, PL, SI, SK.*
Source: *Authors' own calculations based on EU-SILC longitudinal data (2006-2012).*

References

Berloffa, Gabriella, Eleonora Matteazzi, Alina Şandor and Paola Villa. 2016. 'Youth Employment Security and Labour Market Institutions: A Dynamic Perspective'. International Labour Review 155: 651–678

Berloffa, Gabriella, Eleonora Matteazzi, Gabriele Mazzolini, Alina Şandor and Paola Villa. 2015. *Youth School-To-Work Transitions: From Entry Jobs to Career Employment.* STYLE Working Paper WP10.2 Youth School-To-Work Transitions: from Entry Jobs to Career Employment

Burchell, Brendan, Kirsten Sehnbruch, Agnieszka Piasna and Nurjk Agloni. 2014. 'The Quality of Employment and Decent Work: Definitions, Methodologies, and Ongoing Debates'. *Cambridge Journal of Economics* 38 (2): 459-477

OECD. 2014. 'How Good is your Job? Measuring and Assessing Job Quality'. Chapter 3 in OECD *Employment Outlook* 2014. Paris: OECD Publishing.

Youth school-to-work transitions: From entry jobs to career employment

Gabriella Berloffa, **Eleonora Matteazzi**, **Gabriele Mazzolini**, **Alina Şandor** and **Paola Villa**

What types of policies promote good employment conditions?
We examine the ways in which some of the labour market policies and institutions that shape flexibility and/or security in the labour market affect the early labour market experience of young people in different European countries. We particularly focus on the type of employment trajectories that characterise the first years of labour market entry, and the possibility for young people of finding good-quality employment within five to six years of leaving education. The central policy concern is whether active and passive labour market policies, in addition to employment protection legislation (with particular reference to temporary contracts), enhance the possibilities for young people to find long-term, good-quality employment outcomes within a reasonable period of time after leaving education. Since a higher degree of flexibility of the labour market implies a higher level of mobility across jobs, we evaluate employment quality and employment security, rather than job quality and job security.

Many pathways into employment
It is possible to identify different types of trajectories from education to the first employment spell. Here, we classify successful and unsuccessful trajectories, and their connections to institutional characteristics.

The relationships are not simple. We find that expenditure on active and passive labour market policies is positively correlated with successful pathways and negatively correlated with unsuccessful pathways. However, once we control for individual characteristics, as well as country and time dummies, these relationships are no longer significant. Employment protection legislation relating to the use of temporary contracts influences school-to-work transitions, with stricter norms appearing to limit the degree of instability of school-to-work trajectories. Such legislation provides some incentives to improve individual employability through a return to education.

From a policy perspective, these results suggest that the current mix of labour market policies is not effective and that new policy tools should be implemented to increase young people's chances of achieving a relevant employment spell within a reasonable period of time. Furthermore, a reduction in the strictness of rules regulating the use of temporary contracts is not an effective policy tool to improve employment outcomes for young people, especially when labour demand is weak, and it may worsen their outcomes.

Young people's medium-term integration

Labour market integration is more than finding a first job and it is important to consider the experience of young people in the medium term – for example, four to six years after leaving education – in order to consider their employment and economic security in terms of their economic success and good educational-occupational match. The empirical analyses reveal that more stringent norms on the use of fixed-term contracts enhance security for both low-educated individuals and women. While an increase in expenditure on active labour market policies (ALMP) is effective in increasing the probability of achieving secure employment conditions for high-school and university graduates, it does not have the same effect for the low-educated and females.

On the other hand, passive labour market policies have no effect on security, but they do improve the quality of employment trajectories for insecure individuals (by helping young people to find, or pushing them to more effectively search for, more stable/continuous employment). However, passive measures seem to have some adverse effects for women – by increasing their probability of being inactive and reducing their likelihood of being always or prevalently employed.

From a policy perspective, these results are in line with those for short-term integration. In particular, they suggest that the current mix of active and passive labour market policies is not effective and new policies should be designed and targeted towards less educated individuals and females. In addition, more stringent norms on the use of temporary contracts should be encouraged, given their effectiveness in enhancing the labour market outcomes of more disadvantaged individuals.

Towards a school-to-work security index

A synthetic index of the overall level of employment security associated with school-to-work trajectories for young people offers a useful tool for drawing comparisons between labour markets. This index is constructed in such a way that it can incorporate explicitly diverging value judgements in terms of whether or not insecurity is increased by the total number of periods of unemployment, their timing and their additive nature. Our analysis shows that there are large cross-country differences in the degree of insecurity associated with labour market entry, and that these differences are generally increased if we give greater weight to trajectories with more than one period of unemployment, or to longer periods of unemployment.

From a policy perspective, the results of this index suggest that policy-makers should move beyond a 'one-policy-fits-all' view for young people. Indeed, new policies to fight youth unemployment should take into account country specificities and whether unemployment is more transient or structural/persistent in nature. Ultimately, a more nuanced view of school-to-work transitions will help policy-makers develop measures that are relevant for young people experiencing difficulties in entering the labour market.

References

Berloffa, Gabriella, Eleonora Matteazzi, Gabriele Mazzolini, Alina Şandor and Paola Villa. 2015. *Youth School-To-Work Transitions: From Entry Jobs to Career Employment.* STYLE Working Paper WP10.2 Youth School-To-Work Transitions: from Entry Jobs to Career Employment

How has the recession affected young people's well-being in Europe?

Helen Russell, **Janine Leschke** and **Mark Smith**

The impact of insecurity on well-being

It is well established that unemployment and insecurity have a negative impact on well-being. Yet it has been proposed that unemployment hits young people less hard, psychologically speaking, because work is not as central to their identity and because they have fewer financial responsibilities than prime-age workers. If this is true, then the high levels of youth unemployment during the great recession may be less damaging than high unemployment among older workers. However, early experiences of unemployment may 'scar' young people's later working lives. Levels of unemployment and employment insecurity differ across Europe, and it is less clear how this societal context affects young people's well-being and how policy interventions may help reduce these negative impacts.

Measuring well-being across countries

Using data from the European Social Survey it is possible to compare the levels of well-being of unemployed young people (under 35 years) with those who are insecurely employed and those who are securely employed. Well-being is measured using a ten-point life satisfaction scale.

The scale of well-being differences by employment status can also be compared to that of prime-age workers (over 35 years). Comparative analysis across 20 countries allows us to test whether well-being effects are influenced by a range of policy and economic indicators such as level of spending on active labour market policies, and levels of youth unemployment.

The results are based on the analysis of two rounds of the European Social Survey across 20 countries (2004/5 and 2010). We restricted the analysis to those aged under 65 years. Institutional information for both time points was collected from a range of international sources and these were chosen on the basis of the balance of flexibility and security policies. Country level effects were analysed using multi-level models.

Unemployment does have an impact

Unemployed young people had significantly lower levels of life satisfaction compared to their employed peers in all but one of the 20 countries analysed. Overall, the satisfaction gap between the employed and unemployed was narrower for younger people than among prime-aged workers, but the effect was nonetheless significant and substantial. Even among those currently employed, past unemployment had a scarring effect on life satisfaction.

Young people in insecure employment were significantly less satisfied with life than the securely employed and this relationship was just as strong as it was for prime-aged workers (Smith et al. *forthcoming*).

The level of economic hardship experienced by the unemployed is an important moderator of well-being effects, it explains a third of the difference in life satisfaction between unemployed young people and those in secure employment. Family support is also important for young people – living with two parents has a positive impact on life satisfaction for under 35s but no such effect was found for prime-age workers.

Country differences and policies

Some measures such as active labour market policies (ALMP) might be expected to reduce the negative effects of unemployment on wellbeing. In fact we find that higher ALMP spending per unemployed person is significantly associated with greater life satisfaction for both the employed and unemployed. In contrast, low levels of spending on unemployment benefits (adjusted by unemployment rate) does not influence life satisfaction among unemployed youth - this may arise in the case of younger people because in many countries relatively few are covered by such income supports (Leschke 2013).

Conditions on the labour market may have an effect on people's overall feeling of wellbeing. The results show that increased rates of unemployment (in the preceding 2 years) are linked to reduced life satisfaction across the population – among young and older, employed and unemployed. Similarly, the higher the proportion of the employed population in a country who feel insecure, the lower the level of life satisfaction. This effect is somewhat stronger for those aged over 35.

Negative impacts from unemployment and insecurity on young people

Our results show that unemployment and insecurity have a negative impact on the well-being of young people, which is almost as strong as it is for prime-age workers. In addition to this individual level effect, high levels of unemployment and insecurity at the country level have an additional depressing effect on well-being. There is little evidence that higher unemployment levels reduce the negative impact of individual unemployment by normalising the experience.

At the policy level, spending on active labour market programmes is positively associated with higher satisfaction, this is not confined to the "at risk" group and so may be a more general effect of a pro-active welfare state on citizens' life satisfaction. The institutional measures are limited in the extent to which they capture the support available to younger people – this is especially true in the case of cash benefits – and policy-makers need quality data to analyse the impact of measures on young people.

Long-term consequences for young people require policy action

Young people have been disproportionately affected by the rising unemployment and job insecurity in the Great Recession. These changes have had a substantial impact on their well-being, measured here by life satisfaction. Even after re-employment, unemployment in the past five years is found to have a scarring effect on well-being.

Economic hardship has a significant impact on young people's life satisfaction and wellbeing and while welfare state and parental support can mitigate these effects, the effects remain significant. Creating secure employment for young people should therefore be a priority for policy. The centrality of labour market policy to the well-being and life satisfaction of the population means that it is important that analysis and measures for young women and men are enhanced to improve policy at the EU and national level.

References

Leschke, Janine. 2013. La crise économique a-t-elle accentué la segmentation du marché du travail et de la protection sociale? Une analyse des pays de l'UE (2008-2010), *Revue Française des Affaires Sociales*, No. 4, Special Issue on "Emplois et statuts atypiques : quelles protections sociales?

Russell, Helen, Janine Leschke and Mark Smith. 2015. *Balancing Flexibility and Security in Europe: The Impact on Young People's Insecurity and Subjective Well-being.* STYLE Working Paper WP10.3 Balancing Flexibility and Security in Europe: the Impact on Young People's Insecurity and Subjective Well-being

Smith, Mark, and Paola Villa. 2016. *Flexicurity Policies to Integrate Youth before and after the Crisis* STYLE Working Paper WP10.4 Flexicurity Policies to integrate youth before and after the crisis

Smith, Mark, Janine Leschke, Helen Russell and Paola Villa. Forthcoming. 'Stressed Economies, Distressed Policies, and Distraught Young People: European Policies and Outcomes from a Youth Perspective'. In *Youth Labor in Transition*, edited by Jacqueline O'Reilly, Janine Leschke, Renate Ortlieb, Martin Seeleib-Kaiser and Paola Villa. New York: Oxford University Press.

Leschke, Janine, and Mairéad Finn. Forthcoming. 'Labor Market Flexibility and Income Security: Changes for European Youth during the Great Recession'. In *Youth Labor in Transition*, edited by Jacqueline O'Reilly, Janine Leschke, Renate Ortlieb, Martin Seeleib-Kaiser and Paola Villa. New York: Oxford University Press.

Is self-employment a solution to young people's employment problems?

Renate Ortlieb, Maura Sheehan and Jaan Masso

Since the onset of the recent economic crisis, there has been a renewed interest among policy-makers across Europe in measures to stimulate self-employment and entrepreneurship, as an alternative to unemployment. However, fundamental questions about policies to promote self-employment, especially among young people, remain unanswered: what is the job-creation propensity of the young self-employed and do such policies create new quality jobs or just promote new forms of precarious, poor-quality employment?

A question of quality and quantity

Despite considerable interest among policy-makers, there is little evidence available concerning the number and quality of jobs that young people create for either themselves or other employees when they embark on entrepreneurial activities. The job-creation potential of youth self-employment can be measured by the flows of young people in and out of self-employment and by the share of young entrepreneurs with employees.

The quality of a job has both subjective and objective dimensions and these can be assessed against a well-founded conceptualisation of job quality developed for the European Union (Green and Mostafa 2012). Since the transition to adulthood varies in duration across countries and has been prolonged by rising insecurity, it is important to consider these dimensions for self-employed women and men aged under 35.

To measure these qualitative and qualitative dimensions, it is possible to use secondary data sources such as the European Union Labour Force Survey (EU-LFS), the European Working Conditions Survey (EWCS) and the European Union Statistics on Income and Living Conditions (EU-SILC). These data sets cover all EU member states.

What job-creation potential does self-employment create?

Analysis of the Europe-wide data shows that across all countries the job-creation potential associated with youth self-employment is very limited (Ortlieb, Sheehan and Masso 2017). Indeed, only a few young people exit unemployment by becoming self-employed, while, on the other hand, a non-negligible share of young self-employed become unemployed. A considerable share of young self-employed are categorised as 'bogus self-employed' – more akin to employees with the lower social charges associated with self-employment – and only a small share of young self-employed have employees.

Talking to young entrepreneurs … A more nuanced story

Europe-wide survey data only illustrates part of the story, and semi-structured interviews with young self-employed individuals in selected countries and industries can shed more light on their experiences. Interviews can capture a lot more information, including the creative and cultural aspects of self-employment, as well as details of the information and communications technology industries, which are important current and future sectors for young people.

The countries examined are useful for representing the range of different labour market regulatory environments, school-to-work transition schemes and levels of self-employment – Estonia, Germany, Ireland, Poland, Spain and the UK. The levels of youth self-employment ranged from 4.3% in Germany to 11.1% in Poland in 2014.

What is the quality of self-employment?

These interviews confirm that a high proportion of young self-employed had 'innovative' products, services and processes (Ortlieb, Sheehan and Masso 2017). Although many did not employ other people, they often had plans to do so, even though they anticipated some barriers and challenges.

The analysis of job-quality measures reveals a mixed picture. On the positive side, the young self-employed report comparatively low work intensity and a good work–life balance. Importantly, young self-employed generally see good opportunities for learning and work experience. Also, they emphasise that despite long working hours, self-employment has the advantage of providing them with autonomy and offering opportunities to utilise their skills. Among the young self-employed, women tend to report better working conditions than men.

However, large shares of male and female young self-employed do not feel well paid for their job and believe that their job offers limited opportunities for career advancement. Moreover, the findings indicate that many of them are under-employed and are concerned about social security risks such as access to sick pay, paternity leave and pensions. These 'personal' risks were of more concern than those related to their business.

What are the policy implications?

There are several policy implications of considering the quality and quantity of youth self-employment. Firstly, since the actual volume of jobs created through self-employment lags behind what politicians had expected, further policy measures are needed in order to realise possible job-creation potential in the future. Such policy measures could include mentoring and job-shadowing initiatives between established self-employed and young people considering entrepreneurial activities.

It is also important to consider easier access to seed funding and other kinds of support for aspiring youth.

Furthermore, policies that extend the social security protection associated with salaried employees to the self-employed are needed. This would address concerns around access to health insurance, sickness and disability pay, maternity/paternity pay, unemployment benefits and pension coverage. Many young self-employed demonstrate a lack of awareness of the associated risks of self-employment or have insufficient financial means for contributing to optional insurance schemes. However, in many European countries, young self-employed only have limited social protection (European Commission 2014).

A wake-up call

These results are a wake-up call for national and EU policy-makers who often regard self-employment as a panacea for unemployment and job-creation efforts. Targeted policy actions are required to assist young self-employed create jobs and to ensure that such jobs are of adequate quality. Policy also needs to reduce the significant social protection risks associated with self-employment. In particular, the self-employed in many countries are not entitled to unemployment benefits should their business fail, nor have they access to affordable health care. Overall, given the large amount of resources targeted at promoting self-employment within the EU, there is an important need for policies addressing the current and future well-being of the young self-employed.

References

European Commission. 2014. *Social Protection in the Member States of the European Union, of the European Economic Area and in Switzerland. Social Protection of the Self-employed.* Situation on 1 January 2014. Brussels: European Commission.

Green, Francis, and Tarek Mostafa. 2012. *Trends in Job Quality in Europe.* Luxembourg: Publications Office of the European Union.

Ortlieb, Renate, Maura Sheehan and Jaan Masso. Forthcoming. 'Do Business Start-ups Create High-quality Jobs for Young People?' In *Youth Labor in Transition*, edited by Jacqueline O'Reilly, Janine Leschke, Renate Ortlieb, Martin Seeleib-Kaiser and Paula Villa. Oxford: Oxford University Press.

Sheehan, Maura, Renate Ortlieb and Andrea McNamara. 2016. *Business Start-Ups & Youth Self-Employment.* STYLE Policy Brief No 7: Business Start ups and Youth Self Employment

Smith, Mark, Janine Leschke and Paola Villa. 2017. *Flexicurity, the Crisis & Young.* STYLE Policy Brief No 10: Flexicurity

Flexicurity policies to integrate youth before and after the crisis

Mark Smith and **Paola Villa**

Policy influences and responses

The priorities and focus of employment policy shift over time. An analysis of those policies that have been directly or indirectly targeted at youth over recent decades demonstrates such changes in focus.

Over this period, the European Employment Strategy (EES) exercised its influence on member states' policy-making through the 'open method of coordination' (OMC), by establishing employment guidelines and by setting quantitative targets. Guidance at the national level was provided via Country-Specific Recommendations (CSRs) on individual countries' employment policies. These were issued every year by the Commission and endorsed by the Council.

This was also a period in which European countries were encouraged to make their labour markets more flexible (i.e., more responsive to changes). There was an emphasis on moving from job security to employment security, under the assumption that an increase in flexibility should lead to higher employment opportunities for all.

Emergence of 'flexicurity' as a policy goal

An overview of policy-making before, during and after the immediate effects of the crisis highlights the emergence of flexicurity as a key goal of the EU policy framework of labour market reforms. This goal was translated into subsequent implementation at the national level in the intensity of policy-making and the direction of policy changes. This broad picture provides a lens through which we can consider policies targeted at the inclusion of young people in employment.

It is possible to chart shifting policy models and the underlying implications for youth in Europe by focusing on the CSRs, along with the recorded intensity and direction of policy activity at the member-state level (as recorded in LABREF). The period 2000-2013 (which includes the pre-crisis years) was first characterised by some employment growth and declining youth unemployment rates, followed by the Great Recession – in which young people were among the first to lose their jobs – and concluding with the austerity years when, for many young people, unemployment turned into either long-term unemployment or inactivity.

Rising visibility of young people in policy priorities

From the early 2000s, policy-makers focused on two main labour supply groups: women and older workers. By contrast, young people were not identified as a group in need of specific employment policies, and mention of younger workers was rather rare in the documentation and other mechanisms of the EES. After 2005, there was a progressive shift of attention from gender issues towards older workers, and in the more recent years from older workers towards young people.

Analysis of the content of the CSRs directly and indirectly focused on young people shows that they were centred around three broad policy areas: 'Active Labour Market Policies' (ALMP), 'Flexibility' and 'Labour market segmentation'. There was a limited focus on young people, only rising in 2011-2013. In the early period, a small number of countries received a recommendation explicitly considering young people. As the crisis emerged, some countries received a simple generic mention of young people, without any precise suggestion on what policy action to follow. Surprisingly, high youth unemployment was not even a key issue in 2009, when only three countries received some youth-related remarks. It was only in 2011-2013 that the deterioration of employment opportunities for young people was reflected in an increasing number of CSRs directly focused on policy recommendations for the young.

Increasing rate of policy activity

Analyses of the LABREF database of almost 3,600 policies demonstrate a clear increase in the intensity of policy-making and underlines the importance of ALMP, followed by labour taxation and job protection (employment protection legislation, EPL) across the pre-crisis, crisis and austerity periods. Two policy areas show a marked rise in activity in the austerity sub-period, after limited activity in the pre-crisis and crisis years: wage setting and job protection (EPL). The rising trend in policy-making intensity is visible across all country groups, although it is at a higher level in the Mediterranean countries.

The policy analysis over this period also confirms a limited focus on young people by policy-makers at the national level. In line with the trends observed in the CSRs, policies focused on young people only increased after conditions on youth labour markets had deteriorated significantly. Similarly, the most active policy area focused on youth was that of ALMP, and only in the austerity period was there a greater diversity of policy measures aimed at youth labour markets.

Shifting policy focus over time

The results demonstrate how policies wax and wane over a relatively long period, with the parallel evolution of European recommendations, national reforms and policy responses to changing economic conditions. In relation to young people, we see how the so-called 'reforms at the margin', prior to the economic crisis, led to the implementation of the flexibility policies associated with flexicurity that allowed the entry of many young people into employment when the economy was growing. However, there were subsequent calls to address segmentation and long-term unemployment for young people as temporary jobs turned into something of a boomerang effect when young workers were among the first to lose their jobs in the crisis.

It is important to have a longer-term and stable perspective around policy-making regarding young people that relies on institutional complementarities at the national level. We would suggest that countries with a 'tradition' of youth policy and stable institutional arrangements were better able to cope with the choppy seas of the changing economic and policy environment during the crisis and austerity periods. On the other hand, those with a weaker institutional history were forced into a flurry of more reactive policy-making as they tried to cope with a more turbulent European economic and policy environment. Such results point to the need for a long-term and coordinated policy perspective in order to address challenges faced by young people entering the labour market in Europe today.

References

Smith, Mark, and Paola Villa. 2016. *Flexicurity Policies to Integrate Youth before and after the Crisis.* STYLE Working Paper WP10.4 Flexicurity Policies to integrate youth before and after the crisis

The strange non-death of ALMPs

Magnus Paulsen Hansen and **Janine Leschke**

The old debate concerning the need for a distinct European social model has never been more topical. Trump, Brexit, and the unsurprising rise of Marine Le Pen in the second round of the French presidential election, show that our actuality may indeed be repeating key elements of the 'Weimar moment' some 80 years ago. To the political economist Karl Polanyi, writing when the world was in flames, the rise of totalitarian and xenophobic ideologies and states was a logical culmination of a 'double movement' of, on the one hand, the free market reforms of past decades and, on the other, the disorganised attempts of societies to protect themselves. However, Polanyi also anticipated a more progressive response – not too far from what occurred in the post-war welfare state of social rights, and backed by Keynesian economics. The trentes glorieuses are long gone. The big question today thus lies within the kind of double movement being developed by the current protectionist and authoritarian tendencies.

Since the 1980s, the Keynesian post-war settlement has gradually been challenged by a political project of globalisation and Europeanisation of national economies. Along with economic reforms – backed by a coalition of centrist parties from right and left, the European Commission and the OECD, as well as economists and sociologists – European welfare states have slowly but consistently been reconfigured into what in modern policy-making lingua is labelled activation, describing a drive from passive to Active Labour Market Policies (ALMPs): these cover a great variety of instruments including job placement with basic training courses, targeted and temporary hiring subsidies, start-up support, public work schemes, upskilling and training, and economic incentivising and sanctioning. The common denominator is a will to reintegrate 'excluded' people in the labour market rather than compensating them (which is seen as merely 'passive' support), often with a special attention towards the 'high risk' category of youth. ALMPs can have positive effects where they provide new employment opportunities after upskilling or training, or as an outcome of labour market experience through incentivised employment, in particular.

On a European level, these policies have been intensively encouraged since the mid-1990s, notably through the European Employment Strategy (EES). After the financial crisis and the recession, many commentators expected a return to stimulus and demand-side policies. Just like Polanyi, they anticipated a 'second' movement. The Keynesian economist Skidelsky envisioned 'the return of the master', and leftist movements speaking against 'finance', 'greed' and 'austerity' reached the governmental offices in countries such as France and Greece.

However, the return of stimulus and demand-side reforms was only a short and interim visit consisting of dousing immediate fires in the aftermath of the crisis. Similarly, improvements in unemployment benefit schemes to more comprehensively cover groups such as young people who were formerly under-represented were short-lived. Instead, the reform track of introducing more ALMPs, in spite of mixed evaluation results, has continued at pace in EU countries. The same holds true at the European level, where in the aftermath of the crisis the Commission has tried to strengthen the social dimension through initiatives – in particular, for young people – such as with the 'Youth Guarantee'. Most recently the 'European Pillar of Social Rights' framework has continued to recognise ALMPs as one of the panacea to current socio-economic problems in Europe.

The resilience of ALMPs after the recession thus coincides with 'the strange non-death of neoliberalism'. One explanation lies in the ability of the EU to constrain the budgetary space for manoeuvre for national governments by means of the Euro and stability criteria, keeping them on an 'austere' track. But while this helps to explain the lack of demand-side policies (in spite of the new 2015 package of Employment Guidelines, which reflect the new – but somewhat contradictory – approach to economic policy-making built on investment, structural reform and fiscal responsibility), it is insufficient for understanding why European countries have continued to 'activate' their welfare states and labour market policies.

Here, it is important to look at the moral economy underpinning the reform tracks in many countries. In an ALMP logic, unemployment is predominantly taken to be a 'supply-side' or 'structural' problem. Unemployment is, in other words, not caused by economic recessions and insufficient demand, but by mechanisms that somehow relate to the unemployed person, whether due to inadequate jobsearch efforts and unwillingness to be mobile, skills mismatch, insufficient incentive to take a job or a lack of self-control. ALMPs are thus inherently behavioural in their approach to unemployment and, in that regard, do not recognise a recession in a Keynesian demand-side sense.

A recent study of justifications of ALMP reforms in Denmark and France pre- and post-crisis shows that one of the most effective legitimations is the way in which national populations are divided into two moral categories. Whereas the post-war settlement organised all its efforts around the division of capital and labour, ALMPs divide the population into a worthy group of active (hard-)working tax-payers, and a less worthy group of unemployable, disincentivised and potentially irresponsible and lazy non-working recipients. ALMPs serve a paradoxical double purpose in relation to these two groups. They seek both to redeem the less worthy by making them active, and they implement various obligations and control mechanisms to ensure that these people choose the path towards redemption by punishing those who do not. The preoccupation with 'rights and obligations' and the threat of sanctions thus serve to reassure the 'hard-working' tax-payers of their worthiness. This is perhaps the greatest moral cost of ALMPs. In place of the citizen with universal rights, they view the recipients of benefits as partakers in a behavioural experiment, aiming to redeem them by 'activating' them in a variety of ways. Even in supposedly 'egalitarian' countries like Denmark, ALMPs, supported by the vast majority of political parties as well as by the population, have led to intensified control and sanctions, and public mistrust towards benefit recipients, and have gone hand-in-hand with reductions in benefit generosity. Rather than questioning the diagnosis, the recent recession seems merely to have led policy-makers to increase the dosage.

The relation and tensions between the centrist programme of more ALMPs and the rise of the populist right could not be more evident than in the second round of the presidential election in France. On the 'ALMP' side, the globalist Emmanuel Macron claimed to be neither on the right nor the left. He proposed to 'modernise' the French labour market by bringing it closer to the Scandinavian model, which implies tackling the problem of unemployment by increasing skills and strengthening the control and obligations of the unemployed. On the other side, stood a protectionist, xenophobic, authoritarian nationalist in Keynesian clothes who replaces the 'blaming of Frenchmen' with an 'economic patriotism' that blames the immigrant (and the EU) for all malaises.

Compared to the latter, the ALMP stance is certainly preferable, but the proposed programme implies several limitations. The first is the individualistic rather than solidaristic interpretation of unemployment as residing in the behaviour and morality of the unemployed. This risks turning the governing of unemployment into a technical problem of how to make the jobless do the right thing. The second danger is that ALMPs see redistributive issues as a problem that can only be solved indirectly by reintegrating people into the labour market. Finally, there are future social and economic challenges to which ALMPs seem of little value. What about, for instance, the growing geographic inequalities within countries in between thriving centres and the de-industrialised periphery, as well as between North and South in Europe? These trends exist in spite of the 60th anniversary of the European Social Fund, which targets disadvantaged regions. Can mobility within and between countries and upskilling as propagated by the European Commission solve these challenges? Another risk concerns the phenomenon of automation, which radically calls into question the assumption of all ALMPs that more work is the self-evident key to a better life as well the key component of the social cohesion of societies. Despite its many inherent moral and pragmatic problems, the growing interest in Universal Basic Income provides a space for questioning the benefits of the pathway along ever more active labour market policies.

This article was first published in *Social Europe* on 13 June 2017: ***https://www.socialeurope.eu/2017/06/strange-non-death-almps***

Work please, but poverty no thanks: How to avoid the rise in the working poor?

Mark Smith and **Genevieve Shanahan**

As the 1980s rock group The Smiths famously sang 'I was looking for a job and then I found a job, heaven knows I'm miserable now'. The rise of the working poor calls into question the adage that work is the best way out of poverty. With radical changes on the labour market, the types of jobs available and new threats such as robotics, old sureties can no longer be counted upon. What can society do when faced with a rise in the share of in-work poor?

So what is in-work poverty?

Though definitions vary, the European Commission considers the working poor to be people who are employed for over half the year but whose household income falls below 60% of the national median. This definition captured almost one in ten of the EU working population in 2015. The working poor are especially concentrated among single-earner households with children (19.8%), while dual-earner households with no kids have the lowest risk (6.2%).

In-work poverty has arisen from changes on the labour market and in who works, compounded by social protection systems that are not well adapted to the new realities of the economy. A range of new contracts, pseudo self-employment, and precarious work forms have replaced stable jobs that previously provided security for a worker and 'his' family. The diversity of labour market participants has also increased to include more women and more single parents, as well as young people struggling to find a foothold in work.

And where are the working poor?

Young people are over-represented among the working poor because their jobs tend to be lower paid and more precarious. Yet the official rates of in-work poverty may be complicated by the nature of household-level statistics. For example, in-work poverty among young people is less pronounced in Southern Europe, where young adults tend to remain in the family home (Berloffa et al. 2015).

These statistics illustrate the household effects inherent in the working poverty measure: poverty is defined at the household level, yet people are employed as individuals. In this way, poverty is hard to disentangle from household composition.

This feature, in turn, renders working poverty a tricky problem from a policy perspective – at which level should it be tackled?

Is the 'sharing' economy driving more workers into poverty?
The growth of new forms of self-employment provides an additional dimension to the in-work poverty challenge. In almost all countries, in-work poverty is higher among the self-employed. A recent study on self-employment showed that there is greater polarisation in incomes for the self-employed than for employees (Hinks, Fohrbeck and Meager 2015).

The rise of the so-called 'sharing' economy has further highlighted ways in which the low-paid self-employed are vulnerable: they shoulder much of the risk, yet enjoy a relatively small portion of the fruits of these new markets. Research from Germany suggests that low-paying self-employment tends to be concentrated amongst already economically marginalised groups – 'youth, women, part-time workers, single parents and self-employed [workers] with health problems' (Ortlieb and Weiss 2015).

A new definitional problem?
Part of the problem of the new economy relates to the question of whether workers are really self-employed or are just employees without the benefits. While truly independent workers set their prices to account for the cost and maintenance of equipment, low-demand periods, sick days, etc., prominent 'sharing' economy players like Deliveroo and Uber deny their workers this control. Uber has been subject to challenges on this point in many countries, with a potential impact upon worker entitlements in terms of wages, holiday pay and sick pay.

The problem of definition extends to the variability of incomes in the sharing economy. The risk borne by the workers means that they can be managing one week, yet working poor the next. In addition, as pseudo self-employed workers, they are at risk when they face periods without work, such as for health reasons.

What kinds of policies could help improve the lot of the working poor?
One of the challenges for policy-makers is to adapt social support in line with precariousness on the labour market and incomes that fluctuate week by week. The problem is complex and may in fact require action on many fronts. From the labour market perspective, policy-makers require new tools to tackle the reality of the modern-day employment situation, which calls for social support to protect against irregular or low incomes and measures to deal with the negative consequences of some 'innovations' in the new economy.

For social protection, making benefits unconditional, or universal, is one option to provide a floor below which earnings are guaranteed not to fall, mitigating the risk of in-work poverty. A number of countries have experimented with forms of negative income tax, whereby workers receive additional income to compensate for low wages.

However, these can be expensive to implement and are not necessarily adaptable to short-term income fluctuations. Minimum wages are another way to provide an hourly floor, but short or irregular hours mean that a minimum rate does not necessarily guarantee a living wage each week. A Belgian study of policy options for countering in-work poverty concluded with a call for universal measures, suggesting that they could bolster rather than undermine work incentives, when compared with more targeted measures (Marx, Vanhille and Verbist 2012).

In relation to labour markets, policy activity in recent years has been towards reducing legislative protection rather than increasing it, with the aim of raising employment and promoting flexibility (Smith and Villa 2016). In the new economy, traditional forms of collective action by unions are difficult because workers are often transient, young and mobile – all factors that do not help union recruiters. However, there are signs of new forms of mobilisation – for example, among Deliveroo riders and fast-food workers on so-called zero-hours contracts.

In any case, it is vital not to underestimate the risk of allowing in-work poverty to continue unabated – when people feel that they are losing out despite playing by the rules, the risks to society extend beyond precariousness to decreased social cohesion and increased populism.

References

Berloffa, Gabriella, Marianna Filandri, Eleonora Matteazzi, Tiziana Nazio, Nicola Negri, Jacqueline O'Reilly, Paola Villa and Carolina Zuccotti. 2015. *Work-Poor and Work-Rich Families: Influence on Youth Labour Market Outcomes.* STYLE Working Paper WP8.1 Work-poor and work-rich families

Hinks, Robin, Anna Fohrbeck and Nigel Meager. 2015. *Business Start-Ups and Youth Self-Employment in the UK: A Policy Literature Review.* STYLE Working Paper WP7.1 UK

Marx, Ive, Josefine Vanhille and Gerlinde Verbist. 2012. 'Combating In-Work Poverty in Continental Europe: An Investigation Using the Belgian Case'. *Journal of Social Policy* 41 (1): 19-41.

Ortlieb, Renata, and Silvana Weiss. 2015. *Business Start-Ups and Youth Self-Employment in Germany: A Policy Literature Review.* STYLE Working Paper WP7.1 Germany

Smith, Mark, and Paola Villa. 2016. *Flexicurity Policies to Integrate Youth before and after the Crisis.* STYLE Working Paper WP10.4 Flexicurity Policies to integrate youth before and after the crisis

Do young people want Universal Basic Income?

Mark Smith and **Genevieve Shanahan**

Around the world, experiments in universal basic income are taking place. The question of affordability has dominated much of the debate, but a focus on young people, as was proposed in the French presidential campaign, is important to examine.

It's not so easy being young

The International Labour Office estimates that the unemployment rate for young people was 13% in 2016 – a new high representing 71 million people, with little prospect of improvement in 2017. As outsiders looking for jobs with limited professional experience, young people are at a serious disadvantage.

In recent years, the Great Recession has exacerbated the consequences of young people's weak position on the labour market in terms of joblessness and the quality of work. Recent STYLE research has shown that policy responses towards young people have been inconsistent and at times incoherent, demonstrating an on-going reliance on reducing employment protection and limiting income protection (Smith and Villa 2016; Leschke and Finn 2016).

The impact of basic income on youth

A number of pilot studies around the world offer some evidence on how basic income schemes can impact the lives of young people. The effects on participation in education are particularly important – young people are more likely to complete their secondary-school education when the pressure to earn is eased. The effects regarding employment and entrepreneurship specific to young people, however, have not yet been studied.

According to a preliminary report, two subsets of young people were excluded from the recently launched experiment in Finland: students, because the trial was intended to study short-term effects on employment; and economically inactive young people, because their existing benefits are lower than those of adults over the age of 25 (Kangas 2016).

The fact that trials have not yet focused on young people suggests any policies aimed only at this group must be developed carefully. Yet the fact that there is a lack of evidence of the benefits of basic income for young people does not mean that those benefits are unlikely. Rather, this dearth can be traced to the fact that results of basic income studies for young people remain thin on the ground and any such results are likely to vary across groups. For young people, especially, these impacts may also emerge over a longer time period.

The challenges for youth in Europe and elsewhere

The characteristics of the labour markets of France and some other European countries create a number of challenges for young people. For those who drop out of school without an adequate qualification, access to work is difficult. While it is predicted that a universal basic income scheme might support young people's decisions to forgo greater earnings in the short term, whether through third-level education or internships, apprenticeships and voluntary work, there are multiple reasons why people drop out. Furthermore, in countries with well-protected permanent contracts, like France, Spain and Italy, the segmentation between permanent and temporary contracts is perhaps the greater challenge facing young people.

Churning between short-term jobs is certainly a source of insecurity and precariousness, and it is especially prevalent among young people. This is a point highlighted in a French Senate report on basic income, which notes that only 44% of job transitions are direct, involving no period of unemployment between the two. Such vulnerable indirect transitions, it further notes, are concentrated among the young (Percheron 2016).

Being young is also about finding one's way in life, and this group's tendency towards short-term positions might be attributable, in part, to their exploratory approach to employment, whereby low-paying or 'gig economy' jobs are taken to meet short-term needs, to gain experience or to get a taste of a given industry. However, we can also see it as part of a wider trend in which job security is experienced by workers, alongside a rise in the frequency of retraining and periods without work (Eamets et al. 2016).

A universal or conditional income for young people?

One candidate in the French presidential election, Benoit Hamon, had proposed extending income support to young people under the title 'universal income of existence'. Though only a first step towards a true, unconditional basic income, such a proposal could help those un- and underemployed young people who currently do not qualify for income support because means-testing is based on parental income.

A common worry is that providing a basic income for young people would, perhaps more than for other demographic groups, encourage worklessness and dissuade integration into the labour force, with severe long-term effects. In this light, a 'participation income' may seem more palatable.

A participation income would involve imposing conditions on the receipt of a basic income – for instance, that the young person would have to commit to performing voluntary work in their community, pursue training or take steps to establish a business. An immediate difficulty is that the definition of such participation could be problematic. Furthermore, administration of such a conditional scheme would involve expenses that may outweigh any increase in participation relative to an unconditional scheme.

A Dutch experiment, known as Know What Works, is planned for later in 2017 and will go some way towards answering this question by investigating the relative expense of various conditional and unconditional benefits.

A 21st-century solution for 21st-century youth?

As the nature of working life changes, it seems fair to say that workers will need to be agile and ready for retraining and new opportunities. Those people entering the labour market with limited experience bear the brunt of this new reality and the associated risks. Addressing these risks is one core argument for basic income – a secure floor that does not require form filling and applications each time one falls below an income threshold. Such an approach could make sense for young people in a world of job uncertainty and flexibility.

References

Eamets, Raul, Miroslav Beblavý, Kariappa Bheemaiah, Mairéad Finn, Katrin Humal, Janine Leschke, Ilaria Maselli and Mark Smith. 2015. *Mapping Flexibility and Security Performance in the Face of the Crisis.* STYLE Working Paper WP10.1 Mapping flexibility and security performance in the face of the crisis

Kangas, Olli. 2016. *From Idea to Experiment: Report on Universal Basic Income Experiment in Finland. Kela Working Paper* 106. Helsinki: Kela. ***https://helda.helsinki.fi/bitstream/handle/10138/167728/WorkingPapers106.pdf?sequence=4***

Leschke, Janine, and Mairéad Finn, 2016. *Tracing the Interface between Numerical Flexibility and Income Security for European Youth During the Economic Crisis.* STYLE Working Paper WP10.1a Tracing the interface between numerical flexibility and income security for European youth during the economic crisis

Percheron, Daniel. 2016. *Le Revenu De Base En France: De L'utopie à L'expérimentation.* Rapport d'information no. 35. Senat. ***http://www.senat.fr/rap/r16-035/r16-035_mono.html***

Smith, Mark, and Paola Villa. 2016. *Flexicurity Policies to Integrate Youth before and after the Crisis.* STYLE Working Paper WP10.4 Flexicurity Policies to integrate youth before and after the crisis

'Career opportunities the ones that never knock': Are some employers more 'youth friendly' than others?

Jacqueline O'Reilly, **Raffaele Grotti** and **Helen Russell**

Research questions

Surprising little attention has been given to understanding which employers recruit young people. Valuable cross-national comparisons of differences in training and recruitment show that where young people are better integrated into employment, employers are more actively involved in providing apprenticeship schemes (Hadjivassiliou et al. forthcoming). But, can we assume that all employers are equally looking to employ young people, or are the jobs open to youth concentrated in particular sectors?

What has happened to job opportunities in these sectors during the Great Recession? Have young people lost their jobs, or job opportunities, because the sector shrunk as a result of the Great Recession? Or, did the fall in youth employment come about because employers were less inclined to employ young workers? And, have youth job opportunities continued to deteriorate as suggested by Blanchflower and Freeman (2000)?

Research Methods

Using a shift-share analysis based on European Union Labour Force Survey (EU-LFS), we look at where young people (aged 16–24) have been employed and how this changed between 2007 and 2014 (Grotti et al. forthcoming). This allows us to decompose aggregate changes in total employment resulting from different driving forces: the structural change in the overall size of sectors (growth effect); the change in the proportion of youth workers in each sector (share effect); and the interaction between these two forces (interaction effect).

In the decomposition analyses, the categorization of the sectors is based on the NACE statistical classification of economic activities in the EU (Eurostat 2008). Shift-share analysis furnishes descriptive understandings of the shifting trends over time and allows us to investigate whether changes in youth employment are driven by structural shifts in the growth or shrinkage of particular economic sectors or whether they are attributable to changes in employers' propensity to employ young people.

In which sectors are young people employed?

The highest youth share is found in the accommodation and food sector, which is particularly high at 46% in Denmark and the Netherlands. The youth share in this sector is much lower in the subprotective countries, like Spain and Italy, although young people are still over-represented compared to older workers. Over time, however, the reliance on youth in this sector decreased in the majority of countries.

Wholesale and retail is also a youth-intensive sector: in 2007, young people accounted for over one-fourth of those employed in this sector in Denmark, the Netherlands, Ireland, and the United Kingdom, but for less than 10% in Italy and Hungary. Over time, the youth share of employment in wholesale and retail decreased in almost all countries, and particularly in Ireland and Spain, again suggesting that youth are particularly exposed to a hiring freeze or labor shedding in this sector in some countries.

Ireland and Spain also experienced the largest decline in the youth share in construction (17 pp and 10 pp, respectively). Notable decreases of between 3.5 pp and 5 pp are also present in France, Italy, the United Kingdom, and the Netherlands (Grotti et al. forthcoming).

Beyond these marked changes, and with the exception of Denmark and Sweden, the decline in the youth share was observed in all sectors, reflecting young people's declining employment share across the economy as a whole. This evidence substantiates the argument made by Blanchflower and Freeman (2000) that there is a long-run tendency of employers to lower their propensity to employ young people, and part of this trend has been the dissolution of temporary contracts (Boeri and Jimeno 2015).

Shift-share analysis

The heterogeneity in the experience of youth employment among countries could be a result of several different factors. It could be the result of an overall shrinkage in the sector in question (shift) or of a declining share of youth employed in the same sector. Using a shift-share analysis, we decompose changes in the total share of youth employment in 2007–2010 and 2010–2014 by sector. This method enables us to measure how much of the changes in youth employment are due to changes in the size of sectors (growth or sector effect), to changes in the utilization of youth labor within sectors (share effect), and to the interaction between these two forces (interaction term) (figure 1).

Figure 1. *Decomposition of changes in youth employment as a share of total employment in 11 EU countries, 2007–2010 and 2010–2014 (percentage points)*

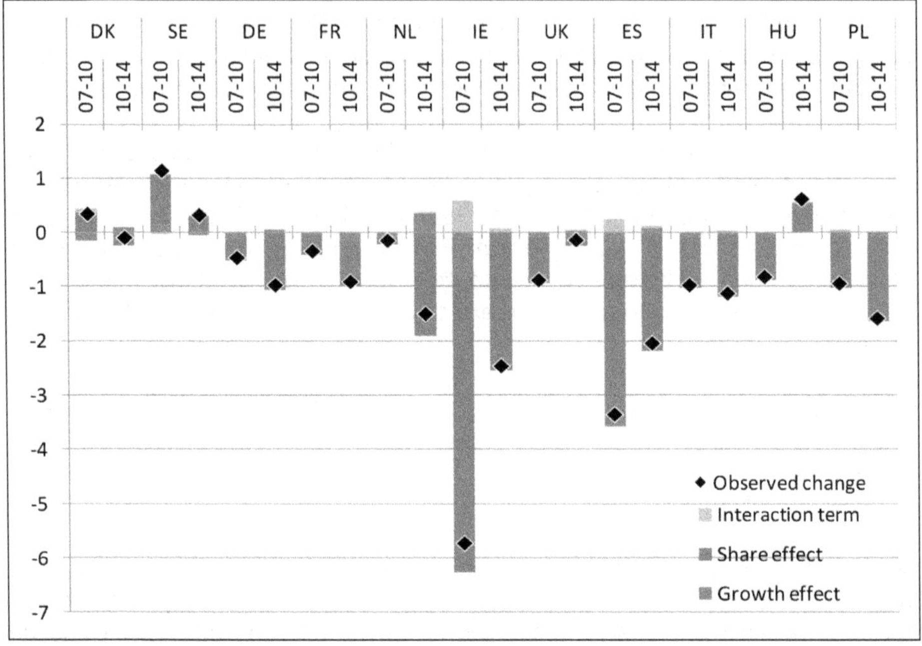

Source: *EU-LFS, authors' analysis. Figure 2.3 in Grotti et al. forthcoming.*

The first thing to note is that, in all countries and in both periods, changes in youth employment are driven by the share effect, namely by the fact that during the recession young people are more likely to be dismissed (or less likely to be hired) compared to older people. For example, the great decrease in youth employment that we observe for Spain in the first phase of the recession (–3.35) is almost entirely due to the share effect (–3.31). This supports the argument that employers have lowered their propensity to employ young people, both by imposing a hiring freeze and through the dissolution of temporary contracts.

In some cases, we observe growth and share effects operating in opposite directions at the same time. For example, in the Netherlands in the second period, the growth effect increases youth employment (+0.35) but the share effect decreases it (–1.91). We could interpret this as being the result, on the one hand, of the expansion of some sectors that traditionally give employment to youth and, on the other hand, to a decline over time in the use of youth within these sectors. This is what has happened for the wholesale and retail sector in the Netherlands.

Although differences between countries exist in the contribution of each sector to the total share effect, the overall changes have been mainly driven by construction, manufacturing, and wholesale and retail.

Gender differences

When youth employment changes are disaggregated by gender, a clear and unique pattern across Europe does not emerge (figure 2.4 in Grotti et al. forthcoming). On the one hand, changes in overall youth employment were driven by changes in female employment in the universalistic (Denmark and Sweden) and employment-centered countries (France, Germany and the Netherlands). On the other hand, in the subprotective (Italy and Spain) and postsocialist countries (Hungary and Poland), the overall changes were driven by changes in male employment. Whenever we observe increases in the share of youth employment, these are often driven by an increased share of female employment.

Has the quality of youth employment deteriorated?

Overall, changes in the share of youth in employment are driven by declines in the share of youth in permanent employment. However, in the few cases where we observe the youth share increasing, this comes from increases in both permanent and temporary youth employment, with the creation of permanent jobs driving the changes (see Grotti et al. figures 2.5 and 2.6).

Manufacturing, construction, and wholesale and retail are the sectors that have driven the decline in permanent employment for youth during the recession. This has occurred both via the shrinkage of sectors and via the declining utilization of youth within sectors. There are a couple of caveats that should be underlined. First, in interpreting the sizes of the decomposed changes, we have to keep in mind that these changes also reflect the sizes of the groups. For example, if we observe the largest contribution of part-time employment in the Netherlands, it is probably because the Netherlands is the country where part-time employment is more widespread. The same holds for temporary employment in Spain.

Second, we have to consider that changes in the share of youth are also a product of the inflow/outflow of those aged 25 years and over into and out of employment (Flek et al. forthcoming). For example, Boeri and Jimeno (2015, 3) observed that a characteristic of this specific recession is that the employment rates of older people increased in most countries as pension reforms progressively increased the retirement age. This, also, is a factor that contributes to accounting for the heterogeneous experience of youth unemployment across countries. Therefore, at least in principle, we might observe changes in the share of youth employment even in cases when youth employment does not change but older people's employment does. In this sense, these analyses furnish a picture of youth employment from a different perspective—looking at the composition of employment—and complement the pictures provided by the study of the unemployment and labor force participation rates (Grotti et al. forthcoming).

Conclusions

One of the clearest findings from this research is the need first to understand that youth job opportunities are very specific to sectors and that this applies regardless of country. Second, the engagement of employers is key to improving youth opportunities for work. Our research evidence indicates that employers have lowered their propensity to employ youth (combining a hiring freeze with the dissolution of temporary contracts), possibly for some of the reasons outlined by Marsden and Ryan (1986) with regard to wages, productivity, and training costs. But closer attention needs to be given to understanding how wage rates, labor market policies, and the costs of training make employers less disposed to recruiting young people. Hadjivassiliou et al. (forthcoming) illustrate how countries perform better where employers are closely engaged in STW transition regimes and VET systems. Here, employers see an incentive to participate. In more fragmented regimes where there is greater inertia in the ability to involve employers through different policy channels, the outcomes for youth have been devastating, especially in subprotective countries (Petmesidou and González Menéndez forthcoming). One of the key challenges in terms of policy learning and transfer requires mobilizing employers and professional bodies within multiagency forms of governance to deliver effective programs to overcome some of the deleterious consequences for youth that have become evident in the past decade.

References

Blanchflower, David G., and Richard B. Freeman. 2000. 'The Declining Economic Status of Young Workers in OECD Countries.' In *Youth Employment and Joblessness in Advanced Countries,* edited by David G. Blanchflower and Richard B. Freeman, 19–56. Chicago: University of Chicago Press.

Boeri, Tito, and Juan Francisco Jimeno. 2015. *The Unbearable Divergence of Unemployment in Europe.* CEP Discussion Paper 1384. London: Centre for Economic Performance, London School of Economics.

Eurostat. 2008. NACE Rev. 2. *Statistical Classification of Economic Activities in the European Community.* Luxembourg: Office for Official Publications of the European Communities.

Flek, Vladislav, Martin Hála and Martina Mysíková. Forthcoming. 'How do youth labor flows differ from those of older workers?' In *Youth Labor in Transition*, edited by Jacqueline O'Reilly, Janine Leschke, Renate Ortlieb, Martin Seeleib-Kaiser and Paola Villa. New York: Oxford University Press.

Grotti, Raffaele, Helen Russell and Jacqueline O'Reilly. Forthcoming. 'Where Do Young People Work?' In *Youth Labor in Transition*, edited by Jacqueline O'Reilly, Janine Leschke, Renate Ortlieb, Martin Seeleib-Kaiser and Paola Villa. New York: Oxford University Press.

Hadjivassiliou, Kari P., Arianna Tassinari, Werner Eichhorst and Florian Wozny. Forthcoming. 'How does the performance of school-to-work transition regimes in the European Union vary?' In *Youth Labor in Transition*, edited by Jacqueline O'Reilly, Janine Leschke, Renate Ortlieb, Martin Seeleib-Kaiser and Paola Villa. New York: Oxford University Press.

Petmesidou, Maria, and María González Menéndez. Forthcoming. 'Policy Transfer and Innovation for Building Resilient Bridges to the Youth Labor Market'. In *Youth Labor in Transition*, edited by Jacqueline O'Reilly, Janine Leschke, Renate Ortlieb, Martin Seeleib-Kaiser and Paola Villa. New York: Oxford University Press.

Further reading on flexible employment and precariousness

Sheehan, Maura, and Andrea McNamara. 2015. *Business Start-Ups and Youth Self-Employment: A Policy Literature Overview.* STYLE Working Paper WP7.1 Business Start-Ups Youth Self-Employment Policy Literature Review

Ortlieb, Renate, and Silvana Weiss. 2015. *Business Start-Ups and Youth Self-Employment in Germany.* STYLE Working Paper WP7.1 Germany

Masso, Jaan, and Kadri Paes. 2015. *Business Start-Ups and Youth Self-Employment in Estonia.* STYLE Working Paper WP7.1 Estonia

González Menéndez, María C., and Begoña Cueto. 2015. *Business Start-Ups and Youth Self-Employment in Spain.* STYLE Working Paper WP7.1 Spain

Sheehan, Maura, and Andrea McNamara. 2015. *Business Start-Ups and Youth Self-Employment in Ireland.* STYLE Working Paper WP7.1 Ireland

Pocztowski, Aleksy, Beata Buchelt and Urban Pauli. 2015. *Business Start-Ups and Youth Self-Employment in Poland.* STYLE Working Paper WP7.1 Poland

Hinks, Raul, Anna Fohrbeck and Nigel Meager. 2015. *Business Start-Ups and Youth Self-Employment in the UK.* STYLE Working Paper WP7.1 UK

Masso, Jaan, Marya Tverdostup, Maura Sheehan, Andrea McNamara, Renate Ortlieb, Silvana Weiss, Aleksy Pocztowski, Beata Buchelt, Urban Pauli, María C. González Menéndez, Begoña Cueto, Raul Hinks, Nigel Meager and Anna Fohrbeck. 2016. *Mapping Patterns of Self-Employment.* STYLE Working Paper WP7.2 Mapping Patterns for Self Employment

McNamara, Andrea, Maura Sheehan, Renate Ortlieb and Silvana Weiss. 2016. *Case Study Findings.* STYLE Working Paper WP7.3

Sheehan, Maura, Andrea McNamara, Renate Orlieb and Silvana Weiss. 2016. *Policy Synthesis and Integrative Report.* STYLE Working Paper WP7.4

Smith, Mark, Janine Leschke and Paola Villa. 2017. *Flexicurity, the Crisis & Young.* STYLE Policy Brief No 10: Flexicurity

Eamets, Raul, Miroslav Beblavý, Kariappa Bheemaiah, Mairéad Finn, Katrin Humal, Janine Leschke, Ilaria Maselli and Mark Smith. 2015. *Mapping Flexibility and Security Performance in the Face of the Crisis.* STYLE Working Paper WP10.1 Mapping flexibility and security performance in the face of the crisis

Leschke, Janine, and Mairéad Finn, 2016. *Tracing the Interface between Numerical Flexibility and Income Security for European Youth During the Economic Crisis.* STYLE Working Paper WP10.1a Tracing the interface between numerical flexibility and income security for European youth during the economic crisis

Berloffa, Gabriella, Eleonora Matteazzi, Gabriele Mazzolini, Alina Şandor and Paola Villa. 2015. *Youth School-To-Work Transitions: From Entry Jobs to Career Employment.* STYLE Working Paper WP10.2 Youth School-To-Work Transitions: from Entry Jobs to Career Employment

Russell, Helen, Janine Leschke and Mark Smith. 2015. *Balancing Flexibility and Security in Europe: The Impact on Young People's Insecurity and Subjective Well-being.* STYLE Working Paper WP10.3 Balancing Flexibility and Security in Europe: the Impact on Young People's Insecurity and Subjective Well-being

Smith, Mark, and Paola Villa. 2016. *Flexicurity Policies to Integrate Youth before and after the Crisis. STYLE Working Paper WP10.4 Flexicurity Policies to integrate youth before and after the crisis*

Villa, Paola, Janine Leschke and Mark Smith. 2017. *Policy Synthesis and Integrative Report on Flexicurity.* STYLE Working Paper WP10.5 Policy synthesis and integrative report on Flexicurity

Ortlieb, Renate, Maura Sheehan and Jaan Masso. Forthcoming. 'Do Business Start-Ups Create High-Quality Jobs for Young People?' In *Youth Labor in Transition*, edited by Jacqueline O'Reilly, Janine Leschke, Renate Ortlieb, Martin Seeleib-Kaiser and Paola Villa. New York: Oxford University Press.

Smith, Mark, Janine Leschke, Helen Russell and Paola Villa. Forthcoming. 'Stressed Economies, Distressed Policies, and Distraught Young People: European Policies and Outcomes from a Youth Perspective'. In *Youth Labor in Transition*, edited by Jacqueline O'Reilly, Janine Leschke, Renate Ortlieb, Martin Seeleib-Kaiser and Paola Villa. New York: Oxford University Press.

Leschke, Janine, and Mairéad Finn. Forthcoming. 'Labor Market Flexibility and Income Security: Changes for European Youth during the Great Recession'. In *Youth Labor in Transition*, edited by Jacqueline O'Reilly, Janine Leschke, Renate Ortlieb, Martin Seeleib-Kaiser and Paola Villa. New York: Oxford University Press.

Inspirational music and film

Music

Here are some of the tunes that have accompanied us on this journey.

Macklemore & Ryan Lewis
'Growing Up' (2016) https://www.youtube.com/watch?v=6mhtJduoCZ0

Adele http://adele.com
'When we were young' (2015) https://www.youtube.com/watch?v=DDWKuo3gXMQ
'Million Years Ago' (2015) https://www.youtube.com/watch?v=1m0iZETAjTc

Sherika Sherard www.sherikasherard.com
'Give me a job' (2014) https://www.youtube.com/watch?v=lQ1La7yCrqg

Tinie Temper http://www.tinietempah.com/
'Pass Out' (2014) https://www.youtube.com/watch?v=yhBiybONjVk

Caparezza www.caparezza.com/
'Non me lo posso permettere' (2014) https://www.youtube.com/watch?v=umUmQgkgFT8

Rizzle Kicks www.rizzlekicks.com
'Lost Generation' (2013) www.youtube.com/watch?v=iL51Tsh6Sdg
'When I was a Youngster' (2011) www.youtube.com/watch?v=Rs2HHYtGhP0

Dizzee Rascal http://raskit.co.uk/
'Bonkers' (2011) https://www.youtube.com/watch?v=Ci40ae8BlcE

Ed Sheeran www.edsheeran.com
Galway Girl (2017) https://www.youtube.com/watch?v=87gWaABqGYs
The A Team (2010) https://www.youtube.com/watch?v=UAWcs5H-qgQ&list=RDUAWcs5H-qgQ#t=75

Plan B http://www.time4planb.co.uk/
'The Defamation of Strickland Banks' (2010) https://www.youtube.com/watch?v=Po_ArckLTXg

Beyoncé http://www.beyonce.com/
'Single Ladies' (2008) https://www.youtube.com/watch?v=4m1EFMoRFvY

Beastie Boys http://blog.beastieboys.com/
'Girls' (2007) https://www.youtube.com/watch?v=hmoHDfXcm_M
'Ladies' (2009) https://www.youtube.com/watch?v=Naf5uJYGoiU&index=5&list=PL HNtS7VIZlyZYrh0s6DUrZ7VwWj5JWdlB
'Sabotage' (2009) https://www.youtube.com/watch?v=z5rRZdiu1UE

Eminem
'Lose Yourself' (2002) https://www.youtube.com/watch?v=_Yhyp-_hX2s

Prozac+
'Angelo' (2000) https://www.youtube.com/watch?v=SC0Lc4N2FOU

Paul Weller
'Broken Stones' (1995) https://www.youtube.com/watch?v=N_M8m4Yr7vc
'The Changingman' (1995) https://www.youtube.com/watch?v=0v9WhRpQw8E

M People
'Moving on Up' (1993) https://www.youtube.com/watch?v=zkHOVJINRD8

Mano Negra
'Mala Vida' (1988) https://www.youtube.com/watch?v=qWV2kM1laIc

Gwen Guthrie
'Ain't Nothin' Goin' On But The Rent' (1986) https://www.youtube.com/watch?v=kAdtfkoRJ2s

The Pogues www.pogues.com
'The Old Main Drag' (1985) www.youtube.com/watch?v=cjW8PSan3-o

Billy Bragg www.billybragg.co.uk
'The Saturday Boy' (1984) https://www.youtube.com/watch?v=2CBWDp71UPM

UB40 www.ub40.org
'One in Ten' (1981) www.youtube.com/watch?v=MbMQTs1P_6U

The English Beat www.englishbeat.net
'Get a Job' (1981) https://www.youtube.com/watch?v=2J2GvipKEwE

The Undertones www.theundertones.com
'Teenage Kicks' (1978) https://www.youtube.com/watch?v=wAtUw6lxcis
'My Perfect Cousin' (1980)https://www.youtube.com/watch?v=Pgqa3cVOxUc

The Jam
'Eton Rifles' (1979) https://www.youtube.com/watch?v=wy3RtGRxQGE

X-Ray Spex www.x-rayspex.com
'Germ Free Adolescents' (1978) https://www.youtube.com/watch?v=G5vwQuuO52I

The Clash www.theclash.com/
'Career Opportunities' (1977) https://www.youtube.com/watch?v=8JM8C49pf40

Johnny Cash www.johnnycash.com/
'Green, green grass of home' (1968) http://www.johnnycash.com/

Lalo Schifrin
'Mission Impossible' (1967) version from The Piano Guys (2013)
https://www.youtube.com/watch?v=9p0BqUcQ7i0&list=RD9p0BqUcQ7i0#t=0

Bob Dylan
'Forever Young' (1974) https://www.youtube.com/watch?v=P1fSVbBwVX8
'Lord Protect My Child' (1983) https://bobdylan.com/songs/lord-protect-my-child/
I Was Young When I Left Home' (1961) https://vimeo.com/216157949

Dinah Washington
'What a difference a day makes' (1959) https://www.youtube.com/watch?v=OmBxVfQTuvI

Film

A short selection of some classic films about youth transitions.

A Taste of Honey (1961) A young girl growing up in Manchester has an unconventional relationship.
https://www.youtube.com/watch?v=2M_pfoHgUjA&index=6&list=PL4CK2suoh0UYMSsiBvQaeJiRu7w_Ao2-v

The Loneliness of the long distance runner (1962)
A young man growing up in the UK in the 1950s
https://www.youtube.com/watch?v=4asUxvijYQ8

The Graduate (1967) A disillusioned, award winning scholar makes his way through some tangled love affairs.
https://www.youtube.com/watch?v=acEh0kEL7_E

Harold and Maud (1971) A suicidal young man gets a new lease of life through his relationship with an 80 year old woman
https://www.youtube.com/watch?v=5mz3TkxJhPc

Scum (1977) Life in a prison for young offenders in the 1970s.
https://www.youtube.com/watch?v=A6rlV9gP8Fs

Quadrophenia (1979) A young man's journey from London to Brighton in 1965.
https://www.youtube.com/watch?v=QmxcW23nWho

La Haine (1995) Three young men living in the suburbs of Paris.
https://www.youtube.com/watch?v=okNJUr6Adf8

Hackers (1995) Young hackers are blamed for capsizing five oil tankers.
http://www.imdb.com/title/tt0113243/

Cresceranno i carciofi a Mimongo (1996) the quest for work and love of an agricultural student
https://www.youtube.com/watch?v=69L1QwDC3LE

Trainspotting (1996) Young people growing up in Scotland.
https://www.youtube.com/watch?v=8LuxOYIpu-I

Tutti giu' per terra (1997) the story of a reluctant young student in Turin
https://www.youtube.com/watch?v=mOBxK_UWe40

Kevin and Perry Go Large (2000) Kevin and Perry go on holiday to Ibiza.
https://www.youtube.com/watch?v=mlagpKaoxuk

Inbetweeners (2001) Four young 18 year olds go on holiday to Malia.
http://www.imdb.com/title/tt0217570/?ref_=fn_al_tt_1

Legally Blonde (2001) Elle goes to law school.
https://www.youtube.com/watch?v=E8I-Qzmbqnc

Bend it like Beckham (2002) Jess wants to play football, but her family don't.
https://www.youtube.com/watch?v=Z7Pt_GMDdGo

Million Dollar Baby (2004) A young woman wants to become a boxer.
https://www.youtube.com/watch?v=4B0zmj0-lac

Kidulthood (2006) Life of a 15 year old finding his way.
https://www.youtube.com/watch?v=9uIauoMugTw

This is England (2007) A young boy becomes a skinhead.
https://www.youtube.com/watch?v=H0jkv2bRFgQ

Tutta la vita davanti (2008) a young graduate woman working in a call centre while searching for employment security and a career
https://www.youtube.com/watch?v=v5_Hr1tAuU0

C'e' chi dice no (2010) a story of three former high school companions facing uncertain employment prospects, creatively trying to oppose a biased referral system of entrance into employment
https://www.youtube.com/watch?v=QM7lZm-kdjo

Get a Job (2010) Unemployed and living with the 'mother-in-law from hell', Will and Terry open a comedy club.
http://www.imdb.com/title/tt1753860/?ref_=fn_al_tt_2

The Social Network (2010) A Harvard student with few friends creates Facebook.
https://www.youtube.com/watch?v=2RB3edZyeYw

Eat, Sleep, Die (2012) A young Swedish woman struggles to find a new job and look after her sick father.
https://www.youtube.com/watch?v=q1sKX6m5nlA

Goob (2014) A young man in rural Norfolk fighting, womanizing and stock car racing, falls for a pretty foreign field worker.
http://www.imdb.com/title/tt3009070/

Smetto quando voglio (2014) Comedy around precariousness, and the attempt of three (former) researchers to pursue employment success
https://www.youtube.com/watch?v=seEhOShK0cc

Top Boy (2014) Young men growing up in London.
https://www.youtube.com/watch?v=qIkEmW1PkYE

Girlhood (2015) Young women growing up in the tough suburbs of Paris.
https://www.youtube.com/watch?v=lJudaZEY-Uc

The Intern (2015) A retired man becomes a senior intern at an online fashion house.
https://www.youtube.com/watch?v=ZU3Xban0Y6A

I, Daniel Blake (2016) A 59 year old carpenter fights to get Employment Benefits, and support a young family. https://www.youtube.com/watch?v=ahWgxw9E_h4

Get a Job (2016) After college, life doesn't go to plan as Will and Jillian take on increasingly strange jobs. https://www.youtube.com/watch?v=eXmOmdzsQVs

Che vuoi che sia (2016) Comedy around uncertain prospects and difficulties in forming a family
https://www.youtube.com/watch?v=qp8qrJy3KTk

T2: Trainspotting 2 (2017) The original crew twenty years later.
https://www.youtube.com/watch?v=IGdiACWiMAM

Nadia (2017) A British school girl with a difficult family who is made homeless.
https://www.youtube.com/watch?v=ffqp6f0_rzw

Eviction (2017) A young man loses his bike with serious consequences
https://www.youtube.com/watch?v=P4Fl3Biz9Eo

MYM: Million Youth Media
https://www.youtube.com/user/MillionYouthMedia

Fully focused: the fastest growing youth media platform in the UK using the power of film to challenge perceptions, raise awareness and transform lives.
http://www.fullyfocusedproductions.com/

Lightning Source UK Ltd.
Milton Keynes UK
UKHW021921070521
383341UK00003B/129